GOD, I LISTENED

**To my babies
Burnie and La-Doris**

GOD, I LISTENED

By
Eula Hendrick McClaney

Editor-in-Chief
Mark Taylor,
Ph.D.

Editor
Anthony Sweeting

Copyright © 1989 by Dr. La-Doris McClaney
First Printing 1989

Printed in the United States of America

"Amazing Grace" by Reverend John Newton
Copyright © 1963

Library of Congress Cataloging in Publication Data.
McClaney, Eula Hendrick, 1913-1987

God, I Listened
Autobiography
Library of Congress Catalog Card Number: 88-092420
ISBN: 0-9621422-0-4

Published by
Dr. La-Doris McClaney
Post Office Box 1157
Beverly Hills, California 90213

ACKNOWLEDGEMENT

A grateful acknowledgement to my almighty God who spoke to me — and I listened.

TABLE OF CONTENTS

*"For I was hungry and ye gave me food;
I was thirsty and ye gave me drink;
I was a stranger and ye took me in."*

Matthew 25:35

FOREWORD

Eula

Eula McClaney is a woman whose uniqueness lies not in the fact that she came out of the cotton fields of Alabama to become a multi-millionaire. Hers is not just a rags to riches story, because it is not the first nor last such story. What is important about her story is that it reveals how she embodies in her life, attitudes, and thoughts, the central message of the world's great gospel: *"I and my Father are one."* She has lived that message in terms of the Christian faith and in demonstration of its wonderful promise: *"It is your Father's will that you inherit His Kingdom."*

The kingdom Eula inherits is truly the kingdom of heaven — of loving and trusting in God, of reaching out to help others, and of loving her fellowman unconditionally. Her Holmby Hills mansion, her world-famous neighbors, her hundreds of friends — both great and ordinary — possessions of silver and gold in the form of cars, clothes, furniture, real estate holdings, bank accounts, and all which glitters to the eye, are mere outward signs of an inner richness of spirit which has sustained her every day in her life.

I know Eula, and I know that you could take away every single one of the outward trappings of wealth and prestige, and she would still be rich. For Eula doesn't think poor. She thinks rich, she thinks abundance, and she thinks gratitude in terms of God's abundant love and goodness, which knows no limits of manifestation.

One of the most touching things I know about Eula is that she is first and foremost Eula, "just a plain, common, ordinary person," as she puts it. Well, it takes a pretty remarkable person to become a multi-millionaire, faced with the heavy odds of being a woman, being Black, being raised in the backwoods of the Deep South, and having only a minimal education. Yet she looks on herself as plain and humble and gives the credit to her Maker, and not to herself; although with His help she was courageous, determined, hardworking, and always resourceful. So when you are around Eula, it is alright not to be rich and famous, just as it is alright to be rich and famous. The way she measures you is by your honesty and willingness to do the best with what you have.

Eula told me something about herself that sums it all up. It belongs here, right at the beginning, so that you will have no doubt as to the kind of person this book is about. Here is what she said:

"In order to make me sure not to forget that God, with the help of all kinds of people who supported me, got me to where I am today, and to keep me reminded of my past days of old, I walk out on this estate barefooted.

"I just leave my shoes in the house, because I can remember when I was a very young person and didn't have what we call everyday shoes. So I just do a lot of things to remind Eula of where she came from. Sometimes I just lie down on the floor, just to remind myself . . . Only, I have here on the floor good soft rugs that I didn't have a long time ago. My mother always taught us, when we were children, that a bird can fly high, but it must come to the ground to get food. So never fly too high and forget that the earth is where you came from and must come back to. It's a shame to give less than your best. Always give your best. I know it pays."

It does pay! It pays best in those treasures that are better than silver and gold and high-placed friends and huge bank accounts. It pays in *knowing,* deep deep down, that you are a blessed child of an abundant universe whose value is measured in terms of the spirit. That is the true reward Eula has achieved for herself. Her loving example and her plain-spoken words telling of how she has lived her life thus far make all who know her feel certain that they, too, can claim and receive their own good bounty, just as she has claimed and received hers.

I am as pleased as I can be to have the privilege of helping her send out her loving, courageous, high-flying spirit to all who read her story which is, in its way, a gospel — a telling out of the good news!

This is Eula, the lady who listened, who listens, and who *"keeps on stepping!"*

Mark Taylor, Ph.D.
Los Angeles, California

INTRODUCTION

Take the Good

I have been thinking about this book for a long time. Why would I want to write my life story? After all, I am a person who has always stayed in the background. All through the years I have stayed in the background, and I have never had any desire to be on the front doing things. I'm not a special person. My education never went above the sixth grade, and that was only in an on-and-off way in a little one-room school in the backwoods of Alabama. You could call me a sixth-grader from the backwoods.

So why have I written the story of my life? Well, I promised my God years ago that if He would just show me the way to bring myself out of poverty, I would share His guidance with others. I know there is somebody out there that will read my book, somebody who feels like she or he has it worse than anybody in the world. I want them to read and say, "Not true! Eula McClaney had it tough. Here's a lady that had it hard, too."

Friends have said to me, "If I were you, Eula, I would not tell about my life and the poverty and hard times. I would just keep it to myself, because anyone who is doing as well as you're doing doesn't need to tell that stuff. You don't need the money, so why tell it?

Mainly, I'm telling it because it may help someone else. Many a day I needed help, needed encouragement, needed to know that somebody else before me had walked this same road and was able to make it. I needed to know that. People who have watched me on television, listened to me on radio and heard me talk in public have told me how much encouragement they got out of what I said, how it just touched and inspired them. And, I came to see that it could be worthwhile for me to sit down and tell the truth so that I might be able to help somebody, maybe save some youngster that just wants to let himself or herself go on down to nowhere. If what I have to tell will save one or two people, I will feel it was all worth living and telling. Also, I feel that the truth is worth telling and I am going to tell the truth, because I **know,** "the Truth will make you free."

This present time in my life is really beautiful. I've always just been going along, working, trying to do what I thought was right. And I never knew, really and truly, that I had done anything exciting. The hardest thing for me to get in my head has been to see my life as something special enough to interest others. Sometimes now I sit down and say, *"Eula, what have you done more than anybody else has done?"* I have talked it over with some friends and my family, and they have said to me, *"What you have done with your life is wonderful. Just to hang in there through thick and thin, through all the obstacles, and not throw your hands up and quit, that was wonderful! How many people do that?"*

Do you know? — I hadn't even thought of throwing my hands up and quitting. I have just **always** thought that you don't turn loose, you hold on. When you turn loose, you fall down. But if you hold on and keep on stepping, you get where you want to go. I just took my stumbling blocks and stepped on them for stepping-stones to higher places, to higher heights — just used them for a betterment of my life and never let them get me down. I knew that on the other side of the rainbow there was something better. I had faith that life could not stay the same, that there was a turning point somewhere — never knowing just where or when. But I knew that life could be beautiful if you keep on keeping on. Yes, it's just beautiful when you take your lumps and bumps and make stepping-stones out of them, stepping-stones for a better future.

These days I live in Holmby Hills, California in Los Angeles County. I have some of the most wealthy and famous people in this city for friends and neighbors. I keep company with the top people, the in-between, and then the very common, ordinary people like me. What I'm trying to explain is that it's not your education that makes the difference. It's where you're coming from, what you believe, how you deal with problems, and how you treat others that makes the difference. I want to be plainly understood about this. Education is very important, but educated or not, you've got to be a person who is **honest** and straight with others and with yourself. I want to inspire not just one segment of people, one color, or one creed, but everyone who reads this book, because I was inspired by God.

Whatever the adversities may be, don't be fooled by them or think that's the way life will always be. Behind every stormy day there is sunshine. I've been through lots of stormy days, and I know the truth of what I'm saying.

God has always spoken to me when I needed to hear something in order to change and improve my life. Now it seems He's speaking through me on many occasions. And He surely still does speak to me now and then through others. I remember that Rosa Parks, the civil rights activist, came to see me once. She said, *"I just had to come to see you. I haven't done anything myself."* Can you imagine Rosa Parks coming to me and telling me that? Look at what this great woman has done! *"I'm the one who hasn't done anything,"* I said to her. But there was this other lady sitting there, looking at us both, and she said, *"You are two pioneer women in your own right. You're both pioneers and you're both from Alabama. It just fills my heart and fills my eyes with tears to see two women sitting down, side by side, and both of you pioneers in your own right — two great women to go down in history."* And I said, *"Not me. Miz Parks will."*

Well, I think that was God's way of getting me to understand that I should tell my story. I used to tell my husband that I wanted to help others, and he used to say, *"How can you help somebody, if you have nothing yourself?"*

"But if I can just do something," I would say, *"just lead the kind of life that will give others a good example, maybe even make a big success, then I could say, 'If I can do this, you can, too.' That would be a help."*

So, it seems now God wants me to do that — make myself an example. Now you know why I am telling my life story. I'm telling it as truthfully as I can, so the bad and good things are all here. But, I want to emphasize the good things, because they are still happening, more and more. What's true for me can be true for anybody. I have often told my daughters, *"When someone that you see is doing good, take that good. Take the good things you see out of other people's lives and pattern yourself after that. Learn what's good in anyone or anything and pattern yourself after that."* That's what I want my readers to do. The bad you see in me, or my life, or anyone, or anything, don't take notice — just ignore it. But . . . *". . . take the good."*

Eula McClaney
Holmby Hills
Los Angeles, California

PART I
Orion, Alabama

1.
My Family

I was born in the backwoods of Alabama during the year 1913. I grew up in the cotton fields of Pike County, which is located in a place called Orion. The nearest big city was called Troy. My birth name is Eula Hendrick; after marriage it became Eula Hendrick McClaney. During my childhood, I was affectionately called *"Bie"*.

My parents were Joe Frank Hendrick and Joanna Holt Hendrick. I was brought up with an older sister, Georgia Mae, an older brother, Joe Frank, Jr., called *"Bae,"* and two younger brothers, Jimmy Lee and Tommy Louis. I also had a brother named George that I never knew who was Georgia Mae's twin. He died when he was six months old. Also, a part of our immediate family were my paternal grandparents, Warren and Johnann Jones Hendrick. They lived in a house close by ours.

We were poor share croppers, who rented from a white man, a Doctor Murphy. Although cotton was our primary crop, we also raised corn, peanuts, hogs, and chickens. We worked very, very hard. We not only worked our farm but we performed practically all of the work on my grandparents' farm as well. They, too, rented their farm. However, my grandfather did not like farming and preferred doing other things. My grandmother, who was always a hard-working lady and always helping out people in our area, had other things to take up her time besides working in the fields. However, for that place and time, my grandparents were fairly well-off. Even so, we planted and picked their cotton for no pay.

Then there was Cousin Clarence Farrier whose farm we also worked. He lived about a quarter of a mile from our house. Cousin Clarence had no wife and no children during the early years of my childhood, but that changed later. Eventually, he did marry, but soon after his wife left him. I always loved Cousin Clarence. He was a kind, good-hearted man. I remember that he would pay us fifty cents a day to work his farm. He gradually raised it to a dollar a day and sometimes up to a dollar and twenty-five cents.

Actually, I cannot tell much about my maternal grandparents, great-grandparents, and all their offspring. Tracing my family tree is not too easy. However, my paternal grandparents, Warren and Johnann Hendrick, were born soon after the end of the Civil War during the days of Reconstruction. Their parents were born in slavery when record-keeping was never complete or accurate. Families were often separated and lost track of one another. So, my knowledge of relatives and ancestors is vague, and I have only hearsay and a few recollections of people like my mother to go on. For me, my family is mostly comprised of people of my paternal grandparents' generation — aunts, uncles, cousins, and their children, as well as my own immediate family members.

My mother was a lady who had lost her mother, my grandmother, Sophronia Burkett Holt, when she was quite young — just a little girl. Her father, Elder Tom Holt, was a minister. He would go around preaching all over the South. When my Grandmother Holt died, most of her children were grown. However, she left behind three young children yet to be raised: my mother, a boy, two or three years older than my mother, and a baby boy. Grandfather Holt, I understand, wanted to keep his children with him, although that would have meant they would have to travel all the time. It was the only life he knew. But my mother had asthma very badly and was in poor health, so one of her older sisters, Aunt H., begged Grandfather Holt to let her take care of her sick sister. Aunt H. was married and had children of her own, but both she and her husband, Henry Williams, whom we called Uncle Tobe wanted my mother with them.

"You can take the two boys," Aunt H. told my grandfather, *"but let me keep my little sister and take care of her. She can't take what them boys can take, 'cause she's sickly and has such a bad case of asthma. Let me keep her. I know how to wrap her up to get her through these spells of asthma. I can try my best. You'll be traveling from place to place with nobody to care for her like I would care for her."*

So, Grandfather Holt agreed to let my mother's sister keep her. Aunt H. raised my mother as if she were her own daughter. Mother grew up a very nice, mild-mannered lady who felt that she had no right, under any circumstances, to speak up for herself, no matter what anyone did or said to her. She was a very passive person. Many times, as a child, I felt like saying to her, *"Why don't you stand up for yourself more than you do?"* But she always remained very passive.

Sometimes she would say to me, *"I didn't have no mother, and I didn't have no father, and I just learned to swallow and take things and go on and do the best I could."*

My father was a different sort of person. I probably take some of my characteristics from him. Dad was *the* man in our home. When I say he was *the* man, I mean he was *the* man! Right or wrong. And many, many times he was so wrong! I could hardly stand it. Mom just took it, though. She just put up with nearly everything my father said or did.

Dad was a good man, but not easy. He was often a source of embarrassment to both his mother and his wife. He tended to be a little reckless, especially if he had been drinking. Dad had a liking for that corn liquor. He wasn't an alcoholic, because he didn't drink it all the time or everyday. But on weekends, he liked to go around with a gang of fellows who were pretty rowdy — drinking and carrying guns in their pockets. Nothing had ever happened, but it did upset mom and Grandmother Johnann that dad kept that kind of company.

Dad and his brother, Uncle Mitchell, were my grandparents' only two children. Dad was younger and spoiled. My grandparents treated them both well and loved them, but I think they showed favoritism to dad. Even as a child, I could see that they loved dad more. It seemed to me that dad stayed in more trouble and caused the family more heartaches than his brother. Uncle Mitchell was a bit more refined than dad and his attitude was completely different. He avoided the kind of people dad went around with. Dad just seemed to love lively people and the more lively they were the more he thought he was having a good time.

When my father wasn't working hard and being pretty much the boss of the family, he had a tendency to drink and cut up. There were numerous occasions when his drinking and his recklessness caused us a little more excitement than we might have cared to have — sometimes just plain disaster. For example, on at least two occasions he drank too much, got careless, and set our house on fire.

Uncle Mitchell, on the other hand, never gave anyone any trouble. He was really a ladies' man, what we would now call a *"playboy."* He was certainly the playboy in our area. When I first came to know him or have my earliest recollection of him, he had already been married and divorced. His wife, I was told, had been a very beautiful lady. Anyhow, Uncle

Mitchell seemed to be afraid to marry anybody after his divorce, so he just stayed single for years. He was a smart man who dressed elegantly. He had been away to school as a boy and I can remember that he was well spoken. There was something about him that told you he was a fairly well educated man.

One of the things I best remember about Uncle Mitchell is how he took an interest in getting teachers for our little school, Corner Flat. Most of the teachers, as I recall, were young, single women. They would always be looking for Mitchell Hendrick. Even though I was a child, I thought they were probably his girlfriends.

We had a different teacher every year. One would teach for two semesters and leave. Our semesters were short, to allow for all the work we had during planting, growing, and harvesting time. The next year a new teacher would come, largely through the efforts of Uncle Mitchell. Sometimes these young teachers would not stay long, not even the full length of the two semesters, because the State of Alabama would not finance them and the local people could not pay for them. But we did get our schooling, thanks in part to Uncle Mitchell.

Uncle Mitchell was the only close uncle I knew. He lived with my grandparents a lot of the time. He would also go away to Florida or Montgomery, or somewhere else. He worked for a while and then he came home. We were always glad to see him. He also had a farm of his own at one time. Occasionally, we helped him out, just as we helped our grandparents and Cousin Clarence. Eventually, Uncle Mitchell got married again and went to farm north of Montgomery. His wife was a smart, hard-working, capable woman. She could do just about everything from cooking and canning to using a tractor in the field. She and Uncle Mitchell bought seven-hundred acres of land and built themselves a nice home. She would go to Hollywood in the fall, work for such celebrities as the Barrymores, and save her earnings to furnish her home. She also managed to receive gifts such as television sets and home appliances from her employers. So, Uncle Mitchell had a very successful second marriage.

Now, my paternal grandparents, Warren and Johnann Hendrick, were very special people who had a big influence on me. I never knew my other grandparents. Aunt H. and Uncle Tobe certainly seemed like grandparents, and I will always think kindly of them. However, by living so close to my paternal grandparents all those years and having them put my sister up on a pedestal, it was inevitable that they made a big impression on my life and character.

As I've thought about telling my story, I've come to see that it's impossible to put in all the "facts" or give everybody equal time. My life has been filled with all kinds of people, the very good, the very bad, and all the in-between. Even now, all kinds of wonderful people, some of them very famous and distinguished, keep coming into my mind. I will do the best I can to tell it the way I see it, feel it, and remember it.

I find looking back on my family in those days a little like looking at an old patchwork quilt made a long time ago. You see this patch and that patch and you remember where some of those patches came from. The memories they bring up are all like bits of patchwork themselves. Other patches are just random pieces you remember working with, but don't connect up in your mind to anything of importance. One patch can remind you of a dress you wore and the times and places you wore it. Another patch reminds you of nothing but a patch. So, what I often remember are events that go with some of those feelings. Some events are like still pictures just lingering in my mind, reminding me of the many words spoken and deeds done. I'm sorting out those early patches, because they are patches of my life and of me. They tell something about who I was and who I am — but not all of it.

My Grandmother Hendrick was a special lady. She was *"Grandmother Johnann"* to some of us, *"Cousin Johnnie Ann"* to others, or *"Aunt John Anne"* to still others. She was the one person in the neighborhood that people would turn to in times of illness, death and tragedy. She had her own troubles, too, but she was always available. She was a very religious lady. The one thing she and I had in common was our love of God. She had her faults just as I have. I've never pretended to be perfect and neither did she. Things she did hurt me very deeply and hurt me for many years, yet she was probably the best example of a good woman I've ever known. She was a real missionary-type lady who loved people, loved God, and did all she could to serve Him. She was a very ambitious woman. For instance, she was the first one in our neighborhood to buy a cream separator (a machine which separated the milk from the cream). Ultimately, she sold the cream for a good price.

Grandfather Hendrick was a most interesting man. He could not read nor write, but he loved the Bible and could quote it better than anyone around. He had what we called a great *"remembrance."* He also loved my grandmother's church, the Primitive Baptist Church, but wouldn't join it. Grandfather was against all of their *"holiness"* (which my grandmother loved). Moreover, he enjoyed others reading the Bible to him. Scriptures seemed to stick to his mind like glue.

Grandfather Hendrick was known to be the stingiest man in the area. For added insurance he kept his money in silver dollars. (The silver dollars were placed in old cotton stockings hidden behind the headboard in the bedroom.) He didn't believe in banks. I guess he didn't think anybody knew where he kept his silver dollars hidden. But I learned in later years that two people did know — my sister and my father. He let them know about it, so my sister told me. Whenever Georgia Mae needed money, she could always get it. She would ask me sometimes if I needed anything to wear. Sometimes she would offer to buy me something extra special. I would say, *"Where are you going to get the money?"* And she would say, *"I'm going in grandfather's bag and I'm going to get some money out of it."* I would never have dared to do that, but she dared and I got a few new things. They were never expensive, because almost anything a poor person got in those days was inexpensive. But, I was grateful anyway just to get them.

Although Grandfather Hendrick was stingy and disliked farm work he had many good qualities. He was an excellent fisherman and he knew the best places to fish. People could fish in the same place as he did and they wouldn't catch a thing. But, grandfather would practically just pull the fish out of the water. He claimed he did it by spitting on his bait. Grandfather was creative, too. He loved to make beautiful baskets which he wove out of strips of white oak.

Grandfather raised Plymouth Rock and Rhode Island Red chickens and sold their eggs. He also raised several fancy breeds of chickens for the fun of it. When he sold his eggs, he always tried to get a higher price than anybody else. He wouldn't take anything as exchange for the eggs. Grandfather claimed his eggs were better, and sometimes people would actually pay his price. He just knew — he had a knack, you could say — how to get money and hold on to it.

Grandfather had one of the loveliest rose gardens I have ever seen — especially for those times. He loved roses, and seed companies used to send him color catalogs with pictures of light yellow, gold, red, and dark red roses. Grandfather would have Uncle Mitchell order this kind and that kind of rose from the catalogs. His rose garden was so beautiful that people would come from miles around to see it. The word would get out to go and see Uncle Warren Hendrick's roses.

My grandfather also kept a well groomed orchard with peaches, apples, walnuts, and two great pecan trees. He was particular about his pecan and fruit trees. He didn't want anybody to pull a peach until he pulled one off first. That was hard on us, because those peaches would start looking luscious long before he'd pick them. He should have given over the trees to us to pick when the fruit was ripe, but he didn't. We had to do so much hard work to keep his farm going, yet he begrudged us even **one** peach. But, my brothers were adventurous and determined. They would go through his orchard, find out which peaches were getting ripe and swipe some of them. Then grandfather would come up mad, so mad!

During the years I lived in Alabama, my family raised horses. My grandfather started it all. While I was still very small, my grandparents bought themselves a fancy two-seat carriage called a surrey. It was a beautiful surrey with upholstered seats, fringe around the top, and a long whip to goad the two horses. There were lap robes, too, that I loved to play with, except I was never allowed to. They had tigers embroidered on them, with real glass eyes. Those tigers' eyes fascinated my brothers and me more than the surrey itself.

When my grandparents got dressed up and went off somewhere in the surrey — and they would use their best horses — people would see them and say, *"That Mr. Hendrick has money."* It was true. Even though my parents were poor and we had to work very hard, my grandparents, as I've already stated, were fairly well-off. It is strange, now that I look back on it, to realize that my grandparents had enough money to own horses, a surrey, and help send my sister away to school, while the rest of us were poor and had to do hard work to get by.

I recall very well the day I went over to my grandparents' house and noticed how peculiar they acted when they finally let me in. Two or three chairs were covered over, but I knew there was something hidden. I knew something was going on. Then, I noticed some old dirty bags lying on the floor. Well, somehow I managed to see that what was covered up were piles of silver coins — quarters, half-dollars, and dollars. There were lots of them. And what my grandparents were doing, when I interrupted them, was counting their money! It upset them that I knew, and they told me, *"Don't you tell anybody that you saw this money here!"* Well, I had enough sense not to go around talking about it, but as of that day I thought, *"They do have money!"* I snickered to myself, laughed, and went on my way. I think that is when I had my first sense of what you call irony.

My sister, Georgia Mae, my brothers and I were all very close in age. George and Georgia Mae and Joe Frank, Jr. are now deceased. The three of us who remain are Jimmy Lee, Tommy Louis and myself. We all try to see each other as often as possible.

We called my older brother, Joe Frank, Jr., "Bae," because that is what Georgia Mae called him when he was a baby, when she was still too young to talk very well. Bae was the quietest of all. He was a good-hearted person who shared whatever he had. Other children, as well as adults in the community, would borrow things from him. Often, they would not return what they borrowed or pay him for what they owed, because they knew he wouldn't press them. He was just easy-going. At home, too, he was very kind and would easily yield in an argument rather than dispute someone.

Bae worked very hard in the fields. You could always depend on him. He would be the first one to jump up in the morning, bring in the water, and go do the chores. After Georgia Mae was married, he would ride a horse and visit her more than the rest of us. He just loved her baby boy and would bring him to stay at our house for a day or two. He even did the same for me when I was married and had my first child, my daughter Burnistine. When he was only twenty-one, he became seriously ill. The doctors were unable to determine the problem and he passed away. It was sad for us all.

Tommy Louis and Jimmy Lee were very close, real buddies to each other. They were the last two children, and Tommy, whom we called Louis, was younger. Even as young men, they bought their clothes together and dressed alike.

Louis, as a young man, sneaked off and joined the Civilian Conservation Corp (CCC) camp just before the Second World War. He would send my parents twenty-two dollars every month. They could then hire help for the farm for about ten dollars a month, which left them twelve extra dollars to purchase food items.

When Jimmy was seventeen, he hitchhiked his way to Anderson, Indiana, where he knew some people. Like Louis, he went off without telling my parents beforehand, so they wouldn't get upset about it. He, too, sent money home. After a year or two up North, he came home to help out on the farm. Later, Louis, also, came home to help the family. Finally, Jimmy couldn't take living in the South any longer and went back to Indiana, where he is now retired and living in Anderson.

Jimmy told me years later about his first experience of going to Indiana. He decided to leave Alabama with no preparation and few belongings. He left one night without saying a word to anyone. When he didn't come home that night, or the next night, or the next one, mom figured that Jimmy had left home and that he hadn't wanted her or dad trying to stop him. In Alabama it was not unusual for a boy to leave home. Some boys would settle for a conventional farm life — marriage and family. But not Jimmy.

He said he walked and walked and just figured out the right highways. At night he would get off the highway to keep people in cars from bothering him. He would walk out into a cotton patch on the side of the road and keep in the same direction. On one occasion, while walking through a field, he heard a couple of men talking. One of them said, *"I see somebody out there in the field."* *"Well let's shoot,"* said the other man. It was a pretty scary time for Jimmy, but he managed to get out of that situation and other situations like it. One night a man gave him a ride and directed him to an old, abandoned house where he could find shelter and sleep. But, when he got there he found hoboes. When he overheard the men discussing how they would rob him, he couldn't sleep. Later, he eased himself out of there and spent the rest of the night walking. Finally, he met a man who gave him a ride to Indiana.

Today, my brothers and I share a lot of laughs over the old days and some of the silly things we did. When they come down on me too hard I remind them that I learned faster than they, and this included Georgia Mae. For example, I learned to walk at an early age. In fact, before I could really walk, I could dance! My mother tells me she thought I was very smart, that I caught on fast to things and that I laughed a lot.

I do know that as a small girl, my family told me, *"You talk too much, you're too fast, you're too flip. Shut up!"* There was something driving within me even then. Whenever I was able to explain myself I would tell it like it was.

Now, looking back, my mother will say to me, *"You know, when you were young, I thought you were so fast. I thought you talked too much. Now I can see some of the results of your ideas that have come out of you in your lifetime. I guess all of that was working in you then, but, I didn't know it, because I never thought that you had so much going on in you."*

Well, I had a lot going on in me. And I still do. However, there is a difference now. Things that I had to keep inside me then can be released today — especially those things related to my older sister, Georgia Mae. Although she was not directly responsible, Georgia Mae was the cause of much of my childhood pain and anguish. Never! Never! Never will I understand why my family singled her out for the utmost in preferential treatment — sometimes to the detriment of my brothers and myself. Never will I be able to comprehend that. Never!

2.
Georgia Mae

Some women possess an inner beauty that seeps through their pores and radiates a loveliness that engulfs them and enraptures all who step into their realm. I have heard people call this "a glow." Even as a child, Georgia Mae possessed this rare gift, and it was hers until her death. My sister was a lovely child who became a beautiful woman. It is ironic that so many of the ugly feelings left over from my childhood revolves around her, when she, personally, personified love and beauty. Strange — but true!

There was a situation in our family that was not right. It had to do with the way my sister, Georgia Mae, was treated by my parents, compared to the way they treated my brothers and me. All of us kids, except for Georgia Mae, had to work hard in the fields and get our schooling from the few months we spent each year at the one-room school, Corner Flat. But, Georgia Mae never had to work in the fields. Also, my grandparents and my father sent her away to school where she could get a better education. This was completely unfair. My mother might suggest now and then that Georgia Mae should stay home and work with the rest of us, but no one listened to her.

"No — Georgia's going to go away and the rest of the kids will stay here and work the fields," is more or less what my father told her.

Well, mom would just sit down and accept it. She was the kind of woman and wife who never spoke up for herself or argued for what she believed in. Anyone who knew her and knew me in those days could probably tell I was **not** going to grow up to be like my mother. I could never be so passive and put up with things that weren't right. It was hard on me as a child to endure the unequal treatment given to Georgia Mae. But, even though I had to put up with the situation, that made me think for myself and probably helped make me a determined person and have great faith in the power of God.

If Georgia Mae got tired of one school, my father and grandparents would see to it that she went to another, a *"better"* one. She would visit us, now and then, but she was always invited to stay with friends in Montgomery and other places. She often got to travel on the train to visit other people. Sometimes Grandmother Hendrick would go away with her. It was an easy and enjoyable life that she led.

In contrast to the favoritism shown to Georgia Mae, I was aware that my brothers and I had to work in the fields, walk to our one-room, country school (four miles — one way) and never go traveling. As for clothes, most of the time I had to wear hand-me-downs which I was glad to get. I never experienced the pleasure of sitting around wearing nice, new clothes, going away to visit friends, or getting what I wanted. Georgia Mae, of course, couldn't do much about that even had she wanted to. This was very hard for me to accept. Sometimes I felt like Cinderella, even though I had but one sister.

It was this particular situation that taught me to pray. In my young days, my parents didn't allow us to express our unhappiness about anything. They would tell us to hush, that children were to be seen and not heard.

Georgia Mae could say, week after week, when she was home, *"I'm sick. I don't feel like going to the field. I don't want to go to work,"* and she would stay home.

I could never do that. When I was sick and really did feel bad I was told, *"You go on to that field."* So, I had to get up and go. I was only able to stay home if I was burning up with fever or truly showed sickness. This was true for my brothers, too. In fact, I was really one of the boys and was treated that way. I was never able to talk about it with my brothers, because they did not react to Georgia Mae's privileged treatment the way I did. After all, as boys and brothers they were all treated alike. If one of them got some blue jeans, all of them got some. They were satisfied. But I felt like the one who was denied.

My father would use the boys' money, mostly to buy my sister her dress material when she came home from school. The boys and I would work so hard to earn money by working for Cousin Clarance, and then dad would use the money to help pay for Georgia's tuition at school. He would tell me that he would send me away to school when I was old enough.

"When Georgia finishes school," he would say, *"I'm gonna send you to school."*

I was so happy thinking my day would come, but as time went on and on, I began to lose faith because my sister would stop going to one school and get sent to another.

I remember one summer, when times were hard, my father came home one night from a trip to Troy and brought back a beautiful piece of material. I thought, *"Oh, now that Georgia Mae is home with all her pretty clothes, I know that dad has bought this material for me."* Yet, when Georgia woke up, dad said to her, *"Did you see what I brought you?"*

Well, I was very hurt. As hard as I had worked and as many pretty clothes as Georgia Mae already had, even that piece of material, which was bought when money was scarce, was for her, not for me. I didn't want to let them see me cry. I went someplace to cry and pray, pray and cry.

Never could I feel within myself that my sister was that much better than I or that she should receive all the good things and I just be thought good only for my hard work and nothing else.

I said, *"God, I know that you know I'm here and I want you to bless me and one day do these same things for me. Let me be able to enjoy some of the beautiful things that my sister does."*

Some people may get the idea that I didn't like my sister or that I resented her. That is just a foolish notion. I want to make it clear that I loved my sister. I never held anything against her, because Georgia Mae was good to me. She was sweet. She wanted me to be happy and have nice things. Sometimes, she would get a chance to set aside some money while she was away at school and would buy a cute little hat or something and tuck it away in her bag and bring it to me. *"Look what I brought you, Bie!"* she'd exclaim. Since I was not able to have my hair done professionally like hers, the hat just didn't look good on me like her hats looked on her. She would also tuck away a little something for my brothers. She had a good heart and she would not let my parents know what she had done.

Because I was the daughter who was slighted and denied certain things, I was forced to look deep in my soul and find my strength, a strength which God gave me as I needed it. I turned to God as my guide. Being the favored daughter, Georgia Mae looked to things and to people for what she needed and wanted. So, she let others control her life. I let God control mine. But, we were loving sisters and at her request, she spent her last years with my mother and me in my home in California. So, even though I have brought up the Cinderella theme, let no one think Georgia Mae was like one of Cinderella's sisters, ugly and mean, or that I was like Cinderella, beautiful and passive.

In later years when Georgia Mae was home, she and I got together and decided on the material and style for our dresses. We would go to a local seamstress. Even though newspaper was hard to come by, we would get some, and the seamstress would cut out the pattern we indicated — you know, map out *something* from what we described and then make it. People thought we were the cutest and most well-dressed girls that were down there in Orion. We would have maybe a couple of dresses for the summer, and they would be worn mostly on what we called *"big days"*. We would figure out, too, what color shoes to wear with them. Those moments were happy times. There were happier moments to share as adults, but even as children, Georgia Mae and I had our good times together.

When Georgia Mae was about sixteen, she told my parents that she was tired of going to school. They were very disappointed to hear this, but she just said, *"I'm tired of it and I won't go to school anymore."* She never finished school; she just came home. I had gone as far in school as I could, since the school at Corner Flat only went through the sixth grade. I had been through the sixth grade twice (there wasn't much else I could do) and promoted to the seventh grade twice. So, I quit that foolishness of going over and over the same ground. I just stayed home, working on the farm and helping mother do chores. I pieced quilts in the wintertime and worked in the field in the summertime.

Well, the time came when Georgia Mae decided to get married. She was going to run away and get married to a man my parents had met, without letting them know. She said to me one day, *"I'm getting married, and I'm not going to tell mother and them that I'm getting married to this man, because I know they don't want me to. I'm gonna run off with him and get married."*

I said to her, *"Don't you think you've hurt our parents enough? They've been so good to you and I don't see how you could treat them like that. Why not let him ask for you, and if they don't give you up, then run away and get married if you must. Run away, walk off, or whatever you might call it."*

"No," she said. *"If I allow him to talk to them about it, then they will watch me, and I will have a harder time to get away. I can't do that. My idea is to just walk away."*

I said to her, *"You better tell them."*

Georgia Mae said, *"If you tell them I will know it, and a lot of trouble will come up and you will be the cause of it."*

Well, at this point I was afraid to say anything. I thought that if I did, my dad would probably get mad. He and the young man Georgia Mae intended to marry might have a real misunderstanding. I knew that the young man, Malachi Noble, was very high-tempered. I thought I'd better let it go, because Georgia Mae always had her own way anyhow. I decided to have nothing to say about it.

What I did say to Georgia Mae was, *"I have one request, then. I would like for you to do this for me. Be sure that he gets the license and brings it home and lets you see it and lets me see it so that I will know he's not playing around and just running off with you without marrying you. Then, be sure that he gets a minister right here in the neighborhood. Go to the preacher's home and get married there, so the family will be sure to be satisfied in knowing that you got married proper near home. Everyone will hear about this and the preacher will verify the fact that you are definitely a married woman. He will be able to say, 'I married them.' Do that for me. Do that for your mother and for your father so at least they will have that satisfaction."*

Of course, it came about that Georgia Mae ran off as she intended to. Before she got married, Georgia Mae cooked dinner while we were working. She was a beautiful cook. While she was staying at home cooking our dinner, she was also getting her clothes and things ready to leave and marry Malachi.

I remember the day she ran off. My grandparents were still alive, and it was a hard day for them as well as my parents. It was also certainly a hard day for me. Malachi came over that evening and Georgia went out of the house to see him. My father knew she had run off as soon as he learned that evening that she had left. Georgia Mae had just tiptoed out earlier. As soon as my dad realized what had probably happened, he was very upset. Now I had guessed, too, what was going to happen that evening when Malachi and his nephew came to our house. I went to bed in order to be off the scene. When dad realized that Georgia Mae was gone, instead of fussing at my brothers he fussed at me.

"I believe you knew it," he said. *"I believe you knew it!"* He didn't allow me to say a word.

Dad didn't give me a chance to talk. I couldn't even have lied about it, if I'd wanted to.

Dad kept saying, *"I've a good mind to whip you. Oh, I am trying my best to keep from beatin' you to death! Oh, if I put my hands on you. You knew she was gonna leave tonight!"*

Dad carried on something terrible. My brothers were afraid he was going to beat me half to death. I laid there in the bed shaking, afraid that he would begin to beat me.

I thought to myself, *"It's just like Georgia Mae said it would be."* If dad had known she was going to run off and get married, he would probably have caused trouble with her husband, and it would have been a big fight. For Malachi was quite a few years older than Georgia Mae, perhaps about thirty years old, while she was about eighteen. But, Malachi was also a very brave man and he had a lot of Indian blood in him. He had high cheekbones, stood more than six feet tall, and was a real nice-looking fellow.

Malachi was also a man that drank some, and was the kind of man who carried his gun with him. He would have it laying on the seat of the car wherever he went. He didn't take any kind of foolishness from anyone. He had an outright way of talking to white people, as if he were saying, *"Now listen here So and So."* That's the way he carried on. He had been born in a place called Midway, Alabama, and he was known to be a very fearless man.

Dad carried on all evening, but by the next day he had calmed down. He got up early, got on his horse and rode off. He went riding around in the neighborhood and finally heard for himself that Georgia Mae had indeed run off and gotten married, but that she had been married right here in the neighborhood. When I heard that, I thanked God that Georgia had followed my advice and that my parents and grandparents at least knew that she was truly married.

Now, I have to digress a bit to talk about The Burial Aid Society, because the next time I was to see Georgia Mae would be at a meeting of that society. A Mr. Bob Lane from Troy had set up the society some years earlier. Mr. Lane, a black man, went to practically every church in our area and to every school, wherever he could get a group of people together to set up this little club. I was told he couldn't read or write, but he could get people organized. Wherever there was a chapter of this society set up, people would get together every so often and collect the money it cost each one to belong. Mr. Lane did quite well by it. It cost twenty-five cents a month for a grown-up and fifteen cents a month for a person under eighteen. This was really a good thing, because it gave our people some way to bury their dead. It provided for a cheap funeral and burial, which cost about fifty dollars for an adult and thirty dollars for a child. It also paid for a cheap casket.

I was the secretary for the children's department of our Burial Aid Society, so my family didn't have to pay for me. My dad was the treasurer for our local club and we would have a meeting of the society on the third Sunday of every month. We would also have meetings that were like conventions that were held at different places. The president of each club would be our representative at these conventions. Because I was secretary for the children's department, I had a chance to go to places like Brundage, Alabama and other little outings. My travel back and forth would be paid as well as my room (we would board with someone in their home). So, I enjoyed these few opportunities to travel away from home. I was glad that I was able to keep the books for our little club.

It was the third Sunday of the month, about three weeks after Georgia Mae had run off, and we were having a meeting of the Burial Aid Society at the one-room school. My dad was there and that's when Georgia Mae came back. I was so happy to see her that my eyes filled with tears. Her husband was with her as they walked into our meeting, laughing. When my dad saw her, he just hung his head and looked sad. He wanted her to feel sorry for him, sorry for how she had hurt him. But, Georgia didn't seem to feel a bit sad about it. She now had her husband to protect her. They could also just get into Malachi's car and drive off if they had to, and dad probably knew that.

I thought to myself that dad would at least say, *"You certainly have hurt us by marrying and not telling us a word."* But, dad had nothing harsh to say to her about it from that day until the end of his life. The only person he was harsh to was me, so I learned then that maybe I was put here to take a few hard knocks. Believe me, I have really taken a lot of them, right on the chin, but, I've just kept on stepping.

Well, after the meeting Georgia Mae, Malachi and I got into Malachi's car and went home to surprise my mother. After Georgia Mae had gone in and spoken to mom, we all later went to my grandparents' house. Grandmother was sick, but she was so happy to see Georgia Mae, because even though she was used to Georgia Mae doing whatever she wanted, she felt that her running off and getting married was the last straw. We were all relieved that things had turned out better than they might have and no one, of course, would have held out very long against my sister. She had just had her own way with them too many times not to have it now.

After she had been married about a year and a half, Georgia Mae got pregnant. It was during this pregnancy that Georgia Mae was related to another painful experience in my life. One day when she was very heavy with her child, Georgia Mae came to visit grandmother. I went to grandmother's with her. When we arrived, we found company sitting around the yard that late Sunday afternoon. I knew how grandmother liked to rave over my sister. After we arrived, I felt in my heart that grandmother would say something that would embarrass me. She always had a way of saying how *"much"* she loved my sister. She would say all the time, *"I just love that one so much 'til I would just fight any of the other kids about this one grandchild of mine."* She talked without thinking about all the work we did for her.

I had hidden myself in the house so no one could see my embarrasment. Then, I heard one of the ladies say to grandmother, *"You don't know what all the kids are going to have to do for you, and I just don't think you should say that."*

"Well, I'm telling the truth," Grandmother Johnann replied. *"This is the way I feel."*

And, I must say she was honest enough to tell it like it was, even though I was hurt and really embarrassed by it. Grandmother Johnann never lived to see her first, great-grandson born — she died about a month before.

When her son was about two years old, Georgia Mae and her husband started having marital problems. Several times she left him, but he always came after her and took her home. Later on, she and her husband had three more children. One of them lived only a few hours after birth. Another child, a girl, now lives here in California. Now, when her fourth child was about a month old, Georgia Mae lost her husband in a very tragic way.

We were never able to find out all the details of what happened to Malachi, so we had to piece the details we had together as best we could. When Georgia Mae and Malachi got married, they went to live in Lynwood, Alabama, However, at the time of his death, Malachi was working in a place near Troy. He would work the week in Troy and then go home for the weekend.

Malachi was a drinking man, and it seems that he had gone to a beer saloon on his way home for the weekend. The story goes that he got into an argument with some white men. Malachi was not afraid of anybody, White or Black, and I suppose that drinking might have made him even more fearless. The report we got was that he pulled out of the argument and left the saloon, but, for some reason or other he went back inside. When he did, a white man shot him in the stomach several times. Some of the other men picked Malachi up, put him in his own car, and another white man drove him to the hospital in Troy in his car. The man left him in the car there and disappeared. No one knew who brought Malachi and his car there. He was operated on right away, and word was sent to Georgia Mae that her husband was in the hospital in Troy.

The next day, Georgia Mae managed to get somebody to take her to Troy. When she got to the hospital, Malachi had regained consciousness, but he was so sick he couldn't talk. Georgia Mae said to him, *"Are you hurt bad?"* He could only reply by bowing his head. Soon afterwards he died.

Georgia Mae now had to go back to the house from which she had run away. My mother and father took her and her three children in to live with them. (By this time, I was married and living in my own place.) Georgia Mae lived with them for two years or so. During this time a cousin of ours, who was living in Detroit, came back to visit her family. Georgia Mae asked our cousin if she could go live with her in Detroit until she could get a job and make a home for herself and her children. Our cousin readily said, *"Yes,"* provided Georgia Mae would leave her children with my parents until she got settled. Georgia Mae begged mom to accept this plan and promised that as soon as she had a job she would send for her children and our parents. She wanted to take mom and dad out of the fields and bring her children to Detroit where they could receive a good education. And, this is what she finally succeeded in doing.

When she went to live in Detroit, there were lots of people who admired her beauty and her warm personality. I knew it would be that way and I also figured that it would be easy for her to find another husband.

Well, one day I received a letter from her. *"Bie,"* she wrote. *"I met a man that I love. There is also another man who loves me very much, and I know he would make a good husband and a good father. He is somebody I know wouldn't give me any problems. But, the guy that I seem to think I really love — well, I have no faith in him. But, I am going to get married, and I'm wondering what I should do — already having three children. I know I'm the type to have more children. What would you do?"*

I wrote back that she should do her best to forget the man she thought she loved but had no confidence in. I said, *"Try your best to find love and admiration for the one that you have faith in and know will be nice to you and your children. He would be a better choice than someone who is not dependable. You are not a teenager! Think about your future and the fact that you have children to raise. You have another problem, too. You're going to have our parents live with you to care for your children while you work. They'll need to be able to live in peace. I would think about loving someone who would love me and would be good to my family."*

That is the gist of what I wrote to her. Georgia Mae was a long time in writing me back, but when she did, she wrote: *"I thought about what you said and I'm working on it. I'm going to marry the fellow who loves me."* She sent me his picture and it was one of a nice-looking man. She married him soon after and I had the most lovely brother-in-law that anybody could ever want. Sure enough, the two of them sent for Georgia Mae's children and my mother, and later my father went to Detroit, too.

Georgia Mae and her new husband soon had a child, a girl. Altogether, their marriage produced three children. My brother-in-law was a good husband and a good father. Georgia Mae couldn't have done better in selecting herself a mate. They had a beautiful home and, in time, came to live fabulously well.

On April 21, 1977, Georgia Mae's life came to an end. Several years earlier, she had come to live in California with one of her daughters. She had come to live with her for the rest of her life, but somehow she grew unhappy and came to me one day and said, *"Bie, I want to live with you and mother."* Georgia Mae had been ill for three or four years from a stroke. So, she came and lived with me until her death. She developed cancer and we knew for a year or better that she had it. And now, as I write this book, my mother, an old lady in her nineties, is still alive and living with me. But, my beautiful sister is gone.

For Georgia Mae, the beautiful child we all loved, the ball had come to an end. Many of the other dancers are gone, too, and for me, who felt like a Cinderella, the ball goes on, with beautiful and wonderful people coming to dance with me. The music keeps changing and like Cinderella, I do not know what will happen next. I miss the other dancers. But, right now the music keeps playing. As a person who has kept on stepping, I am going to hold all those dear ones in my heart and in my memory because with the help of God, that's what I've learned to do best!

3.
Hard Work

I am no stranger to hard work. In the backwoods of Southern Alabama hard work and hardship were constant companions. My parents' farm was what we called a *"three-horse farm."* Grandfather Hendrick had at least a one-and-a-half-horse farm — sometimes a two-horse farm. Cousin Clarence Farrier had a little over a one-horse farm, too, with a mule as well. It was very hard taking care of those three farms.

We put in a lot of hours and endured a lot of discomfort to get almost nothing. But, that was our way of life. We would start preparing the ground and planting sometime in March. The first thing we had to do was to arrange to get money to start farming. We needed money all along to buy some of the things we couldn't do without, such as equipment for the fields, seed, plow points, and gear for our horses and other livestock. Sometimes, we wouldn't have enough feed for the livestock, so we had to buy that. Getting that money was the first goal. The owners of those farms, the *"boss man,"* would lend us the money which they referred to as *"letting you have money to run your crop."* We would also need money to purchase sugar, flour, shortening, meat, and those other necessary items that our family required and would run short on. The owner — in our case, Dr. Murphy — would let us have a little money each month, for maybe four or five months, while we were *"making the cotton."*

"Making the cotton" was the term we used for growing the cotton, corn and other crops to maturity. When the corn had grown enough that we could begin to pick what we call *"roasting ears"* (corn that was ready to eat), the owner would cut off the money. But, by then we would start picking the cotton and could sell the cotton seed and buy the things we needed. The boss-man, of course, would take much of the cotton in payment for what we owed him, since that's what made the real money.

During those days, black people who rented the farms had to deal with the fact that no bookkeeping was kept.We would have to go along with what the boss-man claimed we owed him. Many times the boss-man claimed we owed him a lot more than we actually did. All this went against us. Many people had everything taken away from them, because the boss-man pretended they owed him more than was the case. That was typical of the kind of thing we were up against throughout my years in Alabama.

I can remember when my dad would say, *"Oh, cotton is such a good price now!"* They considered twenty-five cents a pound as the best price in history when we were farming. Only seldom would the cotton sell at this price. It would usually sell for fifteen or eighteen cents a pound — or less. I would hear folks complaining. *"Cotton is so low now. We can't get nothing for it. We're not even gonna come out of debt this time."* Families had to go up against very trying times. Many people had large families and many times the larger families had the tougher time.

When it was cotton picking time, we would pick the cotton and take it to the gin mill. The mill would **thresh** the seed from the cotton and then it would be baled. Once the seed was removed and the cotton was baled, we would be left with five-hundred pounds or so of lint or plain cotton which would be ready to be put on the market.

We would also have the cotton seed and it could be put to many uses. For example, some of the seed might be used for cattle feed. It could be sold to be processed into cotton seed oil and other products. So, while the boss-man made his big profit off the baled cotton, we would take our earnings from the remaining bales we sold as well as the cotton seed sales. We would pay off as many of our creditors as we could — the merchant who sold us fertilizer, the boss-man for what he lent us in order to make our cotton crop, as well as the rent for the farm. Nearly all of our hard earned money went to pay our debts and if we had done well enough, we could pay off all of the debts that we owed. If we didn't make enough money the balance of the debts would be added to the next year's expenses, so we'd owe even more.

We also had our corn to provide us with food for our own needs. We would remove the husks from the ripe corn, shell the kernels from the ear and bag them. Then, we would take the kernels to the corn mill to be ground into meal, mainly to make cornbread. But, we would have to buy our flour (wheat flour), because we didn't raise wheat in that part of the country. So, between the cotton and the corn, we would manage with hard work and good luck to pay our debts and have a basic food commodity. Sometimes, we even had some money to buy food items we couldn't raise for ourselves and money for other small expenses.

Cotton simply dominated our lives and economy. If the boll-weevils were very active, the crop output would be much less. (We used a kind of soda to spread in the fields. It would make the cotton grow faster and work against the boll-weevil.) When picking cotton, I would prick my skin and my fingers, especially around the fingernails. My fingers would get very sore. I will also never forget how my back would pain me from being bent over picking cotton all day long. I can remember many little children wearing flour or cornmeal sacks on their heads to protect themselves from the hot sun. Their mothers would take empty, twenty-five pound, flour and cornmeal bags and wash the flour and cornmeal dust from them. They would then roll the sack down like paper bags just deep enough to put on the children's heads for hats. We would get up picking cotton and go to bed picking cotton. Day after day, week after week, we would pick cotton and usually have little to show for it when it was all over.

In fruit season, we would go out into the woods looking for blueberries and blackberries. Sometimes, we would go miles away from home to find them. We would go and pick them, making sure not to mix them, and bring them home. The blackberries were easier to find than the blue-berries. We would gather pails and pails of berries, take them home and can them in jars. Canning was a big activity while it lasted. We would save all our jars from one season to the other and my parents would usually manage to buy more as well. We would can the berries whole, but some-times mom would make jams and jellies out of them. The berries of course were one of the foodstuffs that we preserved for our winter need.

Then there were the chickens. Raising them was not always too successful. Sometimes, mom would have good luck raising them. As time went on, she learned how to raise them properly. She learned how to keep the chickens up off the ground. Somebody also showed her how to make a food mix for the baby chicks with the proper biddy mash and such things. So, she eventually was able to raise chickens successfully.

Now, I must confess that I was never good at raising chickens. I tried my hand at it when I was first married. What few chickens I did raise were fat and very wild. I could hardly ever catch one whenever I wanted one for dinner. (They were very smart, I must say.) But, my husband and I had a little dog that solved this problem. All I had to do was show that dog which chicken I wanted and he would chase that chicken until he caught it. That was the way I would get my chicken for dinner.

During the summer, when the water would get very low in the well and start running muddy, we would go to the artesian wells in the neighborhood to get our water. We were blessed to have artesian wells in our community. They ran the most beautiful, clear, white water. I guess they had been running like that for thousands of years. The water just ran and ran in them, clear and clean. Anybody could use them. People who were very old and had lived in that area all their lives said those wells had been running ever since they could remember.

The two artesian wells that I knew in my childhood were close to where we lived. They had a settling pond around them, so when our wells ran dry in the summer, we would not only carry our drinking water from these wells, but we would take our clothes, our washpots, everything that needed washing, and wash them there at the wells and the pond. Other people would also come with their loads of clothes and children and do the same as we did.

I am sorry to say that those artesian wells have been allowed to deteriorate since my childhood. People down in Orion have told me that the woods have grown up thick around the wells, and the iron pipes through which the water used to run have all rotted away. Now what remains is an old, dark pond of water, spread out so wide that you can't tell where the water for it comes from. And the road is so overgrown that it's hard to go back in there. It's a shame this has happened to those wells, but they are still there and in my memory they run fresh and clear.

Some grown-up was always saying to us, *"Don't go in the cane patch, don't get no sugar cane yet or the cane's not ready to eat."* Once in a while my brothers would go into the cane patch, break down some cane and eat it. They would try to find a place where no one could detect their intrusion. Some of the old folks would catch on by seeing where they had broken off a few stalks of cane. They would get after them, but my brothers would deny it. My father would get so mad — mostly because they denied doing what they had done — and give them a good whipping.

My brother, Jimmy, was always doing things he had no business doing. On several occasions I remember, he would admit to what he'd done. *"Yes, I did that, I sure did that,"* he'd say, and he would get a real silly look on his face. As he told me in later years, *"I would tell them I had done something I shouldn't have, because I knew that they had caught me, so I might as well admit it."*

My brothers worked very hard, even though they were boys, and I think getting into trouble now and then by stealing grandfather's peaches or breaking into Aunt H. and Uncle Henry Williams' cane patch was their way of letting off steam and grabbing some enjoyment for themselves — in spite of the consequences. All three of my brothers were clever and always finding new ways to do things. They just sort of worked together easy, like a team. I remember they trained two steers to pull a plow and wagon. I don't know quite how they managed it, but they did. They would put the same working gear on the steers as they did on the horses. Those steers would work in the same capacity as the horses! My brothers used those steers to do a lot of the work on the farm instead of the horses, so the horses got quite a bit of rest. The boys even learned to ride those steers bareback.

I recall a tragic thing that happened to those two steers. In the South, we had severe rainstorms with the sharpest lightning and the loudest claps of thunder. It was so frightening that when we had a thunderstorm, I wanted to get away from our raggedy house. You could look up at the sky through the holes in the roof and see the lightning zig-zag through those black swirling clouds. The lightning would zig-zag through the house, too, while the thunder would rumble and rattle so loud that the house shook. It was so frightening that I would run and hide underneath the bed. Well, after one such terrible rainstorm, a bad one filled with lightning, my brothers went out to look for any damage. Out in the field, they found that both steers they loved dearly had been killed. They were standing by a tree when lightning struck. We were all upset and it increased my fear of bad storms. I don't believe I can adequately express the terror I felt during those storms. I am glad to report that since I left Alabama to live in the North and later on the West Coast, that the storms don't seem to sound nearly as bad as they did in the South.

I have only partially indicated the nature of the never ending and tiring work we had to do when I was a child. Of course, we were not exceptional in having to work hard and being poor. Because there was so much hard work in my childhood in addition to all kinds of unfairness and bad times, I was determined to make my life better. I knew, even very early in my life, that I could only improve my life with God's help.

Not so long ago, I bought a Rolls-Royce, a beautiful car that I love riding in, something I wouldn't have dreamed of owning fifty years ago when I was still filling a cotton sack. But, I am a true believer, and I'm still learning more and more how to trust in God for everything I want; for all good things come from Him. Ask whatever you will and have faith, and it will come. So, I want to make it clear that I didn't only ask God to show me how to escape poverty and what kind of business to get in, but I even asked Him to give me a Rolls Royce — to make it possible for me to get it, to show me the way. And I want to report, right now, before I write another word, that He showed me the way. He opened the door and blessed me so that I could pay **cash** for it and I'm truly thankful. It lets me know more and more, and makes me testify more and more to the fact that God is able to do anything to give you the desires of your heart, if you trust in Him and really believe in Him.

I'm always going to hold up his name and tell the people who hear me that God will deliver you and deliver the things into your hands that you want, if you trust in Him. Not just one thing will He deliver, but all things. He'll deliver you anything you want, as long as it is something good and you're not hindering or hurting your fellow man. He will bless you with it, if you want it. Trust in Him, and *"Do unto others as you would have them to do unto you."*

I can't say any of this too often, because I know that so many people want to believe it, but they hold back — just hold on and accept this wonderful truth. Whatever you want is not too big for God. Just *"call him up"* and tell Him what you want. Just have faith, have patience. He will not answer you the very moment you ask Him, but just have patience and continue to look forward to having what you want. It will happen one day, in it's own time, and it will be on time, in time, and at the right time.

Personally, I know that it is faith in God that is the most important thing. But, you must be willing to work for what you want. You've got to be willing to work and keep on working and keep on keeping the faith — working and going in the right direction. You can't work and throw away your money. I must keep stressing that. You can't have your cake and eat it too. You can't get the Rolls-Royces, Cadillacs and all these material things and at the same time spend all of your money on the roulette table in Las Vegas. You've got to make sacrifices and you've got to do very positive things. You can't spend your money on uppers and downers and get your head all mixed up so that you can't think clearly and just end up doing a lot of silly things. You've got to be a positive person, thinking and doing the right thing, and treat your body right so your head will think right. You can't maneuver too well when your head isn't right; your mind needs to be clear. Also, you can't do too well when your heart isn't right or when you're doing mean things to somebody else and trying to outsmart somebody for their things. For instance, not paying your bills, getting more than you can pay for, trying to slip and slide and rip somebody off, and trying to be slick — that won't pay.

Yes, I know what it is to work hard and to be tired. I know, too, that hard work can be rewarding. It's not enough, however, just to work hard and keep your eyes to the ground. You've got to look up and look ahead. You've got to trust in God and listen to His voice, take His direction. Like many others, I dared to look up from my hoe. I trusted God. I walked away from that cotton patch. It took hard work to do that, but I kept on. *Keep on steppin'* is the way I like to put it. I will always keep on stepping. When you listen to God, you can do it. You can look up from your hoe, from whatever kind of cotton patch you are in, and with your hard work step right on to something better.

4.
Home Life

"Into every life a little rain must fall" . . . I don't remember where I first heard this adage, but it has always stuck with me. Believe me, it is true! I don't think that any of us is privileged or special enough to leave here unscathed. Like wounded soldiers, we all nurse our battle scars through this some-times long and hard journey called life. Nothing is all one way in anybody's life. Life is a series of ups and downs, hits and misses, mountains and valleys, hills and dales — and for many of us — a long stretch of rocky roads. The magical key is to persevere, to keep putting one foot in front of the other until you get where you want to go. I know because that is what I did. Today, my life is enriched with lots of sunshine, and I thank God for it. I'm not just referring to California weather, because even here in Holmby Hills it rains on occasion. I thank God for that, too, along with the birds, trees, flowers and all that grows. Rain can't be avoided, but what you make of it is up to you.

I was about four years old when we left our first house. Well, the truth is we really didn't leave that house. It left us! What happened was one of the first of several disasters that occurred during my childhood.

Now, this house that I lived in was quite small. It had a large room with a fireplace which we used as a living room and bedroom, a kitchen and a porch. The porch was partitioned into two parts with one part serving as a large clothes closet. The main room contained all our furniture, including two beds, a dresser, a washstand and several chairs. Most of the furniture had been given to my mother by her sister and brother-in-law when she got married.

There was a small creek between this house and the one next door. That house next door eventually became the house we lived in through-out my childhood.

As I remember, early one morning my daddy went into the clothes closet on the porch of our first house to look for something, while momma was getting breakfast ready. We were still in bed. Since we didn't have electricity, daddy used a lamp in order to see. He tended to be careless about things quite often, and on this occasion he somehow set something on fire in the clothes closet. It was a smoldering fire which he failed to notice. By the time anyone did notice, that little room on the front porch was all on fire with a lot of smoke coming out.

There was a lot of commotion and my parents were concerned about getting us out of there. They managed to get us out, and my mother hollered at us not to go near it. Daddy began to bring water from the branch in a bucket. We children were too small to be of any help, and the fire got ahead of him and moved so fast that the house burned up. We lost everything!

Mom stood by the ashes, crying and crying. I recall her crying, but I also recall how beautiful she looked, even at such a time as that. My mother was a very pretty women. She came from a family known for its good-looking people. My grandfather and father both used to tell me, as did other people, that she was one of the country's most beautiful girls. My girlfriends would tell me later on that they thought my mother was one of the two most beautiful women in the neighborhood. The other woman was my cousin, Vinnie, Cousin Clarence's sister-in-law. Cousin Vinnie was dark-skinned and my mother was light-skinned. I had never really thought about who was the prettiest woman in our community, until my friends began to mention it. I did know my mother was a pretty women and I also knew that Cousin Vinnie was a beautiful woman. She also had a family of about six or seven children, most of them girls. She had two sons, and one of them looked almost exactly like her. Sometimes a child does not look like his parents. I know that I, for one, did not. I am not good-looking the way my mother is.

With our house burned down and all our possessions gone, we went to live with my grandparents. We had nothing to move, so we walked right into Grandmother Johann's home. Grandfather Hendrick didn't object. People gave us a few things as time went by. I was too young to remember who gave what to us. Momma would look at some little thing and say, *"Cousin This one gave me that, and Miss So-and-So gave me this."* People would send word to come by their house because they had something for us. We got some old beds together and a few other things. Eventually, we moved into the house that we called Tolbert House, because it was where one of my grandfather's half-brothers had lived. It was Uncle Fred Tolbert's former house we moved into, next door.

Our new house was an old farmhouse. It was really a very old shack. The roof was covered with rough, handmade shingles. You could see the sunlight through that roof and you could catch the rain through it, too. Sunlight or rain, they came right through. When it did rain, we would have to move the beds out of the way as best we could and set pots and kettles around to catch the dripping water (which always managed to leak on the stove). Well, if you could see the sunlight through the roof, you could see the ground through the floorboards. And, not only did rain come through the roof, but cold air came up through the cracks in the floor — especially in the winter. The house sat on four corner blocks that were made of sawed-off logs, so it was fairly high off the ground. It had four rooms originally, with two fireplaces. Later in my childhood, my father added two more rooms, a kitchen and a dining room. We used a water based paint called "Kemtone" to paint inside the entire house, which made it look better. It was a house that was muggy and hot in the summer and cold and drafty in the winter. Even though we had two fireplaces and a cookstove, we mostly kept warm in the winter with lots of quilts and blankets. I lived in that house until I got married.

I have discussed helping our Cousin Clarence Farrier with his farm-work and being paid by him. Well, the money he paid us would help us pay for clothes we sometimes ordered through the Sears Roebuck catalog. We mostly did our shopping through the Sears catalog. Georgia Mae and I would buy material to make our clothes and my brothers would buy blue jeans, white jeans, duck caps, and polo shirts that buttoned down the front and had short sleeves. The boys would also get little white tennis shoes — I would too — and we thought white looked clean for the summer and for church-going.

My mother was always particular about her things, whatever little she had, and would try to keep them in good condition. One thing that was her pride and joy was a pretty little oil lamp with a pretty shade on it. We all thought it was pretty. It was made to look somewhat like a lamp with a Tiffany shade. To tell the truth, it was just a plain lamp with a milk-glass shade that had ordinary coloring on it, anything but a Tiffany. Well, mom had gone someplace one day and when she came back home the lamp-shade was broken. I was about seven at the time. I guess my brothers had been playing around, little boys being little boys, and had accidentally broken the lampshade. I didn't even notice or even know that the lamp-shade was broken, but mom came home and noticed it right away. After all, that little lamp was the only lamp she had that looked like anything special.

Mom began raising sand. She would always get angry when anything that was especially hers was disturbed. *"Which one of you kids broke my lampshade?"* she hollered. *"I'm going to whip all of you 'til you tell the truth."* There she was, carrying on, and we were all scared. I was definitely not going to say anything, because I didn't know who did it. Even though I was as likely as anyone to get whipped, I would have taken it, because I didn't know who broke the lamp. So, there was mom, her lampshade broken, just blazing away. She finally got the strap, or switch, or whatever she was going to use to whip us, and that really scared all four of us (Georgia Mae was away at school at the time). I preferred to get a whipping with the strap, if I had to get one, than with one of those peach tree switches, because those keen switches really hurt. And momma had a way of sticking your head between her knees and what she did to your backside — it really hurt! She was young then and could really lay it on you.

My oldest brother, Bae, who was a little bit easy going and easily frightened, said, *"Well, Bie did it. Bie broke that shade."* I guess he said it in order to save himself and my brothers. But, if mom had been using her head, she would have realized that if he could not tell the truth until after she got angry and got out the switch, *he* probably was the one that did it. Still, she grabbed me and gave me the whipping of my life. So, even though I had nothing at all to do with that lampshade getting broken, I was the one that got the whipping.

As with other children growing up in most families, life was full of ups and downs. We got our whippings, and had our chores. One pleasant memory I have is of our pet goat, Billy. He was black and white and we could sometimes ride him. Billy would get so tired of us always pestering and playing with him that we'd have to work to catch him. We would get on his back and he would go running to the house. He wouldn't give us time to get off, so when he got close to the house we would have to hold our hands up so they would hit the house, and that would slide us off the goat. He knew exactly how to get us off, too. Sometimes, he would come up on the porch and we would get on his back. Then, Billy would run to the edge of the porch and jump down. We'd have to grab the bannister in order to stay on the porch and keep him from jumping off with us. That goat didn't have a care at all and he had no class about trying to protect you. Even so, we loved Billy and we kept him until we were too big to ride him at all. I think Billy was glad of that. By that time we were big enough to ride the horses. We had plenty of horses to ride. We finally gave Billy away to a family that had some small children so that they could have pleasure with him.

There were lots of nice things that we enjoyed on our farm. One of them was syrup-making time. We would grow our sugar cane and when it was time to harvest it, we had to do what was called *"stripping the cane."* That wasn't too much fun, getting off all the leaves and branches, but once it was stripped and cut down, we would cart it to the syrup mill. It seemed that we were travelling in one big circle, from the cane field to the mill and back again. Like the horses and the mules, we became obedient travellers of the same weather beaten paths.

At the mill, each of the barrels would be covered with a kind of bag, and the juice would pour out of the cane, as it was crushed, ground and strained through the bags into the barrels. When a barrel was filled, we would pour its contents into a great big kettle. There was fire under the kettle as hot as a furnace, which we fed with wood. After a while, the cane juice would begin to boil. As the juice was cooked, a heavy foam would form on the top and we had to keep skimming that off into another barrel that sat near the kettle. So, we would keep boiling the cane juice and skimming it, and it would boil and boil and gradually turn into a real thick syrup that people liked to use on their pancakes. We also loved the cane juice that went into the barrel right after the cane was crushed. That would make a nice cold drink.

Another good time in our life on the farm was in the fall when we killed our beef cattle and hogs and dressed the meat. Before it was time to butcher, we would make a pen large enough off the ground and out of the mud so that they would stay clean. The pigs were treated very nicely at this point. There would even be sawdust on the floor of the pen. We would leave a trough in the pen all the time and just overfeed the pigs. We would give them corn galore to fatten them up. That way we could get more lard from them. It was beautiful to see our hogs get real fat and lazy. They would eat, lay down, roll, huff and puff. We would wait until the weather got cold enough to kill them. We would tell our mother that we had been to the pen and noticed that such and such pig (we had names for each of them) is looking just so. We couldn't feed them enough!

At last the morning would come when my daddy would say, *"I think it's cold enough now to kill the hogs. I think I'll go out and get Clarence Farrier to come and help."* Dad would go and get Cousin Clarence and also another man, a preacher, who lived in the neighborhood. When I say he lived in the neighborhood, that doesn't mean he lived nearby. He actually lived some distance away, but what we called our neighborhood took in a big area of country and farms and we thought of ourselves as neighbors.

My dad and the others would get a big kettle, like the one we boiled syrup in, and fill it with water and keep it boiling. They would put a little pot ash in it also to help take off hair. But, now that it was time to kill the hogs and do the butchering, we were a little sad. We hated, in one way, to see the hogs get killed. On the other hand, we were glad to think we would soon have fresh meat. In those days, we couldn't run off to the store and buy porkchops, sausage, spareribs, and all that. It was once a year when we killed the hogs and got all our meat ready.

On the morning he picked to kill the hogs, dad would get his twenty-two rifle. They would let a hog out of the pen, one at a time, let it walk around, while my dad took aim. The hog would walk around very slowly, because it was so fat it could hardly move. When dad had the hog in the right position, he would aim right between its eyes and fire. The hog would fall over, kick, lay there and die. Then, they would grab the hog by its front legs and stab it in the heart, because it was important to have the hog bleed so that the meat would taste good. I would try to go about my business and not look, because I hated seeing the hogs killed.

After my dad had killed the hog, two or three men would grab it and put it into the boiling water to make the hair come off. He would bring out another hog to be shot. So, while the hogs were being killed, one by one, those that were put into the boiling water could then be strung up. They would run a cord through the hind feet of the hog and hang each one up over a hole in the ground. Then a man who knew how to do it well would open up their stomach and start dressing them. They would remove all the insides, the intestines and organs, and put them in a big tub that was placed under each hog. And, they would clean all the hair off the carcass. Then they would put the carcass on a big table and cut it up. There would be a lot of fat to trim. Cutting off the fat and drying the lard was a big job in itself. And a lot of people would be helping to do all this.

Several people would cook the dinner. They would cook up a lot of backbones, spareribs, and yams, and then we would have a great big feast.

So, it was a very exciting and enjoyable time, although it did seem too bad we had the feast at the expense of the hogs.

Then, we cleaned the intestines for our chitlins and sausage. It would take us several days to do all of this, grinding up the meat for sausage, seasoning it with all the spices and stuffing it into the cleaned intestines. We used a machine to stuff the sausage. Afterwards, we would hang the sausages up in the smokehouse, make a little fire with hickory wood that would produce a lot of smoke underneath them, and smoke them until we had the best sausages you ever tasted. My mother and grandmother knew just exactly what to do. They seasoned the sausages in certain ways, using red pepper and sage along with other spices.

Dad and the others would pack that meat away and salt it down and cover it up on those cold days. They would let it stay three or four weeks. Then, they would know when to wash all the heavy salt off and hang the meat up in the smokehouse and let it cure. The result of all that was to be seen in the sausages, hoghead cheese, hams, and bacon that we had.

We also enjoyed going rabbit and squirrel hunting. It was the kind of work that was fun. We didn't have to do too much to go rabbit hunting, because the rabbits seemed to grow at our back door, almost. They were the easiest game for my brothers to hunt and kill. The big trouble they had was in getting gun shells. The shells were cheap, but we had little money. Mom would manage to gather enough eggs and would take them to the store and get shells in exchange. When my brothers did kill a rabbit or two, mom would say, "Go take Miss So and So a rabbit." So, they caught rabbits and mom often gave them away mostly, I think, because she didn't like rabbit. I never went rabbit hunting because I didn't know how to use a rifle. But my brothers always got more than enough. The only other time we had fresh meat was when we butchered our beef cattle and hogs, had a chicken or caught fresh fish. Whenever we did our butchering we would always take some of the fresh meat and send it to our neighbors. If one neighbor had a nice garden or something that got ready before the other neighbors, like green peas or butter beans or greens or cabbage, it would be shared with others. Everybody would share whatever he had a lot of, especially with neighbors who had many children. It was a beautiful way to live, taking things to one another and sharing.

My father did most of the squirrel hunting, because he was better at it than my brothers. I never participated in that either, but I did like to go possum hunting with my brothers. I would put on a pair of the boys' overalls and a pair of their shoes and go along. I wasn't too big at that time, so I could wear some of my brothers' clothes. I would dress as rough as I could by sticking my overalls into my shoes in case a snake might get me around my ankles or feet. Nothing like that ever happened, but I made sure I wouldn't get hurt. We would go possum hunting with the dogs and a lantern. My brothers would suddenly say, *"They've got one."* I would ask, *"How do you know that, when we can't even see where they are?"* And they'd answer, *"Because they've stopped barking and started howling."* And, sometimes I would see the dogs just howling up at one tree and we would know a possum was up there. We would rush to the tree, with me having a hard time keeping up with them, and they'd hold up the lantern to see if the possum was really in the tree. *"I can see his eyes shining in this light,"* one of my brothers might say. *"Can't you see him, Bie?"* And sometimes I really could see him. The next thing to do would be to take the ax and cut down the tree. I would try to make sure I was out of the way, but I never was sure which way the tree would fall. It was so much fun!

When we went back home with our possums, momma could do a good job cooking them. We might skip a night or two, but it wouldn't be long before someone would ask, *"Bie, do you wanna go possum hunting again?"* *"Yes,"* I'd reply. And I was ready to go with them and go I would. I really enjoyed possum hunting, and I went hunting with my brothers many a night. Now that's one thing I couldn't ever have done by myself because I couldn't cut the tree down!

We also used to enjoy, to a degree, gathering sweet potatoes because you had only to pick them up. The men would dig a round hole, about ten or twelve inches deep, and fill it with a pine-needle straw to a depth of about five inches. Then, we would pile in the sweet potatoes around it, bringing them up into the shape of a tepee. All around that, we would lay boards and corn stalks. Around that, we would place a lot of hay and pad it all in. When it was finally completed, the men would scoop up dirt and throw it all around. The result was that they looked like tepees or like little hills. Sometimes, we would have seven or eight of them. We would put a fence around them, leaving a little place where you knew you could stick your hand through an opening and fill up your pail with yams. They would last all the winter inside those mounds.

That is how it was for us, working day in and day out to keep ourselves going. There was a lot of plain drudgery and I remember all of it. There were also the good times and thank God we could have good times even when we did not have too much. Our houses were little more than shacks that we fixed up as best we could. We had to work hard to get our living from the land, but we managed to keep on and even to enjoy ourselves. In spite of the poverty and hardship, God was looking out for us and we knew that.

5.
The Gift of Faith

"Amazing Grace, how sweet the sound
That saved a wretch like me.
I once was lost, but now I'm found,
Was blind, but now I see."

I always enjoyed the revival meetings. We sang such beautiful hymns. We didn't have an organ, so people just sang from their hearts. They would pray and sometimes they would get up and testify. We didn't have a church near our home, so we used the little one-room school at Corner Flat. Once in a while a minister would come along and preach in that little schoolhouse. The minister, whomever he might be, would stay in our area for maybe a couple of weeks and live first with one family and then with another.

Far away from home, there was the Primitive Baptist Church. It was the one my Grandmother Johnann usually attended and she was regarded as the *"Mother"* of that church. The members of that church believed in the washing of feet. They would make long towels of sheeting, maybe two yards long, and tie one end of the towel around their waists and use the free, long part to dry one another's feet. In holding their services they would cry, shout, and carry on.

My grandfather did not belong to that church, however, or to any other church. He refused to join any church all the years my grandmother was alive. To have him tell it, he knew more about religion than my grandmother or anybody else. Yet, the day came when he married one of the sisters of grandmother's church and just before he died, he followed my grandmother's path of faith and was even baptized. All Grandmother Johnann got from him was his superior attitude, his ability to quote the Bible from memory and his getting down on her about her religion.

I can remember her getting very *"happy"* as she called it. I would hear her crying in the morning or at any time of the day, screaming with a shrill voice whenever a spiritual awakening happened to her. She would say, *"My soul is happy, my soul is happy this morning!"* I would hear her all the way up at our house. I could feel her sincerity and I would pray, too. Oh, how I would pray!

I would talk to her about getting *"happy"* and praying and she would tell me, *"Little granddaughter, I was converted over forty years ago. I know I'm saved. I know that God has changed my life."* Then, she would tell me the things that God had done for her, this thing and that thing. I began to pray more and more. I wanted God to do some of the things for me He had done for my grandmother. I want to tell you that by praying and seeing what happened, I know for myself that God is truly real. All through my life, I learned to find Him for myself. I went right along with Him until one day He changed my life and ever since then I've been going ahead with whatever I had to do, trusting in God.

I not only learned to pray from my grandmother's example, but I learned to pray from having to deal with all the hard situations in my childhood. I would just pray and ask God to take care of whatever the problem.

My cousin Leona, a missionary lady from Andalusia, Alabama and Elder Jessie Mott, a lady preacher, would occasionally come up to our country to preach in the little school. Cousin Leona could sing the most beautiful songs! Some of the songs that we used to sing were: *Come on, Come On, Come on, Don't You Want To Go; I wouldn't Mind Dying, But I've Got to Go by Myself; My Lord is Getting Us Ready for That Great Day; He's Got the Whole World in His Hands; Amazing Grace,* and oh, so many others. It was a glorious experience to sing and hear those groups. I can say that I get my real consolation from going to God in song and prayer. I'm not that much of a singer, but I get a good feeling from singing and humming those songs.

Others would also come to preach at Corner Flat. Among them was a Reverend Frank Rivers whom I remember well. They would go to the school preaching and teaching holiness. In those days, I felt that I needed all the religion I could get to help me endure the obstacles in my life. Those good people taught me to ask God to fill me with the Holy Spirit as many of them had been so filled. I felt they were serious when they told me to seek the Holy Ghost. I prayed for the Holy Ghost and for God to bless me with the spiritual awakening these people had, if there was anything to it, and for Him to bless me with it. As you know, He did.

One day, I was in the field working with my hoe, and my brothers were with me. All of a sudden this jabbering, the same as I had heard in church, came upon me. I got spiritual and filled up with the spirit and I was yelling, "*Holy, Holy, Holy! Bless God!*" Then my tongue got to jabbering and jabbering. With tears running down my face, I was speaking other tongues as the spirit of God gave utterance. Oh, I was so filled! I was so beautifully filled with the Holy Ghost until I just could not — oh, I don't know how to describe it in any way you can understand! It lasted for days and days. Most days, I'd get up happy and lay down happy. I can hardly describe the beautiful awakening I got.

When I began to simmer down and get used to this beautiful feeling so that I could try to explain it, my grandmother would follow me around and just cry. She would say, "*I know my little granddaughter is not putting on. I know she's for real with what she's doing.*" She would cry and just look at me and say she couldn't understand. When she had been converted, she said, she hadn't reacted the way I had. So, when I settled down, I would try to explain what had happened to me. Finally, my mother said to me one day, "*Bie, do you know they say the devil gives you your first religion?*" Well, mom didn't really understand what had happened to me. She said to me what she should have said. God knows exactly what He's doing, however. So, my mother said to me what she honestly knew to say, but this bothered me. I started to pray all over again. My prayer this time says, "*Dear God, show me in some way. I don't know what way. You know. But show me in some way whether or not I have the Holy Ghost. You show me in Your own way.*"

Well, I prayed and just kept on praying. Every time I'd get by myself I was praying. I remember one evening my mother said, "*Go into the pasture, Bie, and drive the cows up and pen them.*" That was so we could milk them in the morning. I was happy to get away by myself — so I could pray again. There I was praying and walking in this little path. The cows were so accustomed to this routine that you could call them, and they would practically get in line to start up the trail on their own. There I was marching in the cows and praying. I can see that cow trail right now in my mind — the cows marching along and me following them and praying. All of a sudden, I started to speak in other tongues. My tongue got tied up and I began jabbering, talking to the Lord and crying. It came to my mind, "**Look in your hand.**" I knew exactly which hand to hold up. When God tells you what to do, He doesn't have to lead you. You *know* what He's saying when

He speaks to you. He said to me, *"Look in your hand."* I held my right hand up and looked at it. There was *Holy Ghost* written in my hand with the type of print found on the cover of Bibles. *"Holy Ghost!"* I screamed and kept speaking in tongues. I screamed, *"Thank you, Jesus! Thank you, Jesus!"* And the words *Holy Ghost* just stayed there in my hand for a short while, then vanished. From that day to this, I know I truly received the Holy Ghost and will thank God for the rest of my life.

Well, little did I know that my grandmother had started praying to God to show her if I had truly received the Holy Ghost. She had selected a praying ground by a nearby tree. Since we all lived, you might say, right in the middle of a swamp surrounded by woods, it was easy to find yourself a tree or a place in the pasture where you could be alone. Grandmother Johnann had found herself a praying ground and I didn't know it. She was praying secretly and asking God to give her whatever it was that I had. Whatever it was she wanted it, too. She also wanted to know if what was happening to me was truly coming from God. She didn't want her grand-daughter being led on by something false, when she felt definitely that I was serious.

Bless the name of Jesus! Suddenly, Grandmother came one day speaking in other tongues. She was so baptized with the Holy Ghost that she was the most beautiful lady you'd ever seen, and with the same speaking in tongues that I had. *"Holy! Bless God! Holy, Holy, Holy!"* Oh, how her tongue was jabbering just like mine! Everything was going in the same direction for her as it had for me. She couldn't talk for all the tears and she was telling us what she could and testifying. Grandmother said, *"I know I was converted over forty years ago, but this is just a higher step in the Lord. This speaking in tongues is definitely true. I can witness to my little granddaughter and with the people teaching it. I can witness!*

Once she began to speak in tongues some of the members in her church were against her. When she would be out at different churches and talking about it, the people would gather around her to hear about the gift of the tongues. Some of them would come up to her and say, *"You know, I was converted because I believed in you. Now, you're coming up here with this mess."* They treated her so badly that she would almost start preaching, telling them that truly there was something to it. Even my grandfather would taunt her and say, *"I thought you had religion 'til now."* He would go on and on about it and fuss about *"all this holiness"* and the people *"comin' up here and teachin' that stuff and there's nothin' to it."* All of this was hurting grandmother since she was the **Mother** of her church and she didn't want to leave. This was the most hurtful thing for her because it wasn't her intention to leave her church. She wanted to tell her church brethren that there was definitely something to speaking in tongues.

"Now, it's nothing against being converted," she would say, *"but it's something to this, too. God has higher heights and deeper depths that he can take you to!"* She would try so hard to tell them. I used to wonder why it worried her so much that people did not believe her. I was young then and was not bothered by that. But, it bothered her and she wanted them to see the light. And, she would talk and talk. Many times to no avail.

Sometimes, there would be a convention or a revival meeting at my grandmother's church. It was often at the beginning of them that Grandmother Johnann had the ministers come to her home as well as a number of other people. They always enjoyed her hospitality. She scrubbed and cleaned as well as baked for the feast she planned. She would work hard and the house would be so clean. I remember that in those days we didn't have bedspreads, but Grandmother Johnann did. For the top bed dressing she used seamless sheets that she would lightly starch. She could iron things to look as if they had been done in the best laundry. She would put starch in those sheets and iron them and the pillow-cases and have all her beds looking just wonderful. I always thought **her** bed looked the prettiest. Consequently, with all her cleaning and hard work, her home was always a place the ministers enjoyed.

Not only can I remember how Grandmother Johnann would clean the house, but she would cook in a way I will never forget. She loved cooking and she was a **terrific** cook! She would cook up all kinds of meat and bake things. She had a washpot on the outside of the house which she used for cooking on these occasions. She would put a certain type of coal around the pot and cook the meat with onions and various vegetables and things so that it appeared to be cooked in an oven. She also made poundcakes which we all loved. Everybody in her family from the city and country loved to come to grandmother's house. (I think sometimes, when I consider how I also love to have people visit me, that I have a little of my grandmother in me. One of the differences between us, however, is that she loved to cook and I do not. I like to eat.)

Grandmother especially wanted everything to look right for Reverend Frank Herndon, who was the first minister I ever got to know. Those travelling ministers were mostly Herndon people. I often asked her if Reverend Frank Herndon was white, because as an old man he looked just like a white man. But, she assured me that he wasn't. Maybe one of his grandparents had been white. Now, one of his sons, I remember, was Reverend Clarence Herndon. Clarence was very handsome, a beautiful figure of a man, and oh, could he preach! I think he lived in the North somewhere. I was real young, but I could see who looked real pretty and who didn't.

Anyway, the Herndons and other ministers, the Jacksons, would stay at my grandmother's house. When there was a lot of company at these times, we youngsters would have to wait to eat at the second sitting. Fried chicken and gravy were always plentiful — and those wonderful biscuits. My grandfather would often kid me by saying, *"I want another biscuit!"* That was because I had sometimes wanted another of my grandmother's biscuits and started crying when I thought there were none left. **"I want another biscuit!"** had become a kind of family joke about me.

It was at the time of one of those revivals, when the ministers were staying with my grandmother, that my dad did something that really embarrassed her. Dad had been off somewhere drinking, while mom and my brothers and I were at Grandmother Johnann's house visiting with her and the ministers. We were having a late supper. Dad came home. He had been drinking a lot of corn liquor. However, it happened that he knocked over one of the kerosene lamps and set our house on fire. He didn't know he had set it on fire and he laid down and fell asleep. Well, the neighbors noticed the fire and managed to wake up dad. They all began to draw water from the well and throw it on the fire. Those of us up at Grandmother Johnann's heard the commotion and we all came running, ministers and all, to help put out the fire. A lot of clothes hanging in the house had caught fire, and people were throwing them outside, still burning, while trying to save the house. Well, that was a sight to remember.

Grandmother Johnann was embarrassed and so were my grandfather and my mother. The next day, when dad sobered up, he was embarrassed, too. He apologized to the ministers and to grandmother.

Just a word about the revival meetings. They took place during the month of August. Among the churches in our area, each would have a big dinner on Sunday. There would usually be friends and relatives visiting from different towns and cities and far away as up North. Those nightly meetings could be very lively, and the big Sunday dinners were lots of fun — again, with lots of food — meats, vegetables and cakes. Grandmother Johnann's church didn't hold nightly meetings during the week. Instead, they would have their revivals on Friday, Saturday and Sunday. However they organized them, those revivals livened up the month of August.

I also remember another time when dad disgraced us again, especially Grandmother Johnann. It was when he was taking us children to a Primitive Baptist Church meeting. My mother rarely attended the meetings and seldom went anywhere with my father. She was afraid dad would drink and do something embarrassing. She would let dad take us to the revivals when we were older because they were special. When dad drove the horses to those revivals he would often drive real fast. The truth is, my father was basically a shy man, so he would take a drink in the morning or before going on a drive to a meeting, to loosen up. The trouble was he would get too loose! As we rattled past all the other wagons on the way, we were very frightened.

On this particular Sunday, dad was driving fast. Near the church was a little old bridge that crossed a place where the water in the creek happened to be very low. Well, the horses were running, springing up and down, their hooves flying, with the wagon just rocking and bouncing, and dad hit the bridge fast. When the wheels of that heavy wagon bounced onto that bridge, *bam!* The bridge, old and rotten, collapsed and down into the water went the wagon with us kids.

Somehow, we all got dumped out of the wagon and into the creek. Unbelievably, no one was hurt. But we were all screaming and hollering as people came running. They pulled us out and calmed us down. There wasn't much else to do to help us. We just had to let our clothes dry on us, while dad and some men got the horses and wagon out of the creek. I had lost one shoe, so I had to pull off my other one. I had to go with my feet bare the rest of the day and my appearance, shabby.

My girlfriends all said to me, *"Bie, where are your shoes?"* and I had to tell them what a great accident we had had. Even though I was very young at that time and it was a thrilling story to tell, I was still embarrassed.

When Grandmother Johnann got to church and learned what had happened, you can guess how she felt. Once again my father had disgraced her. When mom heard about it that night, she just said, *"I'm glad you all didn't get hurt, but oh, I'm so happy I didn't go!"* For many years mom and Grandmother Johnann had to live with the fact that dad was often doing foolish things. We all had to live with it. But, I loved my dad and even though I was sometimes afraid to go riding with him, I went anyway because I loved going places.

Grandmother Johnann was always helping other people. If she heard that anybody was sick she would go to see about them — *"I got to go see Sister Susan,"* she might say. *"They tell me she's very sick."* She would ride sideways on the horse. She would jump up on the side and ride along with both her feet hanging down. Carrying her little bundle of useful things (little medicines, tea-cakes, baked goods and maybe a hambone), to this or that sick person. She would bathe them, prepare food, cook for any children there might be, wash clothes and look after all the family. She was a **working** lady, a hard-working lady, just the neighborhood missionary.

Grandmother Johnann not only looked after sick people in our neighborhood, but she also helped out when somebody died. In those days for those of us who lived in the backwoods, when somebody died we didn't have undertakers or funeral homes. When a woman passed, for instance, they would come and tell my grandmother that Sister Whoever *"had passed last night and we want you to come right now."*

Sometimes, they would come for her in a wagon. Once there, the body would get bathed, dressed and groomed. Somebody would go to town and pick up the casket, and others would help to lay the body out. Since they didn't embalm people back then the funeral was held the next day.

Grandmother Johnann was an old hand at these funeral preparations. She helped in every way she could. She would go where the father may have died, leaving the mother with a bunch of children. I can remember her taking meat out of her smokehouse, cornmeal out of her barrel, flour, sugar or whatever she had to make meals for the family.

A few years ago, I was back in Montgomery, Alabama visiting some cousins of mine who are now grown and have children and grandchildren of their own. Some of them spoke to me about my grandmother, Aunt John Anne, and about the time their father died. *"Many a day,"* they said, *"we don't know how we would have eaten, how we would have lived, if it had not been for Aunt John Anne. She fed us many a day."* That was the kind of grandmother I had.

Finally, grandmother fell into bad health and was ill for several years. She couldn't go to the fields anymore and she died when I was seventeen. On numerous occasions during those years, whenever grandmother was sick, she would send for all the grandchildren to come and stand at her bedside. She would give us sound advice. She would instruct us all to be good children, never to take anybody's things, always to work and be honest, and if we wanted anything that was not ours, to ask. She would tell us to be kind and obey our parents and to be good to our grandfather after she died. Grandfather's health and comfort were important to her, and she appealed to us to look after him. She loved him so much and had always worked hard to please him.

On one of these occasions, she singled me out to ask something very important. *"Bie,"* she said, *"I want you to be real honest with me. Now, I'm not gonna whip you. This one time I'm gonna give you the privilege of saying whatever you want in your own way. Just tell me what do you think about me? How do you think I have been as a grandmother? Just tell me in your own way 'cause I really want to know what you think."*

I think she did know how strongly I felt about her, how I felt about things, and she especially wanted to know about herself, because she was getting on in age and had become sickly.

Now I called Grandmother Johnann *"Mo."* My sister called her Momma and called my grandfather Papa. The rest of us called my grandfather Pa. That's what we were taught by our parents to call them. So I said to her, *"Well, Mo, I feel within my heart that you love us. You bring us milk, meat, syrup, and any excess thing that you have, butter or whatever. You always, as far as I can remember, have helped my parents along the food line. My mother says as babies you would always take care of us — you washed our diapers. You took care of our clothes and you always took care of mom until she was able to get up and take care of us herself. I have been taught that you were a good grandmother, and I've seen you take care of other people.*

"But for me to tell you how I feel? I feel that you have mistreated me and my brothers when it came to us doing all of your farmwork. You have a cotton field of your own, private, aside from your husband's. We chop your cotton, we plant your cotton, we pick your cotton, and we give it to you. You sell it and keep the money. We take care of Pa's farm and you don't give us anything for that. You always give my sister whatever you have to give. As long as you're alive, you don't ever want to see her work hard.

"You don't seem to care about what we have to do, and I think it's wrong for us to have to work like that, and you take it all and give whatever you give to her. I truly think that's wrong. Now that is my big gripe, when it comes to what I have in my heart against the

way my brothers and I are treated. Georgie Mae gets all the trips. When you want to travel, you take her with you. She's a pretty girl, a very beautiful girl, I'll say that myself. I can see myself she's the most beautiful person in our family. But, we are all your grandchildren, even if we don't look as well as she does. And we probably wouldn't look that well even if we were sent to school and could sit down and not do anything. But, she goes wherever you go. She can sit down. She gets all the good treatment. That's why she can feel and look good; she doesn't have to worry about anything. I have only one sister, but I'm the Cinderella. I know the story about Cinderella that was taught to me. You all seem to forget I'm your granddaughter too. Now, that is the thing that makes me feel bad. I will always feel bad about that."

So, I was able to tell her about how I felt. She cried when I told her. I don't think she could deny anything I said. The tears flowed.

"Well, maybe I was wrong for doing some of those things, but I just didn't know any better," she wept.

Just before Grandmother died, she said that she wanted me to have one of her milk cows. It wasn't a full-grown heifer yet. Grandmother said to my daddy, *"Now, when I'm gone, give that cow to Bie."* But, after Grandmother died, my father was so accustomed to not doing anything for me that he didn't give me the cow. Even the little that my grandmother actually gave to me, I didn't receive.

I was sad when she passed because her house had been the closest house to us, and she was somebody I had known all my life. I was sad and lonely and hated to go to her house or pass by it after she died. I would go around it to go to the field. She was the only grandmother I ever knew. I may not have liked some of the things she did, but I loved her and I deeply missed her.

Grandmother and I were really alike in many ways, especially in our love for God, our faith in Him and our desire to help other people. One of the greatest things I learned from her was honesty. Even though her honesty often hurt, she told it the way it was. God loves the truth. She knew it and I know it. She was gut-level honest. Not many people, no matter how smart and dignified, can be that honest. Even when a person who isn't much to admire is honest and stands up and tells the truth or lets the truth about himself be seen, take it or leave it, even that kind of person I respect. A rat is a rat, but if he's an honest rat — well, there's something clean about that. You can't beat honesty.

Although Grandmother hurt me very deeply, the embarrassment and hurt are gone now, just as Grandmother and Georgia Mae are now gone. And when I look back, I know they did their best, even if some of the things they did weren't right. I loved them both and I would still do whatever I could to help them. By telling so much about Grandmother Johnann, I want to show what a basically wonderful and good lady she was and share the faith and love and plain kindness by which she lived.

My grandfather, what about him? When Grandmother Johnann died, he just carried on. He went on like that for a year. Now Sister Susan, a friend of my grandmother's, had lived with my grandparents for several years. Her real name was Elizabeth Pickett, and she more or less ran the house for my grandmother, who was very fond of her. My grandfather didn't like her too much, but sister Susan lived with them right up to the time Grandmother Johnann died. (I remember she was a very kind lady and short — it would have taken her best to be even four feet tall. She had a son, much older than us grandchildren, who was also very short. He went off on his own while we were still young.) Anyhow, sometime after my grandmother had passed on, my grandfather *fired* Sister Susan. He just sent her away. (The last I had heard, she had gone to Troy where she spent her remaining years.) But, that wasn't all of it. After Grandfather had sent Sister Susan packing, he got married again!

The woman my grandfather married was one of the members of my grandmother's church. She lived with him the rest of his life. I will never forget what she did when grandfather died. After the hearse came and took him to the cemetery, that woman got a wagon and had all the household goods loaded onto it — on the very day of grandfather's funeral. She even took the syrup mill!

When grandfather got sick, before he died, he wanted to be baptized. For years he had refused to have anything to do with church or formal religion. And, he always hated what he called *holiness*, that is, people getting filled with the Holy Ghost and speaking in tongues. But now he was claiming that a quickening power was grabbing him, as he had seen it grab me and my grandmother in earlier years, and he was saying, **"Holy! Holy! Bless God! Holy!"** He was doing the very thing he had always made fun of.

In those days, we didn't have a baptism pool. There had been a pool where I was baptized as a child, but it was gone by then. So, by the time grandfather wanted to be baptized the only place available was the creek near his house. That is how life went for him. He finally came around to the faith that my grandmother had held all her life, which she never lived to see him accept.

I remember when I was baptized. It was in a pool of lovely, clear water from one of the artesian wells. A rich man had come into the country and bought up a great load of timber. His name was R.D. Foley. He gave a lot of work to the local farmers. They would saw down the timber he had bought and take it to his sawmill. It so happened that the sawmill was near one of the artesian wells.

Mr. Foley built a pool near the well and his sawmill. It wasn't very big, perhaps twelve by twelve feet at most, but it was filled with that pure water from the well. Then he brought in a young alligator and put it in the pool. People would come to see it. My parents, also, took us to see it. But the pool wasn't the right place for such a creature, and Mr. Foley's alligator died.

The pool remained for many years, with the water constantly running into it from the artesian wells. It was in that pool that I and many others were later baptized. There was no regular church nearby where we could be baptized; the only other possible place would have been the creek. We didn't even have a river. For years people had gone to the edge of the creek to be baptized, even though it was all muddy and crayfish and all kinds of things were to be found in it.

It was in the little schoolhouse church at Corner Flat that I was the first one to witness receiving the Holy Ghost. I was the first one living in that area to be so touched, to be given the gift of tongues and to cry out *"Holy!"* That was real, my receiving of the Holy Ghost. It is real now, all these years later. When anything is real, it will stand. The truth will stand. The thing that always fails us is a lie.

Many others received and witnessed the Holy Ghost at Corner Flat in addition to my Grandmother Johnann and me. My Aunt H., my mother's older sister who had raised her, and some of her children also received the Holy Ghost there. I thank God that I was the first one to declare the Holy Ghost at that little schoolhouse church. I really treasure the truth that I received there. Now, I'm not one to say I've lived a sanctified and holy life, because I've sinned like anybody else. I have done a lot of things I shouldn't have done. I've said a lot of things I shouldn't have said. I've not been perfect. I am not perfect today. I will never say that I am. I would love to grow to perfection. I'd like to be more and more like Jesus and He was truly perfect, but not me. I haven't grown to that. Maybe I'll never make it, but I would love to.

Out of that little, one-room, schoolhouse, church at Corner Flat, God has brought many blessings. It's still standing there today surrounded by brush, straw, grass and weeds. When I was down there a few years ago, the last time that I drove to Alabama, I went to see the place where I declared my faith and had my schooling. It was hardly the place you could drive a car into, especially a great big car like the Cadillac I then owned. I didn't want to get that car all scratched up trying to make it down a bad road all overgrown with brush. But, that car wasn't too good to go where I had my beginning, found the God who blessed my mind, my life and my soul, where they taught me about the God who put that car in my hand. No, it just wasn't too good for that, so I drove right down that road. The car went in and out of potholes, coming up from each one with a shake, but we went on.

There was a little house down in there, and the people came out and said, *"Bie, don't nobody go down there in no car. People have done stopped driving down in there."* But, I had to see it. I said, *"I'm going down there. I want my children to see where I went to school."*

So, I drove on down to the place. I showed my two daughters where I came from, where I went to school and where I first went to church. We drove in there and we drove out with the car in one piece. Despite the rough road full of holes, the tires didn't blow and the shocks didn't give way. Except for a few scratches on the paint, which didn't really matter to me, the car went in and came out all right. And, we saw Corner Flat as it is now, a kind of holy ground to me you could say.

The little schoolhouse is sort of off by itself now, hidden, maybe **protected** by all the brush and wild growth that surrounds it. Today, not too far away on the main highway sits a little white church with a steeple that replaces our little, one-room schoolhouse — Corner Flat.

6.
Portraits

A lot of people come and go in a person's life, and when I look back on my years in Alabama, certain people stand out in my mind. This seems about as good a place as any to give a few portraits from my life's album.

One person I always loved was Aunt Harriet Pickett. She lived all alone, about a mile from us. She was a good, old lady who was born during slavery time. In our neighborhood, everybody lived far apart. Quite often, we made it a point to visit Aunt Harriet when we could.

Some of the older folks referred to Aunt Harriet as a busybody. Nevertheless, I loved Aunt Harriet. I was seven or eight years old at the time I remember her best. Aunt Harriet always gave us something to eat. She had a pot that she would hang in her fireplace on a hook that held it above the fire. She could cook some of the best meat over that fire! She had a kind of oakwood that would make a good bed of hot ashes. She would open up those ashes, lay sweet potatoes in them and cover them over. They would bake until they were soft, sweet and tasted real good. Oh, how Aunt Harriet loved to feed you! I remember she had an old cast iron skillet. She would roll out dough, cut out small cakes and lay them in the skillet to cook. When the skillet reached a certain heat, she would put a few of the oakwood coals on top of it and let the cakes bake. We call them cookies nowadays, but back then we called them teacakes.

Aunt Harriet could cook a nice meal right there in the fireplace. She had learned to do that in slavery time. She told us about her work and how, as a child, she was made to work in the field and pen the cows. She often spoke of how hungry she was. Sometimes, while penning the cows, she passed her master's smokehouse where she saw sausages, hams, and other smoked meats. On occasion she grabbed a piece of sausage. In route, many times she encountered burning coals left by fieldhands, and she would lay her sausage on them, and continue with her work. When she came back that way with the cows, the sausage would be cooked, so she'd eat it while driving the cows home. By the time she got the cows to the pen she would be about filled up with sausage.

I would say, *"Aunt Harriet, you ate that sausage without no bread?"* Because I was young and thought you ate sausage with bread and other things as part of a meal.

"Yes, honey," she would say, *"didn't have no bread. You didn't have no time to get no bread. You just ate that sausage and you had to do the best you could, 'cause them white people would beat you."*

Then, she told us about how they put children on a slave block where slave-owners bidded for them. She told horrible stories about slavery time. She told how she had been split up from her family and sold to another owner. We children sat around, when we had time, just looking at Aunt Harriet and listening to her. Sometimes Aunt Harriet would visit, talk to my mother and dip snuff. We adored her!

I clearly remember Uncle Senus Thomas. He was an old man that lived in our neighborhood all by himself. Whereas, I loved to go to Aunt Harriet's and eat, I didn't care at all to go to Uncle Senus' house. I thought he was dirty. But, he was just a poor old man who lived alone and took care of himself as best he could. Our neighborhood had any number of older people that were our friends and who we liked to be around, like Uncle Ad Rostick and his wife. Their children were grown, so, sometimes they would call on my little brother to go to the store for them to get a nickel's worth of kerosene or something. It seems that we were always, as kids, running errands and doing whatever little things we could for the various older people in our area.

Sometimes nowadays when I'm out shopping or conducting business, I might stop by one of the beautiful parks in my neighborhood to watch the children at play. More than once I have felt pangs of envy. There was little time for fun and games when I was a child. Our family's survival demanded a great input from everyone, and my brothers and I had to labor hard to earn our keep.

Then, there was another neighbor of ours, Mr. Jonas Tomkins whom we called a preacher. Mr. Tomkins had children that went to school with us, Walter Lee, Grace Lee, Lula Reed and several other children. His wife, Lonnie, and my mother would often visit, back and forth, and take their younger children with them. Therefore, the Tomkins' children and us played together quite a bit. In those days, in the backwoods, children were much more shy than they seem to be nowadays. My father would take advantage of our shyness. He would kid my older brother, Joe Frank, Jr., about having Laura Mae Tomkins as his girlfriend, and he would just sort of match us up that way with the Tomkins youngsters. So, when he was around us, while the Tomkins were visiting, we would know what he was thinking. This would make us feel so shy that we didn't want him to watch us play with them. We would act silly and run away, because dad really did a number on us about it.

Now, Mr. Tomkins didn't have a church, but he would talk at different places. When it happened that a series of murders took place in our area and the murderer was on the loose, people were frightened, and Mr. Tomkins was very disturbed. The situation rested so heavily on his mind that he became depressed and acted strangely. He threatened to drown himself in a nearby creek. Whenever he would actually start running toward the creek, his daughter, Laura Mae, would follow and catch up with him. She would throw her arms around his neck from behind and ride him so that he couldn't make it across the cotton rows. He would try to get her off, but would get so tired from the effort that he'd have to fall down. By that time her mother, brothers and sisters would come to help bring him back. She saved her daddy from destroying himself. I thought she was so brave and clever, because if he made it to the creek they might both surely have drowned, since neither of them could swim. That always seemed to me a good example of how God will often take care of you. He will even send someone to look after your safekeeping when you can't do it for yourself.

When I was a child, Mr. and Mrs. Silah lived in our neighborhood. Her name was Frances and his name was Hope. Mrs. Silah would always speak badly about her husband and say he was lazy. She couldn't stand him. Well, Hope was a good-looking man and I don't know if he was as bad as she claimed.

The Silahs had about six children, three or four small ones and a couple that were married. Eventually, they moved away from our neighborhood, and somewhere along the way Mr. Silah died and Mrs. Silah was a widow for many years. Once in a while, Mrs. Silah would come back to our neighborhood and bring her daughter who was named Schug. I always felt close to Schug and I didn't know why. I remember that one day Schug came by and spoke to everybody and said to me, *"Hi, Bie, how're you?"* It took all I could do to hold my tears back and speak. I got filled up and I didn't want them to see me cry. But, somehow I couldn't help but cry. Schug said, *"You're crying, Bie! Why do you cry?"* I was so full I couldn't talk. I really didn't know what was the matter with me.

Later on my mother told me that when I was a baby, Schug had nursed me. She was my babysitter, and I guess I had loved her through those days and didn't remember her being my babysitter. I had forgotten it. Somehow, that same love was in my heart when I saw her. I just cried and cried. Many a time, even now, I wish I could see her again.

Another person who still stands out in my memory is Mrs. Gussie Prichard. She was a woman I knew before and after I was married, when she was about sixty-five. She was a woman who lived very well and had two children. One of them, her daughter, was grown and had children my age and older.

Mrs. Prichard's son had been killed while in the service. I had never known him. She received checks from the government. She was the only person in our neighborhood who kept a nice car at all times and always lived in a nice home that was well-furnished. She also raised one of her granddaughters, Hattie Ruth, who married Herbert Bean and moved to Pittsburgh. I still know and admire the Bean family to this day.

After Hattie Ruth married and moved away, I was newly married and lived near Mrs. Prichard. We became good friends. She was the kind of lady who, as long as you were respectable, neat, clean, and knew how to wear your clothes and fix your hair well, liked to have you go around with her. As a young, married woman, I seemed to please her. She used to love to take me different places in her car, such as to different churches. Sometimes, she and I would even go to Birmingham. That meant a great deal to me. Somebody in my family would look after my daughter, Burnie (La-Doris had not been born yet), and I got the opportunity at last to go to most of the places I wanted to see.

My father-in-law, Dad McClaney, was not fond of Mrs. Prichard. For one thing, Dad McClaney liked to boss everyone around and it didn't please him that I would do things to suit myself. It was all right for Dad McClaney to go where he wanted, but he felt the rest of us should stay at home. So, to have someone like Mrs. Prichard come and take me away somewhere did not please him. Also, Mrs. Prichard lived well and I don't think Dad McClaney liked that, for whatever reason. But, Mrs. Prichard couldn't care less, because she was truly a liberated woman.

Mrs. Prichard died some years ago, while I was still living in Pittsburgh. Her daughter, Mary Frances Randal, who still lives in Alabama, and I became such good friends that we call each other Cousin Mary Frances and Cousin Eula. She often took care of La-Doris for me when La-Doris was still a baby and very sick. I hear from her every once in awhile, and I always go to visit her when I am in Alabama. I am grateful that her mother befriended me and made my life in Alabama happier than it might have been.

When I think of my Uncle George Washington Holt, I am filled with warmth and pride. As a child, he was a person that I admired and respected. I always felt that his profession made a difference in the world. I'm sure that many, many people have benefited from his services. You see, he was a doctor in St. Louis. And even though he was my mother's brother, I never met him. However, I loved him and love to hear his name.

As a small child, I was fascinated with medicine. I don't think any of my brothers or my sister ever talked about what they liked in the professional life. But, I always thought medicine was a great service to mankind. I never said I wanted to be a doctor, because I never saw a college, not even a high school. Yet, I felt that being a doctor was one of the greatest things in life. In my opinion, the doctor had done something miraculous anytime he could walk into a room and give a person's sick body some ease.

When I was a child, if you were sick, even if you were very sick, you couldn't go to the doctor every time you turned around, as you can now. Finally, when a doctor — a country doctor — would come, if a child was really bad off, he would arrive in a buggy or perhaps a wagon that somebody had sent to bring him. After he had seen the child and left, the mother, at least, was relieved. He'd tell her to give the child the medicine he prescribed, until the fever left. Eventually, the child would feel better.

I remember that in the two or three years before I was married, maybe even before Georgia Mae was married, people began to get their hair bobbed very short in the back and a little long in the front. Even though we lived out in the country, we kept up with the styles as best we could. I remember that we would go to the nearby town of Troy to get our hair cut in the latest style. When we returned home we showed the new style to cousin Tave, who was a barber in Orion. Once our hair was cut, Cousin Tave could keep the style — and that saved us the expense of returning to Troy.

Georgia Mae and I were style setters for all the girls in our neighborhood. Cousin Tave would have my sister or me come and sit while he looked at our hair and tried his best to cut the other girl's hair in the same style. He did a pretty good job, too! The girls were happy with his expertise. So, with Cousin Tave's and our help, all the girls in town had the latest hairstyles.

Now, I will just reach back in time to my early childhood, because I see in my mind a hat in a well! It was Sammy Jane's hat. And Sammy Jane — I see it now — said, I was the one who knocked her hat into the well, and . . . but back to the beginning.

FLASHBACK

There was a real heavy lady named Mrs. Ada Galloway. She had been a school teacher at one time, but lived in our neighborhood now, and made her living sewing. She was creative and could make beautiful clothes. She could draft her own patterns. Often she had too much work to do her best. She raised a boy named Sandy Boswell, her foster child. Sammy Jane, his sister, lived with their grandmother. As children we all went to the same school, Corner Flat. Sammy Jane's mother worked in Montgomery, and we all admired the fine clothes she sent Sammy Jane.

It was the last day of school, and we were having a concert that night. Sammy Jane, Ruby Lee (who was in some way related to Sammy Jane), and I were all friends. We were all dressed up and together. As Sammy Jane looked into the well her hat fell in. She was upset and frightened and didn't know how to tell her grandmother *"My hat fell in the well."* So, on our way back to school, Sammy Jane ran on ahead of us to her grandmother. *"Where's your hat, Sammy Jane?"* And Sammy Jane replied, *"Bie knocked my hat off into the well."*

When Ruby Lee and I got back to the school, we discovered what Sammy Jane had said. And I was shocked! My mother was quite upset. She took me off and said, *"What you knock that girl's hat off in the well for? You know I don't have no money to buy that girl another hat."* And she was about ready to hang me.

I said, *"Oh, Momma, I didn't knock her hat off in the well."*

"You know we don't have nothing," said my mother. *"How we gonna get her hat out of the well?"*

I said, *"No, we don't have a thing."* But thank God Ruby Lee was along with me and saw what happened.

So, when we told Ruby Lee what Sammy Jane had said, she said to my mother, *"Oh, no Mrs. Hendrick. Bie didn't knock her hat off into the well. She was leanin' over the well, lookin' down in the water, and her hat just fell off in the well. Bie did not do that."*

Ruby Lee's telling the truth saved me a whole lot of trouble. My mother believed her and went to Sammy Jane's grandmother and told her how she really lost the hat. Then they arranged to get her hat out of the well. Somebody let the bucket down the well underneath the hat and brought the hat up undamaged. So, that was that. It was a small incident, but at the time it seemed very big to me, and it is still vivid in my mind.

Whenever we had a concert at school, we would feast on the chicken, dressing, rice pudding and homemade cakes that our mothers brought. Everybody would share and it always turned out to be a nice evening.

The children wore their prettiest clothes for the concert. On this particular night at this particular concert that I remember so well (thanks to Sammy Jane's hat), Georgia Mae and I were really dressed very pretty. I had a cousin, Johann Rayford, whom I did not know very well. She was named after my Grandmother Johann. I rarely saw her, but Georgia Mae lived with her while going to school. Cousin Johann had two adopted daughters who were twins, and she dressed them well. Cousin Johann worked for wealthy white people who bought pretty clothes for their children. These people would give my cousin anything that their children had outgrown. So, in getting us ready for this concert, Grandmother Johann had gone to our cousin and borrowed two beautiful dresses, embroidered with beautiful threads. They had a sash that began at the side and tied in the back in a great big bow. Georgia Mae and I wore these identical dresses. I thought we looked beautiful! I was always a little larger than Georgia, but she was taller. I shall always remember that day and night, with Sammy Jane's hat falling into the well and Georgia Mae and I looking so nice for the concert.

Mary Gussie McClaney was the oldest of my three sisters-in-law. When I married Bernie, all of his sisters were single. Mae Gussie, as we called her, was almost like a mother to the rest of the family. And I thought at first, *"Oh, I'm going to have a beautiful, motherly type lady here at home."* But, when I really got to know Mae Gussie . . .! That lady kept more gossip and unpleasant things going than anybody I have ever known. She kept herself and the family in constant trouble.

We went on and on with Mae Gussie. Someone in the neighborhood would come up to us and say, *"She told me such and so . . ."* And we'd find out it wasn't so, not at all like she said. That poor girl stayed in hot water all the time, until at last a young man became interested in marrying her. I guess she was, by that time, around forty years old. One night a young man came over and I heard early the next morning that he had asked for her hand in marriage. I tell you, the word got out all over the neighborhood early that morning, and we were all happy!

When the young man asked to marry Mae Gussie, I was told that Dad McClaney said, *"Yes!"* and gave her up right away. He told the young man he need not even come back to pick her up, that he would meet him downtown in Union Springs and bring Mae Gussie there himself. He quickly told the young man to meet him at the courthouse. I had never heard of a father taking his daughter to get married at the courthouse, and taking her there himself.

The next day, when they were to go to Union Springs, something happened to keep them from making it. I don't remember what happened, but I was dismayed and said, *"Oh, don't tell me something happened and we're not gonna get rid of her today!"* I did feel sorry for the young man, but I thought, *"It's better him than me . . ."* I was just tired of hearing all that stuff from her. But sure enough, the next day Dad McClaney got his oldest son to drive the car and they went to Union Springs with Mae Gussie and witnessed her marriage. I will report that today, Mae Gussie is still with the man she married. I've been told they live in a little house there in Alabama.

7.
Bad Times

I recollect clearly what it was like to be Black, to live in the country and to go to the city. It seemed that white people had a deep hatred for black people. We could not walk on the streets comfortably. You were afraid that if you brushed up against a white person you were likely to get a fist or you might be put in jail for a minor accident. Sometimes, if the street was a little cluttered with white people, we would rather walk on the side of the curb and take a chance that a car might hit us rather than brush up against one of them. And then, depending on who was at the wheel, we might get knocked down as we were walking there on the edge of the street. So, we were on the street, off the street, back on the street or on and off the sidewalk, because we didn't want to be accused of something. It was frightening just to pass by white people who were strangers. And, even though a trip to town was pleasurable, it usually added up to being a miserable, frightening day.

It was sometime in the twenties, when Model T Fords came out, that my father and Uncle Mitchell bought themselves a brand new Model T. To ride around in a new car was really a big step up for us. We now had a chance to go places we'd never gone before. We would go to Troy much more often, and to church and even to Montgomery which was forty miles to the north. Even that was a mixed blessing, considering the way black people were treated by most of the Whites. You would hear of certain black folks who had a car that got beat up or put in jail or had something bad happen to them. Just as you weren't supposed to pass by a white man walking in the street in front of you, so you weren't supposed to pass by a white person driving a car ahead of you. If you did, you'd hear, *"He passed by me . . . that's a uppity nigger . . . that nigger passed me!"* Just anything you did was an insult to white people.

As much as I liked the opportunity to go somewhere back then, it was always pretty miserable if we went where there were white people, especially to town. We had to be so careful about what we said or did. And, coming from the backwoods and being taught by our parents about how careful we must be, I think we had a little more fear than most people. Since we lived in the country and worked on our own farms, we were never around white people very much. We didn't do housework in their homes or work around them elsewhere.

Even while living in the country, we had occasional trouble with white people. Our landlord, Dr. Murphy, had a son, Dean Murphy, who sometimes treated us without much consideration. The Murphys owned some fabulous bird dogs and they would come hunting around our place in the fall. They mostly came to shoot quail, which we called partridge. Dressed in hunting clothes (red caps and all), they would bring their friends, accompanied by their overly eager and vicious dogs. They would come up to our house and tell my brothers, *"I want you to come out and pick up birds for me."*

My mother was afraid the boys would get shot. When the dogs flushed out a bunch of birds and set them flying into the air, the men would begin shooting repeatedly. It seemed very dangerous to mom, all those men, those guns, all the commotion, and shooting. *"What if they shoot my kids?"* she would wail. But, there wasn't much she could do about it. If Dean Murphy and the other men ordered my brothers around, they had to do what was ordered if they knew what was good for them. As a black person you had no say-so. Even though I am getting ahead of myself here, I will say that I always admired my father-in-law, Dad McClaney, for being the kind of black man who stood up to white people and didn't let them push him around. Every Tom, Dick and Harry was not going to come into Dad McClaney's house and tell him and his folks what to do. In that way, he was exceptional, and I admired him for it.

Another time, we had trouble with Dean Murphy was when my brother Jimmy was seventeen. He had become interested in girls and started dating. The only way he could go to see a girl was on horseback. At the time of the incident I have in mind, he was going to a church on Sundays that was about six miles away. So, he would ride one of our horses to make the trip.

Now, it seems that Dean Murphy wanted to go hunting and had told one of the other black men on his father's plantation to tell my brother that he, Dean, wanted to have such and such horse to ride on Sunday. But, the man did not tell my brother. Of course, it wasn't right in the first place that Dean could just order Jimmy around like that and help himself to our horses. But, that's the way white people did, just ordered you around about your own things. And, if you gave them any trouble, they would take your things as if they were their own.

Sunday came, and Jimmy hadn't been told that Dean Murphy wanted one of our horses. That morning Jimmy got up, dressed and went to church, riding the horse that Dean had decided to use. When Dean sent for the horse and found Jimmy had gone off with it, he assumed that Jimmy had ignored his order. So, he sent over one of his men to take our other horse and we never saw that horse again. He had that horse taken away without any word to us. You could raise up your own horse and they could come and take it. This was because most black people wouldn't dare resist that kind of treatment for fear of what might happen. They had been conditioned to put up with it, just as the whites had been conditioned to have their own way.

I also remember one day going to a neighborhood store called Chiney Grove. It was near Troy and the owner was a white man. His niece came stepping out of his big home nearby. I remember she was wearing a white dress. She got into her car and stepped on the gas, but the motor wouldn't turn over. At that point she spoke to us, *"Come on, you boys, and give me a push."* It was just taken for granted that we would do what she said. She didn't ask us; she told us. That's the way it was. Most white people didn't notice black people any more than if they were flies. They didn't speak, say hello or good morning, or anything to show they noticed you. You were nothing.

Well, we gave the lady's car a push and got the car rolling. Off she went, without waving her hand to us to say thank you. I would have been happy if she had done that, just acknowledged that we helped her. Since we were children, she might even have given us a sucker which would have delighted us. But no, she went on without even a word of thanks. We were there to take an order, otherwise to keep out of the way and be ignored.

After I was married and my two little daughters had been born, my husband went up to Pittsburgh to see if he could get work and send for us. It was a period of about six months that Bernie was gone and I was waiting to join him. I lived with my family during that time. I helped them all I could to work their farm and to take care of the house. I was also helping my mother take care of Georgia Mae's three children while caring for my two.

The mailbox was about three miles from the house. I was usually the one to get the mail. It was dangerous for women down there to take a long walk like that alone. Someone might come by in a truck and begin to give you trouble, maybe even a group of white men, who might very well grab you and rape you. The white men never cared what they did to black folks. So, I would take my husband's rifle with me. Bernie had taught me how to shoot. As I recall, it was a twenty-two. Now, even though I knew how to load and shoot the rifle, I could never hit anything with it. But, I looked as if I could handle it. Therefore, I would take the rifle with me, and I'd always take a child along, too. Georgia Mae's oldest son was about six years old. I would take him with me, since Burnie and La-Doris were too small to walk that far.

One day on our way home from the mailbox, we encountered some white men who were a short ways off from the path on the edge of the woods. I don't know what they were doing, but they began to yell at us. I didn't look around and I didn't say a word. I just kept walking. Then, I heard one of the men say, *"She might shoot you with that rifle. You see, she's got a rifle on her shoulder and she might shoot you."* I still didn't say anything and kept on my way. The men didn't bother me. I think they would have, if I didn't have the rifle. They assumed I really knew how to shoot. If only they had known the truth! I carried it and it did look dangerous, but that was about all. I have often thought about that incident and wondered what could have happened to me. And, I have often wondered how many people have had to carry a rifle just to walk to their mailbox!

We all had our share of bad times. I remember my Grandmother Hendrick's father. He was an old minister, a very tall, broad-featured man. I remember he shook a lot because he had "the palsy." His hands shook so much he could hardly pick up his pipe or tobacco. Grandmother Hendrick would take us to see him. She called him Paps. Paps was born during slavery time and he talked to us about slavery and sometimes quoted from the scriptures. The only way he knew the Bible was to remember what people would read.

Paps had children that he depended on, and he lived with some of them. He had a son we called Uncle Buddy Jones. He had two more sons we called Uncle Ben and Dolf Jones. I remember early one morning, someone came over to bring my grandmother some very sad news about Uncle

Dolf Jones. That morning he had been plowing in a field of his that joined a white man's. The white man and Uncle Dolf got in an argument, and the white man killed him.

I heard Grandmother Hendrick hollering. Uncle Dolf was her younger brother and he had been murdered! He had died and left behind his wife, Aunt Tilda, with a host of children to raise. At that time, there was no welfare available nor aid for a woman left alone with children. It would be up to the widow to work and raise whatever food she could, and people would help her out with what little they had to spare. We had to help one another and we often had very little we could help with.

The man who killed Uncle Dorf, Charlie Simms, was put in jail— oh, yes, put in a jail *for a few minutes.* He was soon right back working on his farm. As far as I remember, he was never sentenced to prison or anything. After all, he had only killed a black man and probably felt that he had good reason to do so.Old Charlie Simms may have shot and killed Uncle Dolf, but he just continued plowing, farming and living his life as usual.

I can also recall another tragic thing that happened during my childhood that touched and terrified us all, children and grownups alike. It happened not too far from school and involved some of my relatives on my mother's side of the family.

That day started as any other ordinary day. I got up on time for school and was ready for at least fifteen minutes before mom could shoo my still groggy brothers out the door. I quickly took the lead because we had to stop by Grandmother Johnann's house where our teacher (who boarded at Grandmother's house) would be waiting to join us on our way to school. I didn't want Grandmother Johnann or our teacher to chastise us so I was almost running. My brothers grumbled but they kept up. Sometimes we would pick up other children along the way, and one of them would be our Cousin Willie. He was related on my mother's side of the family.

What happened on this day remains as one of the most terrifying experiences of my life in Alabama. Everybody was scared! Moreover, my family stood at the center of this dismal, backwoods tragedy. On this particular morning, Willie was waiting for us as usual — only this time he was alone with his baby brother.

"Willie, are you going to school today?" we asked him.

"Yeah," said Willie. *"I'm waiting for my mom to get back so I can go with you."*

"Well, she'll be here in a few minutes," we said, *" 'cause we saw her water buckets sitting down there on the road side — two buckets of water."*

We went on to school and left Willie behind, waiting for his mother. Now every morning, before Willie went to school, he would stay at home and watch the baby while his mother went to a well some distance away to get some buckets of water. This way she would have water during the day and not have to leave her baby alone. Willie's parents were Tave and Nettie Williams. Tave was the son of my Aunt H.

On that particular morning, we had come upon two buckets of water sitting by the roadside near the Williams' house. There was no sign of Nettie Williams, and we figured she had just gone into the woods. So, we didn't think too much of it when Willie told us his mother had not come home yet. We assumed she would return soon and then Willie would come on to school. So, we went on our way.

Willie did not come to school that morning, however. I think, in the back of my mind, I knew something was wrong. It was sometime after lunch when my Uncle Frank Gibson came to the schoolhouse door and looked in and asked to speak with Miss Laura Jackson, our teacher. (Uncle Frank and his wife, Callie, lived near the school and had a large family of fourteen children, seven boys and seven girls. Aunt Callie was one of my mother's older sisters.) Miss Jackson went to speak with Uncle Frank and they stepped outside where they talked very quietly.

Miss Jackson came back in and said, *"I have something to tell you, children. A terrible thing has happened. Mrs. Nettie Williams, Willie's mother, has been murdered. Her body was found just off the road this morning, up in the woods a little piece, and she had been tied to a tree with a rope and strangled. You all have to go home now, where you will be safe, while they try to find out who did it."*

We were all very distraught by the news. Miss Jackson walked home with us. That night, the sheriff came from Troy and we got more information about what had happened. They told us that someone's cook had been killed and then covered over with some trash in a ditch. She was found later after a rainstorm. They said that some other woman had also been strangled and it looked as if someone was going around that part of the country killing women.

Well, the rumors and stories began to fly about the neighborhood and people grew very fearful. One of our neighbors told how a strange black man had stopped at his house and they had given him dinner. We country folk had a way of feeding whoever came along. Our neighbor said, *"This man ate dinner at my place the other day. He asked me for some food, so we had him sit down at our table and eat dinner with us. But, that man acted so peculiar and was so restless!"* And, people began to put two and two together and realized that this was the man who was murdering people.

The sheriff and his men brought the bloodhounds out and put them on the trail of the killer. They would trace him just so far and then lose the track. Several times, they trailed him up to the river and would have to begin all over. The murderer eluded the dogs and all the men who were after him for a number of days. In the meantime, he killed several other women by either strangling them or breaking their necks.

We were all scared to death while the killer was on the loose. We and our neighbors never locked our doors. We could go to anybody's house and, if we wanted to, unhook the door chain from the nail on the porch wall and just walk in. Everybody's house was accessible to the next door neighbor or to anyone who wanted to go in. If something happened like a fire or somebody was sick, you could go into people's houses if you had to. We were never afraid of intruders. But now, everyone was fearful. People were carrying their shotguns. Women would not stay at home alone, but would leave with their husbands in the morning and stay where they could be with other people. Everyone was buying locks and chains, fixing their door and hooking their windows. When we came home at night, from the fields or somewhere, my brothers would get a lantern and climb up in the loft and look from corner to corner to see if that killer was in our house. And, we also got out our old guns and got new shells (Momma sold some eggs just so we could buy more). And it was a scary and frightful time we had to live through.

I forget how they caught the killer, but they finally did. He turned out to be an escaped prisoner from a work gang. In those days, prisoners wore stripes. They would be taken out of prisons in gangs and sent to work on the plantations of big white farmers. Of course, the prisoners were mostly black men. While working on the big farms, the prisoners would get the feel of the country and some of them would manage to break free. Now, the man who terrorized our neighborhood had managed to sneak away. After, roving around, he had obtained some civilian clothes and began attacking and killing black women. He killed Nettie Williams. (For a time, Nettie's father thought it was Tave who killed her, since she and Tave had not been getting along too well.)

They took the man to Troy and kept him in the jail there in solitary confinement. Word got around that he said, *"They're not going to kill me. I won't be hung, 'cause they're not gonna be able to hang me. I can tell you they're not gonna hang me!"*

I was just a child and scared to death by all that had happened. When I heard what the man had said, I was afraid that anybody that mean would maybe know what he was talking about. In the meantime, the authorities got ready to hang him. They had a gallows built and had sent out the word that if anyone who had a relative or friend that this man killed, they might volunteer to knock the trigger on the gallows that would release the trap door and cause the prisoner to hang. I don't remember anything about a trial, but I suppose there was some sort of legal proceeding to prove that he was the murderer of all those people. As for volunteers to knock the trigger on the gallows, I don't think they had any from our community. Cousin Willie's father, Tave, could have been one with a legitimate claim to do it, but he didn't have the nerve to kill somebody that way. So, it was the town jailer who carried it out.

I can remember the day of the hanging. A high platform had been built by the gallows where the prisoner could walk out where everybody could see him. I have been told all this, because we children did not see the hanging. People say it was a peculiar looking day, a hazy day that no one had ever remembered seeing the likes of before. They say the man came out and said the kind of things he had been saying, how no one could kill him. But, they went right ahead and knocked the trigger and he fell through the trap door and his neck broke as he fell. And, in spite of all his threats, he was dead.

However, even in the midst of hard work and being poor, we all had our good times, because it's built into people to try and be happy whoever they are, wherever they are, and however they can. It's the good times we hold on to. When you can, let the bad times go. Don't wallow in what was wrong. Just keep on stepping, putting the bad behind you and setting the good before you. Yes, oh, yes, just let those bad times go!

8.
Good Times

"Look, Bie! Look!" Jimmy Lee exclaimed. *"Did you see that man eat that fire?"*

"No," I answered *"Where? I was looking at the tigers and the elephants."*

"Come on!" Jimmy Lee screamed. *"Maybe we can catch up with him."*

We were all overjoyed. The circus had come to town — to Troy! And there was a big parade. Our parents had brought us to see the animals, the performers and the band. This was a wonderful and exciting time. Nowadays you can see all of that and much more on television. But, we didn't get to see any of it, not even in pictures in books and magazines. A giraffe was something you heard about. We had a general idea of how it looked from some black-and-white photograph we might have seen. It was the same for tight-rope walkers, trapeze artists, clowns, and all the other performers in a circus.

A little while ago, I was telling some folks that we used to go to the circus when I was a child. They said, *"That's wonderful, Eula. It must have been a thrill for you to see the circus in those days."* Well, I had to laugh. *"We didn't **see** the circus,"* I said. *"We only **went** to it."* And I had to explain that my parents were too poor to buy circus tickets. I went to the circus several times as a child, but I never **saw** the circus —even though I did **see** the parade.

We would go onto the circus grounds, walk around and look at the people coming to see the show. We would catch glimpses of the performers and the animals as they were hurrying in and out of the big tent. However, we never got to go in the small tent either, the one where they kept the animals on display. My mom and dad would usually manage to buy us each a hotdog, and then we'd roam around and enjoy ourselves. But for us, that was a good time. I don't suppose it would have worked a hardship on the circus owners to let poor, black children in free or at a very little cost, but that was out of the question. So, we were there on our own, looking at the sights, listening to the sounds, smelling the scents of wild animals, sawdust, hotdogs, cotton candy and carmel corn — as I say, going *to* the circus.

Usually, if we went anywhere to have a good time, it was right in our own neighborhood. The little, one-room school house, Corner Flat, was the setting for many of our get-togethers and festivities. That little wooden building served as a school, a church, and a community center. Even though my formal education was meager and confined to the Corner Flat School, a lot of the pleasant times of my life are connected to it. It provided a center around which our lives circled, from the Burial Aid Society meetings to the church socials.

Let me take what we called *camp meetings* as another example of how we enjoyed ourselves. I don't really know why they were called camp meetings. They weren't strictly religious affairs, even though someone might preach or there would be singing. People would go inside and sit down awhile and listen. I always enjoyed that aspect. But, the main action was going on outdoors.

The camp meetings took place on the fourth Sunday in September, before the harvest. They were held at Corner Flat School and my daddy headed them. They might seem unimpressive, social affairs by today's standards, and I have often given parties that would make them look insignificant. But, they were big events for us. I loved them. We would maybe get some new clothes to wear to them, nothing very costly. The girls would get simple cotton dresses and the boys got new trousers. I wouldn't mind going to one of those meetings right now and re-experiencing its simple pleasures.

As head of the camp meeting, it was dad's job to buy up a lot of pig tails, pig ears and fresh fish. Others came and took charge of the cooking. They got big wash pots, the kind we boiled laundry in, and set them up outside over hot fires. They would be half-filled with grease, in which to fry the fish, or to cook the pig tails and pig ears. Dad would also buy several cans of different kinds of sauces, mustard, relish and ketchup. A big wooden stand was built — mainly they were boards laid flat to serve as counters to hold the bread and the sauces. Behind them stood the people cooking the food. We went up to the stands to buy fish or pig tail sandwiches. There would be lots of lemonade, soda and bootleg liquor for sale.

It's funny, but the food always stands out in my memory! So, I naturally remember folks frying the fish and cooking the pig tails and ears. Sometimes, we'd have barbecues going at the camp meetings, with big pits in the ground full of hot coals. I can still see and smell those fish frying in the pot and grease boiling hot with pieces of fish being dropped into it.

My daddy would give each of us kids twenty-five cents apiece to spend at the camp meeting. It was rare for us to have our own money. Georgia Mae, of course, was used to spending more than that and could always find a way to get more than twenty-five cents from our grandparents or someone. But, my brothers and I were glad to have what money our parents gave us. Well, on one occasion, my parents gave me an entire dollar and told me, *"Don't you change this dollar until you can be sure to give your brothers each his quarter."* They knew I loved to eat and just might get carried away. So, there I was with a dollar in my hand and all that food smelling so good! I was talking with some other little girls running my mouth — *and eating.* Somehow or other, I'd forgotten my instructions *and my brothers* and had just bought myself a fish sandwich. Only I think I bought more than one, because when I realized what was happening and went looking for the change from that dollar, I couldn't find it. I didn't have any money at all!

Now, I was at an age where I couldn't count very well. It could have been that someone hadn't given me back the right change. But, I think the truth is that I had spent that dollar on myself, on eating, and was having too good of a time to take notice of what I was doing. I looked for that money in vain. I was so worried about what Momma would do. Momma could look at you and kill you right inside. And, now I was going to have to tell her that I didn't have the dollar, that I'd had something to eat, and that Bae, Jimmy and Tommy hadn't got their quarters. Finally, I was forced to tell my mother the truth.

"We told you not to change that money, until your brothers were around, Bie!" Momma yelled at me. *"You know I ain't got nothing. Now, those other kids ain't got nothing. They ain't even got their money!"*

"But Momma, I don't know where it is!"

"I know where it is," snapped Momma. *"It's in your stomach!"* I was just miserable. Now, I see how funny it was and Momma does too. But, at the time it was a terrible thing. I had gone and eaten what belonged to me as well as what belonged to my poor brothers. But, oh, those pig tail sandwiches were good!

We didn't make as much of holidays when I was young as we all do now.

People were poor. And, if you lived in the country, getting around wasn't all that easy, since most of us walked places most of the time. Roads were poor, too, and we didn't have the cars and the public transportation that we have these days. Also, we didn't read and hear a lot of carrying on about Halloween, Thanksgiving or the Fourth of July. Since we didn't have electricity, radios or newspapers, we were kept out of the mainstream of people who make a big thing over those holidays.

We never observed Halloween, never. It would have been next to impossible to go trick-or-treating down lonely roads and through dark fields at night, and nobody had ever heard of giving a Halloween party. As for Thanksgiving, we usually had to work in the fields. Sometimes, our parents would give us some time off on Thanksgiving, maybe the afternoon. And, sometimes, we'd go and work the whole day. *"The more we do today, the less we'll have to do next week,"* Momma would say at such times. As for Easter, we really did nothing about it. If we were lucky, we might get something simple in the way of clothing, but that was rare. We never celebrated our birthdays. We'd be working and not even know that it was our birthday, or we might remember at the end of the day, *"Oh, today was my birthday."*

But, Christmas was a good time for us. It was so simple! Today's children would hardly know what to make of it. Kids nowadays wouldn't even get out of bed for what we got up for — two apples and an orange. And, we were happy to get that.

At Christmas time, we would look for Santa Claus and we would put out our shoe boxes. Every fall, we would each get a new pair of shoes. We would save the boxes so that we would have our own Christmas shoe box. Santa Claus would put his gifts in our shoe boxes. We always got the same thing — maybe two apples and an orange, a few little raisins, and maybe three or four little pieces of candy. Also, once in a while, if we were lucky, I would get a cheap little doll (a white doll) and my brothers would get a pair of blue jeans.

We would put out our shoe boxes in the one room we called a sitting room, the room that had the fireplace, since all our rooms had beds in them. Our parents made sure we put the shoe boxes on a chair, a trunk, or the dresser. Like most children, we would get up several times in the night to see if Santa Claus had come yet. Our parents would holler, *"You all get to bed now! Santa Claus ain't coming to you, if you get up anymore!"* But, if one of us could manage to find out that Santa Claus really had come, then we would all get up, no matter how early.

We never had a regular Christmas tree or hung Christmas stockings, but we did put up decorations. Momma would order them from Sears and Roebuck. She would send away for paper roping, green and red, and for bells made of paper and cardboard. There would be small bells and then there would be one great big one, the largest one that momma could afford. We would hang the large bell in the center of the room and put the smaller ones on the sides, with the paper roping looped all around. It wasn't much, but it gave a happy feeling to our poor little rooms. It was the way Christmas *looked* to us. Only in later years, when I was practically grown, did we have a Christmas tree, a little artificial one that you could put on a table. It was something to look pretty.

After we got to be larger children, my mother began raising turkeys. When she had good luck raising and selling them, she would use some of the money to buy clothes, as well as better decorations. We would save the decorations, of course, and wrap them up in some old tissue paper and put them away. We were also one of the families who had turkey for Christmas dinner.

My mother and grandmother and people out there in the country did an awful lot of baking at Christmas time. It was nothing for them to bake seven or eight cakes: pound cakes, coconut cakes, and jelly cakes. Often we would have a hog freshly butchered, one that had been saved for the occasion. Then, we might have a turkey, a tom turkey my mother had especially saved. She always tried to have a two-year old tom, and a few weeks before Christmas she would bring it inside, feed it, and let it grow big. She would also cook a ham and there would be lots of sweet potato pies as well as vegetables we had stored or canned earlier.

We would have a feast for the Christmas holidays. All the families around would do the same thing, the best they could. Before Christmas, the mothers would start to save butter and eggs to get ready for all the baking. They would bury their eggs down in salt to keep them fresh. Somehow, by saving and planning, they always managed to make Christmas a wonderful time. We didn't have much, but what we did have we enjoyed all the way.

I remember one Christmas when my brothers, especially Jimmy, were very adventurous and did something that now seems very funny. Sometimes, the boys would get a harmonica for Christmas. We called them **harps.** On this particular Christmas, they figured they would not be finding any harmonicas in their shoe boxes unless they did something about it themselves. Now, whenever those boys needed a little money that they didn't want to let my parents know about, they would catch one of my mother's hens and sell it. Momma never seemed to catch on to what was up. Whenever a hen turned up missing, she never knew the boys had taken it to get themselves some money. Daddy never knew it either. So, on this Christmas, they all wanted to have a harmonica. They thought the best way to get themselves a harmonica would be to sell some chickens, maybe one or two, and take the money and buy their own and just put them in their Christmas boxes.

"If anybody asks how come they're there," said Jimmy, *"we'll tell them Santa Claus brought them. They can't come and say he didn't, 'cause they claim he brings the other stuff."*

Well, when Christmas morning came, Jimmy, Bae and Louis had themselves harmonicas in their shoe boxes. Soon, they were all playing away on them.

Mom and dad were really puzzled by those harmonicas. Dad managed to get around to mom and say, *"Where did they get those harps? Did you put them in their boxes?"*

"No," said Mom. *"I thought you might have given it to them."*

"No," said Dad. *"I didn't."*

Well, Jimmy, Bae and Louis just went on blowing those harps.

Dad said to Jimmy, *"Boy, where'd you get that harp?"*

Jimmy was real devilish and said, *"Santa Claus put it in my box."*

"Boy," said Dad, *"you know Santa Claus ain't . . ."* But dad just stopped from saying the rest of what was on his tongue.

Those boys had my folks in a place where they couldn't give them a whipping, because it was Christmas and everybody *knew* Santa Claus brought you your gifts. Oh, it was really funny. I don't think Santa Claus ever brought my brothers any more gifts after that, however. But, by then we were all pretty well beyond the apple-and-orange stage. I must add that when I was little, Santa Claus not only came to our house, but he also left something for us at Grandmother Johnann's as well. Usually it was the same thing, apples, oranges, and pieces of candy. But, as soon as we had gone through our shoe boxes at home, we would get up early, before daylight, get dressed and go to my grandparents' to see what Santa had brought us over there. I can see us now walking over the hard, frozen ground to our grandmother's house. We never had any snow lying on the ground. Whenever it did snow, the soggy earth would freeze. Part of our Christmas joy was to go to our grandmother's for more gifts. When we were much older, we always got some clothes for Christmas — maybe a coat-sweater, a wool dress or new shoes. One of the neighbors might have a party and there would be a Christmas tree there, perhaps. Someone would **pick on a box,** that is, play the guitar, and there might be some dancing. But for me, as a child, Christmas was our simple little decorations, our Christmas boxes and the knowing that Santa hadn't passed us by.

I have many other random memories of how we amused ourselves. We all had relatives who had gone to live in other cities and other states. Many of them would come to visit; we would all take turns having the visiting relatives come to dinner. My grandmother, my mother or somebody else in the family would have them over. Sometimes, when two or three had come back, we'd invite other close members of the family to come to dinner, too. I was always fascinated to sit and hear our visitors talk about what it was like to live where they lived, especially if they lived in the North. I soon began to realize that life in the North was much better for most black folks than it was in the South.

I had an aunt and uncle who lived in Cincinnati. My aunt always sent us boxes of shoes, clothes and other things. Once I remember receiving a sweater that was so thick that I thought it must be terribly cold up there for people to wear something so thick and heavy. Also, I remember, when I was small, receiving some soft-leather boots that had little heels and laced up — what I thought of as regular little-lady shoes. They hurt my feet, but I insisted on wearing them. One day it rained heavily and I went outdoors wearing those shoes. After the heavy rain, the wet shoes fit more comfortably.

Not many of our folks left the South to live elsewhere, but folks like my grandmother managed to travel from time to time. Grandmother Johnann had a brother, George, who left home when he was a young boy and went to live in Beaumont, Texas. Grandmother was always talking about him. She loved Uncle George very much. So, she went to see him in Texas, stayed with him for a while, and came back home. I remember her telling us about the rabbits in Texas. They were the largest rabbits she had ever seen in her life. She brought us back a pair of dried rabbit ears. She unwrapped them; they were like dog ears. They were so big we could hardly believe it. But, she assured us they were rabbit ears. We were all amazed!

Even though we had flashes of life elsewhere, as we listened to the stories of visitors to our area, our own life remained sheltered and limited in many ways. People just stuck to the old ways of doing things and changes came slowly. What we mostly knew was working in the fields. We didn't have all the games, sports and recreational activities that are now common. Oh, we had baseball games regularly, but it was not real baseball. It was more a game of dividing up sides, hitting a pitched ball and running to a base. That was about the only team game I ever remember. We never had snow to speak of in the winter, so we didn't have winter sports and games. In the summer we didn't have much time to play games. Some of the men and boys would go swimming now and then. But, the creeks were the only places where they could swim and the water was always dark and dirty-looking, and there were likely to be water moccasins and other snakes around. My brothers learned to swim there. Like the other boys and men, they would go swimming without any clothes, because no one had such things as swimming trunks.

One thing I always enjoyed was what they called **bird thrashing.** In the spring, we would clean up the fields by piling up the corn stalks, broken limbs off the trees, leaves and such. On a given night, when those piles of trash were dried out, we would go around and set them on fire. Sometimes, birds would be nesting in them, and as soon as they would begin to fly out of the burning piles, we would swat them down with a little brush paddle. Since they were groggy from all the smoke and heat, we would manage to catch a good many of them. Then, we would take them home and pick the feathers off. We would wash and dress them and then lay them on the hot coals in the fireplace, turning and salting the birds until they were cooked. There would be only a little meat on them, mostly on the breasts, but it was good.

The other good times came from people acting crazy at times or doing outrageous things. For instance, one of my mother's older sisters lived nearby. She had a son who had been living in the North, who had come home for a visit. It was pretty clear to most folks who knew him that he was going to beg or trick some money off his brothers and sisters or mother or whomever he could. When he came home and stopped at his brother's house he told everyone there, *"I've killed a man up North and now I'm running away. They're after me and I want you to give me some money to help me get away."*

They said to him, *"Joe, you ain't doin' a thing but lying. You ain't killed anybody. You're just trying to get some money."*

"Yes, I did too kill somebody," Joe insisted, *"and I want you to give me some money to get away."*

"Look here, Joe," they said, *"you didn't come all this way from up North just to get away."*

So, Joe started over to his mother's house. His brother and sister-in-law began running after him crying out to the old lady, *"Momma, Momma, don't give Joe no money! He is just lying!"*

Before they could get her to understand, she had gotten out what little money she had and given it to him. And, Joe went flying off as fast as he could. By the time they made it clear to her that Joe had tricked her, and he had tricked some others, she began wailing, *"Lord, Oh, Lord, the dirty dog! That dirty dog come in here and got my little money from me!"*

Everybody was laughing about how he had fooled her. Even though it wasn't funny for her and other family members, I recall how folks down there laughed about it. Things like that were a change from the daily dreariness and gave us an opportunity to laugh. I will admit, we sometimes laughed at someone else's expense.

We also had weddings from time to time, dances and quilt-making get-togethers. The weddings were special. We would dress up for them. Maybe the bride would get a new dress for the occasion. A lot of folks would do the best they could to make it a nice wedding. Some brides were able to have an attractive dress and perhaps a veil as well. There would be a little girl to act as the flower girl. The parents would do everything they could to set an appealing table of food. I have to laugh as I think about those weddings, because there would always be a bunch of greedy, old people at them. We could hardly get to the table, because they would be there first, stuffing themselves. A lot of them merely came to weddings to eat.

The gifts the couple received were very modest. Nobody could afford to go out and buy anything new. People would look in their cupboards and take out whatever item they could spare, perhaps a pretty-looking little plate. They would clean and wrap it in any paper they could find.

Sometimes, we would have a special dance. It would be called a supper and was usually held at Corner Flat School. Some people would play guitars and sing — mostly old blues songs — and a lot of folks would get on the floor and dance. My family never danced, however, because my parents didn't approve of that. Dancing and singing were popular, and everybody would manage to have a good time. There was always a kind of **sporting crowd,** even in the backwoods. They would get on the floor and dance in such a way that, in those days, we would have been killed by our parents if we had done what these sporting folks did. Some women, considered to be loose, danced with some of those sporting men. We would sit back, watch, and enjoy being there. Compared to how young people dance and carry on these days, anything that went on at those suppers would seem very tame.

We also had quilting parties. The women would all go to someone's house and piece together a quilt. Then, it would be somebody else's house the next time and so on. It was enjoyable to get together and talk, but oh, that was really hard work! Your fingers would get so pricked up! But, it was the way we all got quilts for ourselves. I don't think, however, it was as quaint or charming as it's been made out to be in stories.

One custom that was still around when I was very, very young was called **plaiting the pole.** We pronounced the word **platting.** Long before I was grown up the custom had been abandoned, but I remember it clearly from my very early years. I've since realized it was what is known as the Maypole Dance. There would be a long pole with long, thin strips of colored calico cloth attached to the top of it. The strips were about eight inches wide. I suppose they tacked the strips to the pole first and then stood it upright in the ground. There was a day set aside for plaiting the pole which I suppose was May Day. People would pick up the end of each streamer. Then, in time to music that had a kind of skipping beat to it, they would dance around the pole, weaving in and out, until they had braided the pole tightly with those colored streamers. The music was provided by a guitar, maybe a fiddle sometimes. I am certain this was a custom that black people had picked up from the Whites and which I understand was a custom that came from England. I don't think any of us knew the true background or meaning of this event.

Years later when my life had become far more complicated and a little more sophisticated, I would look back with yearning for a dose of those simple pleasures we created for ourselves in the backwoods of Southern Alabama.

9.
Marriage

I want to be as truthful and fair as I can about Bernie, me, our courtship and marriage. What I have to say, of course, is only from my point of view, and I find that this isn't the easiest part of my story to tell. We are no longer married, and I don't want it to seem that I am hollering sour grapes. After we were married, Bernie proved to be a very good father and a hard-working man. As the years went by, it became clear that we didn't share the same goals and interests. What had always been true from the time we began going together finally became a fact that couldn't be denied. The truth was that we were basically pulling in opposite directions.

I knew that Bernie came from a good background. Even at my young age, I knew that it was important what kind of parents and home a man had, because I knew that if a man's father was successful and aggressive, he might be that way himself. But, there were some things I didn't realize then.

The time came when I told my father that I was quite fond of Bernie, and that he wanted to be my boyfriend. Dad didn't object to it, so Bernie and I started going together. He lived more than ten miles away, so we only saw each other about twice a month. Bernie would ride down on horseback to see me. He was something of an athlete and sometimes rode our way to play ball with my brothers as well.

There weren't too many young bachelors in our area, so young women didn't have a wide choice of sweethearts or husbands. That is the truth. I am not putting anyone down. Moreover, I think some people probably fell in love with persons they might not have been really suited for, just because they had a limited choice. I was in love with Bernie, no doubt about it, even though our courtship was not easy. It's hard to be cautious when you are in love.

Bernie would write me a letter once in a while and I would write him back. My address was plain and simple: Miss Eula Hendrick, Route #3,

Troy, Alabama. In those days, a letter cost two cents to mail. I was always happy to get a letter. Gradually, through our letter-writing, we decided that we were closer to each other than to anyone else. So, we started going together in earnest. But, you could hardly call that a big romance or a whirlwind courtship!

After Bernie proposed, I had him explain our decision to my parents. I had no intention of running off to get married as Georgia Mae had done. I told my folks that I wanted to get married at home. Well, my daddy was very unhappy about my getting married. He liked Bernie, but he was still unhappy to lose me.

"I just hate for Bie to get married," he told people. *"She was the best working hand I had."*

That was typical of my father in those days. He depended on me — *to work.* He needed me — *to work,* and didn't hesitate to tell that to people. *"Is that all he's ever got in mind for me, just work?"* I thought to myself. *"He never sent me away to school for a good education. He never let me do many of the little things I wanted to do. All he wants is for me to stay here and work, work, work!"*

I did get married at home. Dad kept telling everyone that he wasn't going to give me anything. He acted as if I were letting him down and that he didn't have the heart or money to send me to my new home with a dowry of any kind. Well, my cousins, Allene and Fronie Williams, talked to dad. They told him he couldn't just let me go off to my new family, folks who made something of themselves, with nothing to take. What would they think of me? What would they think of my family? And, how would I feel, with nothing concrete to show my parents' blessings!

Dad finally gave in. Allene and Fronie were not going to take no for an answer. They wore him down so he would listen to reason. So, dad did give me some things: a trunk, an iron-frame bed, bed springs, and a mattress. Consequently, I had my small portion of goods to take with me as a bride after all. But, dad was still unhappy about the entire thing. He kept saying that he wasn't going to do much about my wedding, because he didn't have anything to do with it. He did settle down some, and let mom prepare a nice repast for everyone. I received a few, simple gifts such as cut glass or household items people already had at home. I was very grateful to receive what they gave.

After Bernie and I married, I had the opportunity to see how his father,

Dad McClaney, was an aggressive and successful man. He believed in getting ahead. I would talk to Bernie about this, telling him that I, too, believed in working to get ahead. I didn't tell him about my father's negative attitude, because I didn't want him to copy. Since Bernie liked my father, he might feel inclined to adapt his attitudes rather than his own father's.

Bernie didn't like his own father's attitude too much, because his father had always done more for his older brother than for him, just as my parents had done more for Georgia Mae. Bernie was a smart man and he liked to work. Before we got married, people told me what a hard worker he was and he worked hard after we got married.

It seemed to me now that Bernie was willing to work hard, but he wasn't going to push himself ahead as Dad McClaney had done. I think he also picked up some of Dad McClaney's ways, like being very conservative about his family and household, as well as not wanting anything changed *ever;* like being in charge of everyone and everything because that was the way men were supposed to be.

When we got married, we were very poor. It was right in the middle of the Depression. The only way I could have a dress to get married in was to earn some money and pay for it myself, because my parents had nothing. I taught school at Corner Flat for two months at ten dollars a month. The twenty dollars I earned paid for my wedding dress as well as a couple of other little things I needed. At the time I was planning to get married, some of the people in the community said, *"We want to get Bie to take our little kids and carry them a little bit. We hate for them to come home and just sit."* So, having only gone as far as the sixth grade myself, I became a schoolteacher for a little while.

In 1933, the first year we were married, we lived in a little house right behind Dad McClaney's big house. This was about thirty miles north of Troy near Union Springs in Bullock County. Bernie sharecropped for his father that first year and I went to work in the fields, too. Our house was just a two-room house (a kitchen, a bedroom, and a porch) that Dad McClaney had built for his mother to live in until she died. I made that little house look as nice as possible. There were two beds in the one room, and I got some cheap spreads to put on them. We didn't have glass in the windows, but I put up cute curtains that made them look much better.

During that first year, I learned that whenever I bought some little thing, no matter how cheap and mediocre it was, it would always upset Bernie. He never wanted to get anything new. He wanted us to live with what was already there. I began to wonder if it would always be like that, or if he would always object to my buying anything or making any changes for the better. I thought I might, in time, persuade him that we could do better for ourselves and acquire more things. After all, I was a new bride and I wanted to go back home for the camp meeting and maybe on some other occasion. When I did, I would want to have a new dress or a new pair of shoes. I had hopes that we would make a little money from our crop and have some left over to spend. Bernie soon made it clear that we were going to put the money in the trunk, that he would lock the trunk and keep the key. I began to think, "Oh, I have a miser on my hands," and I worried about what kind of man I had married. Was I going to live with a man who would never spend any money or make any changes or try to improve his circumstances?

That first year, we worked with Dad McClaney on what we called **halves.** Dad McClaney supplied the stock and we were to give him half the return on our crop. After paying what we owed, we came out with a little money left over for ourselves. We had made our crops on three dollars a month — that's the money we borrowed from Dad McClaney to farm with. I had taken great pains to save, especially on our food. Somehow we managed to come out a little ahead. I felt good about that. We had our meat, corn meal, syrup and the few commodities (like sugar) that we had to buy. And, we were even able to buy our own stock at the beginning of the next year! Bernie wanted to be the master of all the money. He eventually started a bank account, but he never wanted me to have access to it.

The next year, we moved from the little two-room house to a large house on about eighty acres of land that we rented from Dad McClaney. We did well farming that second year, and Dad McClaney wanted us to buy that farm. I persuaded Bernie that we should go on renting it. Even though I said nothing about it, I was already beginning to feel that we should leave Alabama. I wanted to go North above the Mason-Dixon line, where life was integrated and things would be better for us and the children.

We bought our own horse from a man who lived near Orion and we also bought ourselves a wagon. Again, we managed to pay our rent and other costs and come out ahead. I had worked hard, but Bernie couldn't be easy with the money and use it to better our lifestyle.

I began to feel that it wasn't right for him to expect me to work and work, helping him as much as possible, and never receive any money to make improvements. It was the cause of a deep misunderstanding between us. Anyhow, we seemed to do fairly well farming, and we got along well whenever we were working together. Before we moved to the larger house on the eighty acres of land, I felt the time had come for us to get a new stove and a piece or two of furniture. The stove we had in the two-room house was Granny McClaney's stove. It was so small that it wouldn't hold enough wood to let you cook one entire meal. It would fill up so quickly with ashes that I would have to clean it out and start a new fire in order to finish cooking our dinner.

After the crop was in and our bills paid off, while we still lived in the two-room house, I told Bernie that I had to have a better stove. *"I'm not going to fight this another year,"* I said.

Bernie was so upset by what I said that he didn't know what to do, except to object.

"Oh, no, Honey," I said, *"we're going into town and we're going to get a stove."*

Consequently, we went shopping in downtown Union Springs. I always had a certain knack for buying things that were quality. The stove that I bought was a wood-burning range that had an oven and six burners. Bernie was against us getting it, saying we should buy something smaller and cheaper. I remained firm. I said I wouldn't have anything else but that stove, nothing smaller or cheaper would I accept. So, we got it and I was able to cook a proper meal in the proper way.

We also bought what we called a **chifferobe,** a very nice vanity table, and another iron-frame bed to match the one we had. Of course, that was almost too much for Bernie! But after that, we always bought something new to make our house more comfortable and attractive with whatever extra money we had left after the cotton was picked and sold.

In our new house, we set up a room that was our **best room,** because we didn't have what could really be called a living room. The room looked far nicer than the average best room, because most people made do with whatever. But, I refused to live the way I saw most people living. (And, I'm still refusing to live like I see a lot of folks living these days, too.) I did things my own way and the best that I could, first in my little two-room house and then in my bigger house.

Our bigger house had a large porch in the front, but we had nothing to put on it to sit in. Usually, people put on their porches first one funny, broken-down old chair, then another such one, and sat in those. One day a man came by in a truck with a set of new porch furniture he wanted to sell. The set consisted of a porch swing, a double settee chair, and two rockers. I had the man set them up on the porch to see how they would look. When Bernie realized I was serious about getting the set, he didn't know what to do!

I told the man I didn't have any money and asked him if he would let us have the set in exchange for some meats, such as hams and shoulders. He said he would. I asked Bernie to bring out some of the meat we had stored. He said, "No!"

"Honey," I said, "we've got to sit on something. We've got a porch and we need to put something on it to sit in."

Bernie kept objecting and I kept talking. Because of my determination, before that man left, I had something to sit in on my porch. I knew that no one in our neighborhood had anything on his or her porch nearly as nice as the set we had gotten ourselves off that truck. Even though Bernie was upset about it, I tried to make him see then, as I did at other times, that it's possible to have some of the things we wanted. It was all too easy to never have anything living in Alabama. I knew in my heart that I didn't have to go along with the status quo and remain poor and down-trodden.

I tried to talk over my ideas about getting ahead with Bernie. "I would just love the day," I said, "when you would come home and tell me you know I want such and such a thing, or that you want a car or something for yourself and that we will find a way to get it. I would just love for you to say that we will increase the things we have, cattle or whatever, in order to improve our life."

Even though it was during the Depression, we were doing fairly well for backwoods farmers in Alabama. Yet, whatever the situation, Bernie wanted to keep it exactly as it was. He seemed to want to stay right there, never making any real changes.

I remember that Bernie wanted a well dug at our place. The well we had was dry. We got our water from a nearby spring. Bernie wanted Dad McClaney to dig a well, but Dad McClaney refused, whereas he probably would have done it for his oldest son, his favorite. This upset Bernie, which was understandable, and once he got mad he could stay mad longer than anybody I have ever known. He could get mad over nothing, and with Dad McClaney he had more than nothing to get mad over. On the other hand, with some people he could get over his anger easily. But, when Bernie got mad at Dad McClaney, he stayed mad so long that I think that was one reason why I was able, later on, to get him to leave Alabama and move to the North.

For the first time in my life, my house was near a church and near a real school. As a young housewife, I seemed to impress people in the church as someone who kept a comfortable home. Whenever the church had visiting ministers come for special days, the people who were in charge would ask me if I would take the ministers and their wives into my home. They took me to be a good cook, too, which is funny, because I've never liked to cook or thought of myself as a good cook. I was always willing to oblige them, and I felt pleased that they saw something in me and my home that was good enough for their visitors.

Always, I would do the best I could to be a good hostess. I would clean and cook and get everything ready for the visiting delegates. There I was, a young housewife, being looked on already as a lady that people wanted to open her home to the ministers and their wives, just as Grandmother Johnann had done. And, when the day came that I left that community, some people were actually sad to see me go. They had come to look upon me as someone special in the community, not a leader necessarily, but certainly someone whose presence was an asset. That was a good thing for me to know.

Dad McClaney was a remarkable man in many ways. His ancestry was part native Indian. I understand that his mother was a full-blooded Indian with long hair and a fair complexion. Dad McClaney had been widowed for many years. He stayed single and raised his family by himself. His last two children were twins and were born right after Bernie. Dad McClaney remained single right up to the time Bernie and I got married. Soon after, he married his second wife.

About two-and-a-half years after Bernie and I were married, we had our first child, a daughter we named Burnistine. I remember that at the time Burnistine was born, our farm was quite a distance from our home. Burnie was born in September, and that was the time when we were busy picking cotton. Well, it meant that when I was near delivery — and who knew if it would be in the day or at night? — Bernie might be away from the house and working in the fields. So, we arranged to have a lady come and stay with me. She would be there to fetch Bernie whenever I came into labor.

When Dad McClaney learned that this particular woman was going to stay with us, he said, *"No, that woman is not coming on my place to stay at your house. I will not allow her to come on my place."*

However, Dad McClaney did not replace the woman with anybody. He, his family and Bernie continued to work in the fields. I thought to myself, *"What a rough man he is! He comes into my house and tells us that this woman cannot stay with me. I don't know what disagreement they have had in the past,* (They have known each other for years, I'm told), *but here I am — alone."*

It looked as if that was the way things would be until Georgia Mae, who was still married to Malachi and living in Alabama said, *"I'll speak to my husband and see if he'll let me come and stay with you."* So, Malachi let her come and she stayed with me for two weeks until Burnistine was born.

We were still living in the house behind Dad McClaney's at the time Burnistine entered this world. When Georgia Mae came to stay with me, she brought her two children with her. Her little son was very handsome. Everybody liked him because he talked a lot and was a bright little boy. Her little daughter was a great big chubby baby and was just learning to walk at that time.

I was the kind of person who was seldom ill. After Burnistine was born, I was soon well enough to take care of my home. No one in Dad McClaney's family ever cooked a meal for me, and somehow we made it through.

I depended on God to help and guide me. Whenever people did not treat me right or show a good attitude, I prayed and kept on stepping. I learned that it was the best way for me to do things. Oh yes, I've learned over and over that God will truly take you through difficult times. He will carry you through as long as you're doing what you know to be right and you are trying to do His will. He will just take care of you.

Now, I don't exactly know how Dad McClaney treated my sister-in-law whenever her children were born. But, I knew that her own family would always come and stay with her and take care of her, just as Georgia Mae stayed with me. We all knew that Dad McClaney was a strong-willed man who had to have his own way. So, we all learned to do what we had to do on our own behalf and everything always worked out all right.

My mother-in-law was a sweet person. She once said to me, *"Sis, you know many times I wanted to do things for you or at least offer you my services. But, you know that I can't do no more than I'm allowed. You know how it is here. So, I just have to go on as best I can."*

"Oh Mother, that's all right," I said. *"I appreciate you anyway. Thanks all the same."*

Dad McClaney, what had he to say? Well, many a time I heard him, when his wife was around, declare, *"I can say one thing about my wife . . . If she ever leaves me, ever walks off from here, she'd better go to heaven or hell."* And, he meant it. After all, he almost always carried his gun with him wherever he'd go. He always went for bad in the neighborhood and people would step back when they saw him coming.

I think that Dad McClaney helped to mold me into the kind of person I am today. Just as I learned from my own father's example of what I didn't want to be or do, so I learned from Dad McClaney's example of what I did want to be and do. In fact, I would say that my father, my Grandmother Johann and Dad McClaney were great influences in shaping my character. I learned from Dad McClaney's example that you could build and look out for your family and for your children, so that others can't simply walk in and say to you or them, *"You go do this and go do that."* I saw that sort of thing being done as I was growing up, but I saw that Dad McClaney did not tolerate it. I was determined to follow his lead.

Although he did not work himself too hard farming, Dad McClaney did the overseeing of the work. He saw to it that all his children knew how to work hard. He even made sure that his daughters knew how to plow. Those girls could do anything the boys could do. As a family, the McClaneys were all hard-working and **smart.** Dad McClaney had raised them well.

Dad McClaney was always busy looking after his properties and his houses. Then, there was the farm work that he oversaw. He also did a lot of logging. Seems like there was always a lot of timber being cut and dragged here and there. So, the McClaneys were always busy. Dad liked to boss his kids, even after they were married. He liked to come up and get Bernie out of bed early in the morning so he could feed the stock and do this and do that. He just kept the whole McClaney enterprise moving along.

I may have admired Dad McClaney's aggressiveness and ability to control his own life, but I didn't really care for his conservatism and his excessive bossiness. He bossed his wife, children and household. The McClaney house was rather meagerly furnished, but dad would not permit anybody to move one single item without his say-so. His wife and children could not change their furniture, such as move a bed into a new position, without his consent. Of course, dad never consented. He wanted everything to sit like it had sat from the beginning of time.

I would say to one of his daughters, *"Why don't you change the bedroom once in a while?"*

"Well, Pa won't allow us to change the bedroom," she would reply.

I soon came to find out that **Pa** wanted to manage and master everybody, which meant me and my home as well. But, **Pa** soon found out that he wasn't able to master me and my little rooms and whatever I had. I did my own mastering.

Bernie took after his father in being conservative and rigid about things. He seemed to have it in his mind, as soon as we were married, that whatever we had started out with in our home should stay just as it had been at the very outset. If we should buy something and put it in a certain corner, then that is where it must stay forever.

I remember that the mantel over the fireplace in our house was so high that it was almost up to the ceiling. At least it looked that way to me. So, I had Bernie replace it. I had him put it down lower so that I could put a little mirror and a few things on it. He didn't want to do it, partly because he thought it should stay as it was, but also because *"Pa won't like it."* Well, I told Bernie what I thought of that, and he lowered the mantel. It was all right for Dad McClaney to boss his own household, but not mine. I did love a lot of things that dad stood for. But, when it came to him bossing our house and our affairs, I thought, *"Well, Pa wants to go too far."* So, I never let him get control over me.

I have the feeling that Dad McClaney didn't like me as well as his other daughters-in-law. He didn't like not being able to order me around. Also, since he was such a conservative man, I know he didn't like me travelling around with Mrs. Prichard, because I showed every sign of becoming a liberated woman like she. I was also a better dresser than his other daughters-in-law, which upset him. He wanted you to wear the same clothes most of the time. But, I enjoyed getting a new dress, hat and shoes whenever I could. One of my sisters-in-law was a lovely lady and she had babies more often than I did, so most of the time she wasn't bothered by not having new clothes. Dad McClaney believed that you had to be very conservative to get anywhere. I would love to have him visit me today and see that you don't have to be rigidly conservative in order to succeed. I would like to show him my way of doing things. I would tell him that I picked up and followed those ways of his that I admired and ignored those I didn't.

I can think of a good many random things that occurred during the first years of my marriage while Bernie and I were still living in Alabama. Even though we were doing better than might be expected during the middle of the Depression, by most standards we were still poverty-stricken. So, I remember well the pleasure I got from being able to subscribe to a little newspaper that came from Montgomery. It came once a week in the mail. Our mailman was Mr. Clint Turner. He ran what was called the Linwood route — Route One, Linwood, Alabama. I was always so happy to get the newspaper. I enjoyed reading *everything* in it, whether it was news or wasn't news. That newspaper was a lifesaver for me, especially while living out in the country without even a radio.

Mr. Turner would also stop at Dad McClaney's house and sometimes talk with my mother-in-law. They would converse near the mailbox. Mr. Turner was fond of saying to her, *"You know that Eula McClaney? Down there at her house it's so nice and clean! Their yard and everything is kept so clean. You know what? That girl is smart as a steel trap!"* It made me feel good that he thought that about me.

I used to get a kick out of baking egg-custard pies for my mother-in-law. As much as I didn't like to cook, folks generally liked what I did prepare and Mother McClaney was really fond of my custard pies. She would have me bake them whenever she had to take something to the dinners at her church.

Looking back now, I see that as a young wife, I was already cutting out a good reputation for myself, as a hostess, cook (amazing though it sounds), housewife and mother. I enjoyed doing my best in those capacities and I liked being able to control my own life. For instance, I got a great deal of pleasure out of dressing Burnie and La-Doris as best I could. When they were very small and we were still in Alabama, they were practically the same size. That made it easy for me to dress them alike. I loved the little two and three strap shoes that were made for little girls. In the summer I would dress them in white shoes and in the winter, black. They also wore dresses exactly alike. My cousin, Allene Blackman, could sew well, and she would make matching dresses for my little girls. People would admire the way Burnie and La-Doris dressed and talked about how cute they looked. I was proud and pleased that my children were coming up in a better way of life than I had.

Even as infants, I found it possible to leave my children in good hands so that I could work in the fields with Bernie or, now and then, take little trips on my own (as I used to do with Mrs. Prichard). When Burnistine was just a baby her great-grandmother on her father's side of the family was still living. Her farm joined the McClaney farm. We would have Grandmother come over to my little house and keep Burnistine so that I could go to the field.

Grandmother was one of those neat ladies who was petite and cute. Since she had two daughters who could sew well, she was always dressed nicely. She would come over every day to stay with Burnistine. I would get everything ready for our dinner at noontime and Grandmother would finish cooking it. She would have it ready by the time we got home from the fields.

When we came home in the evening, Grandmother would go back to her own house. We always came home before dark so that she could safely walk home alone. I remember that Grandmother did not have any social security or any kind of welfare support, so we would always pay her with food. I canned lots of fruits and we had the meats from our butchering.

"I know you children don't have any money," Grandmother would say, *"but I have to have the same things to live on that you do, so I will take my pay in food things."*

I would pay her with all kinds of foodstuffs: meat, syrup, meal, shortening, canned goods and whatever else I could spare. So, Grandmother helped us out for about two years. Later, we moved further away, so she couldn't come to our home any more. The fields on the eighty-acre farm we rented from Dad McClaney were all close to the house, so I was able to work and keep an eye on Burnistine myself.

There is one experience that stands out sharply in my memory. It occurred just before La-Doris was born. It foreshadowed the deeper and more serious problems pending in our marriage. It began on Mother's Day (a few weeks before La-Doris was born on Father's Day). Bernie and I had a real falling out over something he had done. It concerned a woman who had children who were as old as Bernie and I. Because I was in the last months of carrying La-Doris, I was not able to do any field work. This woman was helping Bernie in my place. Whether anything besides work was going on, I can't say. However, I went down to my parents' home to spend the Saturday night before Mother's Day with my mother. Bernie came and picked me up that Sunday evening. When we got back to our house, he told me that a lot of fuss had come up concerning the woman who was helping him. Her boyfriend, who she more or less lived with, had been fussing and fighting with her about her coming and helping Bernie with the work. So, Bernie had gone down to her place to try to help straighten things out, and there had been a regular ruckus.

I think I could have gone along with that without getting too upset, because I know people can make a fuss over nothing. On the other hand, I wasn't all that sure that there wasn't more going on than I knew about. What greatly upset me though was that Bernie had gone down to her place when she and her *"husband"* were in the middle of a heated argument and could have easily had his head blown off by that man. I told Bernie he shouldn't have gone there. It would have been one thing if the man had come to our house to talk to Bernie, but for Bernie, being hot-headed himself, to go there to see about this woman and her problems — and she'd been having problems long before he was born — was pretty foolish. I was upset.

What got to me, however, was what happened the next day. On Monday morning that woman, with two or three of her children, came to our farm and went to work in the field. She completely ignored and defied her *"husband."*

I took Bernie aside and said, *"If she's having trouble at home with her 'husband,' so to speak, why does she keep coming up here to work for you? It seems to me that she should stay home until they get this settled."*

Instead of giving me a satisfying answer, Bernie got real smart-mouthed and said something I disliked. I can't remember now what he said, but I know it hurt my feelings badly. I was as upset with him as I had ever been. So, I just put on my smock, took Burnistine by the hand, and set out for my parents' home.

We lived a good fifteen miles or better from my parents and it was already getting on towards 11:00 p.m. when I started walking. I remember I was wearing two smocks. I had just put one on over the other as I prepared to leave. I put one foot in front of the other, taking it slow, with Burnistine walking by my side.

When I was about three to five miles away from my folks' house, I stopped by the house of some friends of ours. I had to wake them up. Burnie had gotten so sleepy that she was falling asleep while walking through the moonlight. I tried to carry her, but I was pregnant and exhausted. We had just worn ourselves out walking down the road in the dark, through the woods and fields, with only the moonlight to guide our way. I asked the man of the house if we could take his horse and ride to my parents' home.

The three of us made it to my Aunt H.'s house. The man rode his horse with Burnie riding with him. I walked along beside them. When we got to Aunt H.'s house I was so tired I couldn't go any farther. I was so glad to see Aunt H. She insisted I stay there for the night. We thanked the neighbor who had helped me and he went back home. Then, I rested and soaked my feet in a tub of hot water, because they were just burning and aching from that long walk. Burnie was put to bed, because she was completely worn out, too.

"How did you have the nerve to do this while expecting a child as you are?" Aunt H. and Uncle Tobe asked me.

I explained what the situation was between Bernie and me. We all talked a while about my problems. I don't recall now what anybody said, but I know I was glad to be among people I loved and who loved me. I stayed there the rest of that night. The next morning Uncle Tobe took Burnie down to my parents' home and I walked the rest of the way.

I stayed with my family for a month or so until La-Doris was born, on Father's Day of that year. Bernie came to my parents' house the next day to see me. I guess he hadn't believed I would walk all the way home. He expected me to come back to the house any moment that night. Much to his surprise, I didn't. I kept on going, because I am the kind of person who keeps on stepping once I make up my mind where it is I intend to go or what it is I intend to do. I just put my trust in God and keep on stepping. It isn't always easy — oh, no! It's usually hard and it tests your character and spirit. But, I did it. That is probably the real secret of my success.

One day, after I had been at my parents' home for a few days, I was walking across the floor and a plank gave way and I fell down to the ground underneath the house. What a thing to happen when I was expecting my baby so soon! It was miraculous that I didn't hit my body on anything or hurt my baby. As I fell through the floor, a plank did strike me on the right side of my cheek just below my eye, yet it didn't even break the skin. The plank that gave way had always been dangerous and we all knew about it while I was growing up. I don't know why my father never fixed it. It was a short plank. Since it wasn't nailed into place, we would lift it up in order to go under the house for something and then lay it back in place. On this particular day, I forgot about it and the accident happened. I have always felt God's protection around me and that was one instance of seeing it demonstrated.

When La-Doris was born, I was attended by a midwife. We didn't have doctors available there in the backwoods. La-Doris was born very early in the morning. My father got somebody to take him to pick up the midwife. She had granddaughters who were my age, and were my friends. She was a very nice woman I had known for years, and she took good care of La-Doris and me. It was good for me to be able to see her again and to have her help in my delivery.

My father was as happy as he could be when La-Doris was born. He was also proud that he had gone and fetched the midwife. *"This is something I haven't done in twenty-odd years!"* he kept saying. *"I haven't been for a midwife since my baby was a baby."* And, all his life he was happy about this and happy about La-Doris. He called her Babe and she was always very dear to him. He always said what a big thing it was to him when he got that lady for Babe.

After La-Doris was born and the rift between Bernie and me was repaired, I learned that Dad McClaney was very upset with what Bernie had done — getting himself mixed up with that woman. He didn't like that woman and her family anyway, because they were always wanting to meddle in McClaney business and to give trouble. Dad McClaney got after them and gave them a good talking to and told them to stay out of his children's business and said he didn't want them on his place. So, I realized that dad was on my side in the whole affair. Dad didn't tell me this himself, but a man called Prince Prichard told me. After that, I knew Dad McClaney was more for me than against me. I think he would approve of what I've done with my life this far.

In the months following La-Doris' birth, I became convinced that the best thing for Bernie, our children and me would be to leave Alabama and move to the North. I knew we had to give our children a better chance for a good life than we had had ourselves, and I knew we could never do it if we remained in the South. As I said before, I think I had an easier time convincing Bernie we should do this, because he was angry with his father at that time. Also, some of Bernie's cousins had gone North to live, and we knew of other people who had done the same. It didn't really matter to me where we went, so long as we went above the Mason-Dixon line. Besides, I wanted Bernie to have a say in the matter. If he would be kind enough to take me from Alabama and the cotton fields, I thought it was right for me to give him the say-so as to where we would go.

"Where do you want to go if we leave here?" he asked me.

"I'll leave that to you," I said. *"You can go anywhere that you want to go. I'm willing to go anywhere above the Mason-Dixon line. Don't take me anywhere South, because I'm deep enough in the South now. I want to get away from this whole Southern atmosphere. I have heard that every place in the South is alike. I don't want to be bothered with prejudiced people. I don't want my kids to grow up in such an environment."*

Bernie thought it over. He had an uncle who had gone to live in Chicago, and he thought he might like to go there. I said that would be fine with me. Then, he thought about some cousins he had gone to school with who had moved to Pittsburgh. *"Maybe I'd rather go there,"* he said, *"because they're my age."*

I said, *"I wouldn't mind going to Pittsburgh, because I have met your cousins and they are of our age."*

So, Bernie said, *"Well, Pittsburgh then."*

It was all right with me. I thought it wasn't fair for me to insist on him going to where my sister was in Detroit. He might get there and be unhappy, and then figure that I was the one who told him to go there. I was happy just to have him be congenial enough to go anywhere out of the South.

Bernie went to Pittsburgh by himself and got a construction job. He was making very little money, but that was all right because we hadn't been used to making much money anyway. He was at least able to get established in Pittsburgh and save some money to send for the children and me. While he was in Pittsburgh those first months, I moved back in with my parents. Burnie was a little over three-years old and La-Doris was about a year-old.

Bernie left in November, and by the following July he wrote and told me to *"Come on, come on! If you're going to come, come on!"*

In the meantime, Georgia Mae had come back home to get her children, who were living with my mother and father, and also to take mom and dad back to Detroit with her. She had gotten married again and had another child — a baby girl, who was just beginning to walk — who she brought with her. I would have liked to have stayed on at home while Georgia Mae was there and had a kind of vacation with her, but Bernie insisted that I join him in Pittsburgh as soon as possible. I had enough money to go. I had sold four very fine hogs we had raised and had saved some money. Bernie had also sent me the money for my train ticket (there was no charge for Burnie and La-Doris to ride). Therefore, I had about a hundred dollars and was really all set to leave.

I was happy to leave Alabama. We could have all taken the train together as far as Cincinnati, where they would change for Detroit and I would change for Pittsburgh, but my parents were not able to leave until some months later.

Finally, the day came when I left Alabama. Now I will tell what happened to my father after I left for Pittsburgh. Once the cotton and peanut crops were in, my mother left Orion with Georgia Mae and her three children and went to Detroit. My daddy, however, hated to leave the country so badly that he said to them, *"Well, I'm not going now. I'll just come on later."*

"I ain't going now," he kept telling people, even though he was all alone. He seemed determined to stay there on his own. Now, it must be remembered that we lived further in the backwoods than anybody else, deep down in the woods. Also, some of the old houses back there were all closed down, because people like my Cousin Clarence were dead and all their folks had moved away.

Dad tried to stay down there by himself. They say he cried so about it and he kept saying, *"I been here all my life and I just don't want to leave. It's the only home I know."*

They always said that it was very ghostly in those woods. I used to say that if there were such things as ghosts, they would surely look over my daddy. Now one night, when daddy was all alone in our house, something began to make a noise. There were no electric lights there and the noise became so intense that it ran dad out of the house. He said it was in the wee hours of the morning and that was better for him to get up and put on his clothes and leave, rather than to stay. He left the house as fast as he could and walked four or five miles up the road to my Aunt H.'s house. He felt that somebody who had died (could it have been Grandmother Johnann?) didn't want him there alone and made all that noise to frighten him out. He told Aunt H. that he would have to leave and go to Detroit. I must say it took an overwhelming experience to move my father.

Well, there isn't much else for me to say about my life in Alabama. Looking back on those years, and the first years of my marriage to Bernie, I can see how adversity spurred me on to find a better way of doing things. I might never have known my business potential, if Bernie had not been the way he was. I learned that if I had to go on my own I could do it, no matter what. All those hard experiences taught me to pray honestly and to have faith that my prayers would be answered.

I learned a lot from people, positive and negative things. What I have always said to my daughters I would say to anyone.

"Learn what's good in anything and take your pattern from that."

So, I took the good I found in Alabama with me. The rest I left behind.

PART II
Pittsburgh, Pennsylvania

1.
Gone North

The day I left Alabama in 1940 was probably the most important day in my life. When I got on that train that took me from Montgomery to Pittsburgh, I was starting on a twenty-year trip from poverty to wealth, from believing God could help me to *knowing* God can do anything. It takes a lot of climbing, one step at a time, to get high enough up a mountain to look back and begin to see how high it really is. And, when I look back now, I see how high the move to Pittsburgh actually took me, higher and farther than I could have imagined at the time. All I knew then was that I was getting out of the South—thank the Lord!

I didn't have much to take with me. My cousin in Montgomery had checked my one and only piece of baggage, a trunk, through to Pittsburgh. It carried a few quilts, my little supply of linens, some clothes, and things for the children. The rest I carried with me, mostly diapers and a special powdered, malted-milk for La-Doris, a change or two of dresses for Burnistine and myself, and some food my cousin had packed for us to eat on the train. And, I had my purse with our tickets and what little money I had—maybe a hundred dollars. For traveling so far, I traveled light.

The thing I was most concerned about was changing trains in Cincinnati. I just didn't see how I could manage it with two, little babies among the crowds of people and trying to find my way in a big, strange depot in a big, strange city. I was really worried I was going to miss the Pittsburgh train. Then, what would I do? But, it turned out that the people on the train were friendly. They told me not to worry and that they would help me find my way. They reassured me that changing trains was no big deal.

People talked to me and sometimes gave me a hand with La-Doris and Burnie. I told them how I was going to Pittsburgh to live and that my husband would be waiting there for me. Of course, I had to ride sitting up all night, which was hard to do with two little children to look after. I had to hold La-Doris on my lap much of the time while Burnie could sit and lay down on the seat beside me. The other passengers were very nice about making room, if they could, so both of the children could lie down. The porter gave me some pillows and blankets. I was able to lean back and get some rest and cover myself and the children.

It seemed like a long trip, since it took about two days and two nights. The children would get restless, so I would let La-Doris stand up on the seat and on the floor where she could move around some and play. Burnie, too, was very good about playing with La-Doris and helping me look after her.

When we got to Cincinnati, people told me just to get off the train and follow the crowd into the depot. My cousin in Montgomery had also given me the same advice, *"Now, when you get off the train in Cincinnati,"* he said, *"you've just got to follow the crowd. The crowd will be going to the depot and you just follow."*

There I was, in Cincinnati and following the crowd! It seemed like there were hundreds of people getting out of our train and other trains, and walking and walking. I was very nervous and doing my best to carry La-Doris, my purse, my other little bags, and trying to keep track of Burnie who was scooting along beside me. We had all been sleeping and dozing earlier, but when we were almost to the station, the porter woke everyone up. There was lots of commotion from everybody getting their things together. With all of that and the excitement of finally getting off the train, I was just in a kind of daze and trying to keep my wits.

As we were walking along and into the depot, I said to somebody, *"I'm supposed to get on another train that's going to Pittsburgh, Pennsylvania, but I don't know the name of the train or what time it leaves."*

"I'm going to Pennsylvania, too," a man said. *"I believe we're taking the same train. I'll be glad to help you."*

I began to feel better. I was also glad I had enough sense to open my mouth and let people know that I had never traveled before and wasn't sure what to do.

The man who had offered to help me asked, *"Is anybody gonna meet you in Pittsburgh?"*

"Yes," I said, *"my husband."*

"Well, then, you're going to be all right," said the man. *"Once you get on the Pittsburgh train, all you got to do is ride and enjoy yourself. And, your husband will be waiting there at the other end."*

It turned out just as the man said. With his help I got the right train. By the time we got to Pittsburgh, I sort of knew my way around and had learned that riding trains was not so difficult after all. I had already begun to learn new ways and I found out that I could manage.

Bernie was waiting for us when the train pulled into Pittsburgh. A cousin who had a car was with him. He had offered to bring Bernie to pick us up and take us back to his house before he had to go to work. This cousin and his wife were rooming with his aunt and uncle. They had lived in Alabama, too, and by the time I saw them in Pittsburgh they had two children.

Bernie and his cousin took us to the house and then they went to work. The cousin's wife was about my age, but she fussed over us like a little old grandmother. She offered to fix breakfast for me, but I told her I wasn't hungry. I was still too excited about seeing Bernie again, being in Pittsburgh, and getting myself calmed down.

"You got to have a hot meal," she said. *"You got to eat even if you don't feel hungry. And, your kids need something, too."*

So, she fixed breakfast for us. Then, she fussed around and insisted that the children and I have a bath and that Burnie and La-Doris get into bed and sleep. We just followed her orders while she talked on and on. She drew the bath water for me and I washed the children and put them to bed. I was tired, but I was too keyed-up to sleep. By the time she and I had talked and asked and answered all kinds of questions, the day had just flown by.

When Bernie came home from work that evening, he told me about a place where he had arranged for us to room. We moved in that night. It was two rooms in a house that was up on a hill. The house was owned by a Frank Smith and our two rooms were on the third floor. There was no bathroom on that floor, which meant we had to use the bathroom on the second floor. But, that hardly mattered to me. I had never had an indoor bathroom with a wash-basin and a bathtub. It seemed like heaven to me.

Life in Pittsburgh was drastically different from anything I had ever known. For the first time in my twenty-some years I was out of the cotton fields! It seemed as if I had hardly anything to do but to keep our rooms clean, to look after my children and to have my husband's dinner ready when he came home. Added to that, Bernie was regularly bringing home money. Money that we could count on week in and week out. It wasn't much, but we knew it was coming and we could begin to plan our lives. Oh, it was truly like heaven to me, living in a city with its hills, houses, trolley cars, crowds of people, stores, churches and schools. Everywhere I turned there was something new and interesting. Sometimes in the evening, when he wasn't too tired, Bernie would take me and the children walking. He would carry the little ones in his arms when they got tired. We would walk down the streets, walk out and come back home. It was a whole new life for me and it was beautiful. I loved it.

There was one thing I had trouble getting used to, however, and that was the relationship between Blacks and Whites. Many white people in Pittsburgh had an entirely different attitude towards Blacks than what I had known in the South. They actually seemed to think we were human and equal! And, most of the black people obviously had an attitude towards the white people that was far different from what I had known in Alabama. There wasn't the fear of Whites and having to step aside for them.

Near the house we lived in was a little neighborhood grocery store. I think the people who owned it were Jewish people. I would go to this store to buy the small items I needed, a pound of meat, some butter and a few eggs. I wasn't used to this, just buying a little bit of something anytime I wanted or needed it, but it was part of learning how to live in the city.

Whenever I would deal with the lady who ran the store, I would always answer her questions and remarks with "Yes, ma'am," and "No, ma'am."

"Where are you from?" she finally said to me one day.

"I'm from Orion, Alabama," I told her.

"Well, why do you say, 'Yes, ma'am,' and 'No, ma'am' to me?" she asked.

I was embarrassed. I couldn't tell her that it was because she was White and that I'd always been used to speaking that way to white folks.

"I want you to say 'Yes,' or 'No,' " she said. *"Don't say 'Yes, ma'am' and 'No, ma'am' to me."*

Even with her consent, I couldn't say that to her. I couldn't say a simple *"Yes"* or *"No"* to save my life. I would end up saying *"Yeah"* to her. Oh, I would try hard to *"Yes"* and *"No,"* but I would forget and be back to saying *"Yes, ma'am"* and *"No, ma'am."*

Finally, she just couldn't stand it. One day she began saying to me in an exaggerated way, *"Oh, yes, ma'am!"* and *"Oh, no, ma'am!"* I just had to laugh then, because I saw how it sounded.

She was a very sweet and charming lady who didn't want me honoring her just because she was White. She knew my background and that I had been conditioned to be over-respectful to white people. It was important to her that I learn to respect myself and that I just speak directly to other people, no matter what color they were or who they were.

I must say that everywhere I went in Pittsburgh, I also saw that black people didn't seem at all afraid of white people. They would walk down the street not fearing if they would accidentally brush up against a white person, and if they did, no one paid it any mind. When the Blacks would talk to the Whites, they would look at them and not say *"Yes, sir,"* and *"No, ma'am,"* but just *"Yes"* and *"No."* I also noticed that if somebody White would say something nasty to a black person, that person would say something nasty back. In fact, some of the black people got so ornery, they would say something nasty when they had no reason to and nobody White had bothered them!

As it turned out, we didn't stay in our rented two rooms too very long. Frank Smith, the man from whom we rented our quarters, was what I would call a very slick and shiny man. He was a sharp-looking, single man and a very good dresser. He was a kind of man who would always look very up-to-date and *"with it."* But, I had an uncomfortable feeling about him and there was something about him that just didn't seem right.

Frank lived on the first floor of the house and we lived on the third floor. A couple, a white woman and a black man, lived on the second floor. The woman was always complaining about Burnie and La-Doris. She didn't like children and didn't like living where there were children. She was always running to Frank and telling him that my girls were always using and keeping her out of the bathroom. The truth is that I tried to be as careful as I could about our use of the bathroom. I would take Burnie and La-Doris there and bring them back up, and made every effort to see that the bathroom was always clean. But, Frank always seemed to pay a lot of attention to whatever that woman would tell him and he would believe her. I knew he was the kind of man who could get very nasty if he wanted to.

I told Bernie about the situation and that I thought we should find ourselves another place to live. I told him that I didn't think Frank Smith was a man to be trusted. Bernie, as usual, would disagree with me and side with the other people. *"Frank's all right,"* he said. *"You just don't like him. But the man's all right."*

Well, I knew two things. I knew that Bernie was not going to stand by me in this matter and I knew that the Lord always took care of me. I also knew that I was going to have to get out of that house and that situation.

"Look," I finally said to Bernie, *"if you're not going to leave this man's place and if you intend to stay with him and think he's in love with you, you stay on here with him. But, there's one thing I'm going to do. I'm going to get away from here."*

"And, where do you think you'll go?" asked Bernie.

I said, *"I'm going around to Bertha Smith's. She's got extra rooms. She's from down home, too. I'm going to stay with her a little while until I can get my things away from here. Then, I'm going to Detroit and get me a job. I'll leave my two kids with Momma and go to work. 'Cause I can't stand talking with you. You are always for the other side and never pay me any mind."*

When Bernie saw that I was definitely going to leave, he got very upset. He knew that I would go to Bertha Smith's and get a place there.

As much as he liked hanging around Frank Smith, he agreed that we would move.

The night came that we had decided on moving. After Bernie got home from work, a friend of his brought his car around and we were busy loading it with our few clothes and other belongings. While I was out putting things in the car, Bernie went into the kitchen just as Frank Smith appeared. Bernie, of course, just thought that being *kind* was going to work with Frank.

Bernie handed Frank the keys and said, *"Well, Frank, I'm ready to go on. We have found another place to live—better for Eula and the kids. We're leaving this evening. Here's the key."*

Then Frank, who Bernie thought was such a nice fellow, said nothing and hit Bernie, a powerful blow that knocked him over. Bernie hadn't even thought there would be any such thing as fighting. So Frank who was small but mean, was able to topple him with that one blow of his fist. By the time Bernie began to straighten up, maybe to hit Frank back, Frank had grabbed up a chair. It looked to Bernie that Frank was going to come after him with the chair. He didn't waste a minute trying to do anything to Frank under those circumstances. He ran out of the kitchen door and came and told me what had happened.

"I'm so glad Frank hit you," I said. *"Lord knows, I can't knock any sense into you."*

Bernie got mad at me when I said that. He knew I had been right about Frank. He knew he was always misjudging people and taking sides with them against me. Frankly, I was glad Frank had hit him, because it hadn't hurt him and I had hoped it might help him learn to trust my feelings a little more and to stick by me.

A few days after we had left Frank Smith's house, we were nicely settled into rooms in Bertha Smith's house. Bertha and Frank were not in any way related. They were about as different as any two people could be. We lived with Bertha for a few weeks. In the meantime, Bernie and Frank sued each other. I don't recall who sued who first, but they both dragged each other to court.

When the time came for Bernie to go to court in response to Frank's suit, Bernie insisted that I go with him. Frank was there wearing a hat, and I could feel that he was up to something really tricky. At the moment when he was to speak to the judge, Frank stood up and dramatically removed his hat. Well, I had never seen such a sight as Frank's head! No one had. His hair was all different lengths with bare patches here and there, as if someone had pulled clumps out of it.

"Look, your Honor," whined Frank. "Not only did Mr. McClaney hit me, but he did to my hair just what you see!"

"I didn't hit that guy a single lick!" Bernie protested. "Eula, you tell the judge I didn't touch the man."

"I don't want to say a thing," I told the court. "I didn't actually see what happened."

"He hit me, I tell you!" Frank insisted. "And, he grabbed me and pulled out my hair."

It was obvious, however, that Frank's hair hadn't been pulled out at all and was just cut in chunks here and there. The judge didn't believe a word Frank said. He also wasn't too much impressed with what Bernie said. I just kept quiet. I was still glad Frank had hit him, because he'd been easier to get along with since then. The outcome was that both suits were thrown out of court. That was the last we heard from Frank Smith.

As I think about it, that was my first introduction to courts, judges, lawsuits and legal action. I am a peaceful and patient person, and I like to deal honestly with people. I want everything to be open and fair, because I never have anything to hide and never want to take advantage of anyone. But over the years I have had to go to court numerous times, because of dishonest tenants and various other persons who have tried to cheat me and lie about me. These dishonest people will just cause trouble for someone they see who is sincerely trying to get ahead and who is making it. All of this should make me pretty hardened to the lengths people will go to strike out at you and to use the courts as instruments of revenge. But to this day I hate all the legal hassles and never enjoy dealing with courts, agencies and bureaucracy. Yet, it seems that God allows me to have these distasteful experiences, I guess, to keep me from falling into the trap of thinking that everything is a snap to accomplish and that Eula McClaney is somebody better than others. Just because you mean well doesn't mean everything will go smoothly. And, dealing with the rough places in life has given me a legal training I'd have been glad to avoid.

After we had been with Mrs. Bertha Smith a few weeks, we were able to rent a small apartment from a Mr. Davis. Mr. Davis had a lovely apartment building with six apartments, five of which he rented out. He lived in the sixth one himself. He had built the building, having been a successful brick mason in Pittsburgh, and he had made those apartments just as nice as he could. Ours was an apartment with three rooms, one of them a kitchen with an attached breakfast nook. We enjoyed living there very much. Even though it was very small for the four of us, it was the nicest place we had ever lived. La-Doris and Burnie slept in the living room on a convertible sofa bed, which was one of the first pieces of furniture we bought in Pittsburgh.

During the time we lived in what was our first real apartment, Bernie worried me so badly at times that I hardly knew what to do. He was a young man who had always lived in the country. Now, he was living in a big city and making a little money every week with a regular payday to count on. Also, he had been by himself for seven months or so before I came to Pittsburgh and had been able to live the life of a bachelor in a city where there were all kinds of new attractions for a country boy.

Some evenings he would come home, take a bath, put on a pair of dressy slacks, a fresh shirt, shoes and go out for a while.

"Well, I believe I'll go back to Fred and Ailey's place and get me a room. They tell me any time I want to live with them again I can do it," he would say.

"What are you going to do with me and the children?" I would ask. *"What will we do?"*

Of course, Bernie never answered that. He would throw out this threat, but he never gave any suggestions as to what the children and I would do. He seemed to get a kick out of this. The more he could aggravate me and get me to worry, the better he seemed to enjoy it. He was young and I was young, and he wanted to be something special, what you would call *"hot stuff."* That seemed to mean he could just say these things to upset me completely. He acted and talked as if he might just walk off any time. He knew that I wouldn't think of leaving the children for anybody.

One day I spoke to Mr. Davis. *"Bernie's talking about leaving me, Mr. Davis, and going back to live with Fred and Ailey."*

"What's the matter with that boy!" Mr. Davis snorted. *"Why would he think anything like that?"*

"He's one to worry a person," I said. *"He seems to get a kick out of it. But I think he might just go off by himself, the way he keeps talking."*

"Well, the only thing I can tell you," said Mr. Davis, *"is don't ever worry about the children going hungry or anything like that. I would not let them kids sit here and go hungry. You will not have to suffer for food for the kids as long as I can work, 'cause I wouldn't let that happen."*

I realized then what a wonderful man Mr. Davis was. But somehow, by the grace of God, Bernie did not carry out his threats. He stayed with me, and through the next years we managed to improve our way of life and get ahead. Still, I never had a truly easy time, because I never knew what Bernie would or would not do.

We lived in the little apartment while waiting for a larger place in the new federally financed housing project that was being constructed. We put in an application for a two-bedroom apartment on the ground floor. The housing projects were part of the government programs that the Roosevelt administration had started. Because the winters in Pittsburgh could be so cold, the project apartment buildings were very well built of brick. You could also apply for whatever floor you wanted to live on. However, we had to wait, because the buildings were not completed at the time we applied. By the following year, however, we were notified that a project apartment was available, two bedrooms on the ground floor, just as we had requested. The apartment cost us twenty-five dollars a month with gas, water, and electricity included. Charges were based in accordance with what your income was, and in those days just before the war, Bernie was not earning too much at the steel mill.

It was in connection with that housing project that I had my first opportunity to see a President of the United States. President Roosevelt came to Pittsburgh and made a visit to the project where we were then living. The President didn't tour the projects or anything like that, but he drove past it in a motorcade which was very exciting to me. Crowds of people went down to Central Avenue to see him. There he was riding in an open convertible so that everyone got a good look at him. The motorcade stopped at the project. President Roosevelt spoke to us about the project and about how the government was planning and doing things to help get the country back on its feet.

We all loved President Roosevelt, and I was thrilled to think that I was actually seeing him in person. People still had a lot of bad feelings for President Hoover, who they felt had got us into the Depression. But, President Roosevelt seemed like a man who had real feelings for people. Many of us poor folk gave him full credit for such programs as the WPA, which put people to work. He didn't just hand out money while people continued to sit down and do nothing. Also, President Roosevelt was the first President that I or anybody in my family had been able to vote for. We hadn't been able to vote in Alabama. But in 1940 my parents in Detroit, as well as most of our friends who had come North, and Bernie and I voted for the first time. We all admired President Roosevelt. He didn't mind black folks living halfway decently, and he talked about a chicken in every pot. Folks believed in putting something in their pots now and then, since nothing much had been in them for a long time.

We lived in the projects about four years. Along about 1944, I began to feel that we should get out of the projects and into a house of our own. Something within me was not content with merely going on just getting by as I saw so many people do. Like Bernie, many people were content to make do or to reach a certain level and stay there. But I had an inner need to go on improving my lot in life. I expected something better, even though I didn't always know exactly what it would be or how it would come about. I think that the spirit of God stirred within me, reminding me in my heart that we are our Father's children and can dare to expect and ask for and work for the best. After all, didn't Jesus tell the parable of the Prodigal Son whose father said that all he owned also belonged to him? Didn't Jesus tell us to seek and we would find, ask and we would receive, knock and it would be opened? I may not have always thought of it in those exact words, but I always *felt* it.

So, I began to say to Bernie, *"Look, our children are growing up and they are not going to want to go on living here in the projects. I don't want them to grow up with a projects or welfare mentality."*

Then one day a friend of mine, Cora Hough, said to me, *"Eula, if you stay on in that project or rent a house anywhere in Pittsburgh, you and your husband are not going to end up with anything but a handful of rent receipts. You need to get out and buy yourselves a house."*

It was as if the Holy Spirit was talking to me through Cora's lips, using her tongue to tell me what I needed to hear. Besides, as I've said, I had already begun to feel the need to move on and up.

Cora went on, *"Now, I don't care if you buy yourselves anything fine or just some ordinary house, but buy a home to put your children in so you will have something other than rent receipts to show for all your hard work and all your years."*

"Buy a home?" I said. *"How? We've only been in Pittsburgh a few years and all I do is stay home and look after my kids. How much would a house cost?"*

"Oh, you can get a house for about three-thousand dollars," said Cora, as if that was nothing.

"Three-thousand dollars!" I said. *"That sounds like so much money."* After all, I had been used to next to nothing.

"That's no money at all," said Cora. *"You don't have to pay it all at once."* And Cora explained to me what was more or less involved in buying a house.

The idea begun to grow in my mind. I kept talking about it to Bernie. It was sometime during 1944, because the war was still on, and Bernie was now working at U.S. Steel. (It had taken a lot of pushing and persuading on my part to get him to leave the small mill he had been working in for a better paying job at U.S. Steel.)

However, I got to wondering about how we could find the money to make a down payment on a house. Bernie never saved much money, but he had been buying some war bonds, and every time they came in the mail, I hid them. Then, I figured out that we could borrow some money from my father. He was working at Ford's in Detroit, Michigan and living with Georgia Mae. He was earning good money. Also, two of Bernie's sisters were living with us and paying us rent. I had been saving most of the money. One of his sisters had a baby and was getting a divorce from her husband who was in the armed services. I took care of the baby while she was out working. Bernie had objected to the idea of them staying with us, but we needed what little rent money they could afford to pay, so we managed to squeeze them in.

I wrote to my father and asked if he could lend us some money, and he wrote back and said he would. I was overjoyed. The bonds, plus the five-hundred dollars my father loaned us, together with the money I had saved was just enough for us to make the two-thousand dollar down payment on a twelve-room house. It was a great day for us. We had to wait several months for the house to clear escrow, but at last it did, and in 1945 we moved into our very own home! We rented out the third floor, after putting a bath in what had been a large closet. We had the remaining eight rooms on the two lower floors for ourselves, with some rooms to rent out. This meant that the rents we collected would take care of the mortgage payments, so we ourselves no longer had to pay rent for a place to live. We were buying our own house!

That was the turning point. From the time we bought that first house in Pittsburgh, all my prayers and dreams began to be answered and to come true. It took work and patience to make it be so. The years that followed were far from easy. But, when I left Pittsburgh twelve years later, I had already become a prosperous woman. The talk with Cora had started the ball rolling. Sometime afterwards, when the Voice began to speak to me, everything began to happen very quickly. I learned what it means to pray as if everything depends on God and to work as if everything depends on yourself.

By 1945 one thing was clear. I was out of the South forever. I had gone North.

2.
The Voice

It was wonderful to have our own place, not an apartment, not a rented house, but a house which we were buying for ourselves. The days of our paying rent for property we would never own was forever behind us. From now on, rent would be paid to us—Bernie and me. I knew this in my heart and thanked God for it, even though I didn't know how it would unfold. The example given to me by Dad McClaney, to own your own property and expand your holdings, was working its way in me. I wondered if it were the same for Bernie.

As for my good friend, Cora Hough, whose suggestion to buy my own home was the thing that got me started, things turned out differently for her than they did for me. Even now, I still keep in touch with Cora and talk with her on the telephone and have her come and visit me. She still lives in Pittsburgh in the house that she bought. Over the years, she took in many roomers and cooked and cleaned for them. She also served Sunday dinners to church-goers. But, she never bothered to go and accumulate more property. Sometimes, Cora says to me, *"Eula, honey, I could have done the same thing you did and gone just as far."*

"You could have, Cora," I agree. *"But, why didn't you?"*

Well, the answer to that is something more than either Cora or I could truly give. I think it has something to do with the fact that ever since I was a child, something within me just pushed and guided me, and kept pushing and guiding me right up to now. It's still pushing and guiding me. I probably saw opportunities when Cora didn't, because I have always been the kind of person that looks ahead. Whatever led me to buy the porch furniture in Alabama also led me to look for opportunities to step ahead in Pennsylvania. Cora's a good woman and has worked hard, but that inner need to keep on stepping didn't push her the way it pushed me. Besides, I had the Voice. Nobody could control that.

Let me tell you about the Voice. It has done glorious things for me, yet It isn't always talking to me day and night. Only when I really need to hear It is when I really do. Why does the Voice come to me so clearly? It isn't because I'm a better or more deserving person. Maybe it's because I'm just somehow tuned up to hear It. I only wish everybody could.

I realized that not only was Bernie unhappy about the move, he was opposed to making any real effort to improve our life. For instance, he declared that he wouldn't live in more than six rooms, even if he were in a large place. That was fine with me since I wanted to rent out rooms as an apartment anyway. But, when it became clear the house needed a better heating system, Bernie said the house was all right for him just as it was. He said that it was as good as he wanted to live in and die in. He also started up his talk again of leaving us. I began to figure he was always going to be a pain in the neck, not wanting to go forward and always threatening to pull out. With that attitude, getting him to make improvements (even with something so necessary as good heating in winter) was next to impossible.

We lived for four years in our house with the rents gradually paying off our interest and some of the mortgage. But, I knew we couldn't just sit still and let it go at that, because we were still poor. With Bernie everything continued to be negative. I know the reason we're not together today is that he never wanted to go farther. After four years of this status quo, I said to him, *"You just don't want anything and I do. I have ideas to share with you when you come home from work, but you just tell me 'No, no, no,' all the time! How are we ever going to make it together?"*

One bright morning, when the sun was shining so strongly and the drapes were pulled open, something suddenly said to me, *"You do it yourself. This thing you're talking to Bernie about, **you do it yourself.**"*

I was astonished when I heard It. I heard a Voice say those words as clearly as if someone were standing in the room talking to me. I knew that It came from God and I knew it so strongly that I began to cry. I said, *"How am I going to do it? I don't have a job and I've always been against going out to work while my children are in school. They need to be looked after by their own mother. You know children aren't going to act right when the mother's not home. What will I do? Where will I get the money?"*

I began to pray even harder. *"Father,"* I prayed, *"what shall I do? Where will I get the money? I'm willing to do whatever I have to do, but how? I don't have a job."*

I kept praying over that, praying unceasingly and asking God to show me what to do. Then there came to me, in my mind, these words: SAVE EVERY PENNY YOU CAN GET AND THEN GO INTO REAL ESTATE. This wasn't the Voice talking, but it was something that came clearly into my thoughts.

The next thing I had to go pray about was where to get the pennies to save? Then, I began to get some ideas. I could take in a few more roomers and I could bake sweet potato pies and sell them on weekends. I had a beautiful home. There was wall-to-wall carpeting, draw drapes, good furniture, and it all made a very pleasant atmosphere for roomers. Doing these things would surely bring in money that I could save.

It also came to me to begin helping Bernie with his spring time cleaning jobs. Every spring people would hire him to wash their walls and ceilings, because houses were heated by coal in the winter and coal dust and smoke settled on the walls. Bernie got a lot of calls to do that kind of work, and he had to hire people to help him with it. This was something he did in addition to his regular work at U.S. Steel.

I figured Bernie might as well pay me as to hire somebody else to help him with the wall cleaning. La-Doris and Burnie were both in school all day long and didn't come home for lunch, so I had the time to do such work. Bernie didn't want me to do it, but I said, *"You can't make me just stay home while you're paying somebody else, since you hardly ever give me any money. So, let me go to work with you and earn some money for myself."*

Bernie finally agreed to let me work with him, and he paid me. I worked for two or three springs, washing walls and cleaning the interiors of houses. I was working as much as I could while our girls were in school. But, the job required reaching up and stretching which wasn't too good for me, and I began to have pain and trouble with my side. In the meantime, I was selling sweet potato pies and taking care of foster children. The pennies were coming in and I was saving all of them.

During this period of working at anything I could do and saving every penny as I had been directed, I went one day to talk to a real estate agent. I had been working hard and saving for three years or so. I had about twelve-hundred dollars saved. My money was mostly in post office certificates, because Bernie wouldn't let me put my money in the bank where he put his. I think he was angry and jealous about my saving money, because he knew what I intended to do. I wasn't a secretive person and I guess now that perhaps I told him too much of what was on my mind. This might have made him a little more unhappy. I always thought it did more harm to have a lot of secrets and then just burst out on somebody with something, than to have them know already what was going on. Anyhow, Bernie had showed me how to go to the post office and buy the savings certificates. The least amount you could put in was two dollars. I remember well going down to the post office on the streetcar with only two dollars to deposit. I was at first afraid that I would lose my streetcar transfer check or my two dollars, so in the early days those trips were small ordeals for me. But, I continued to buy certificates and in time I had twelve-hundred dollars saved and deposited with the post office.

When I spoke to the real estate agent about buying a piece of property, probably a house, and asked how much money I might need for a down payment, he said, "Oh, you've got to have at least fifteen-hundred dollars, Mrs. McClaney. Something in that amount at least."

That was a blow to me. It seemed I had worked so long and saved so much and yet, I needed at least another three-hundred dollars. I had followed the words of the Voice and I felt that the time was at hand for me to go into real estate. I wrote to my father in Detroit and explained to him that I had been saving money to buy a house, even one that was run-down, in order to start out on a new path. When he learned that I needed another three-hundred dollars, because the real estate agent said I should have at least fifteen-hundred dollars to work with, he wrote to me and said, "If you find your house before you get the rest of the money, I'll loan the other three-hundred."

I was so happy when I got that letter! I was just jumping and screaming. Imagine, my own father telling me that! The real estate agent hadn't yet found me the house I could buy for fifteen-hundred down, however, so I just went on until I saved enough money to buy a house when one turned up. Knowing that my father would help me out gave me the inspiration to keep on stepping.

At last, a house was for sale that required a fifteen-hundred dollar down payment. I bought it. That's when my career in real estate began, as well as my education in business—buying, owning and managing property, and enduring the ups and downs that go with it. Make no mistake, it was up and down for a good many years, but after each down I always managed to go farther up. If I took two steps back, I always learned from it so that I could go three steps ahead afterwards.

When I bought the house, I inherited a tenant on the third floor. She was a woman who wouldn't pay her rent. So, I had to start off immediately to have her evicted. I also started immediately to get the house cleaned up, the walls papered, the woodwork painted, and made all kinds of general repairs and renovations that I knew would make it more profitable for me. I did as much work on the house myself as I could, although I did hire someone to paper the walls and make repairs I couldn't handle. I also got some tenants in there as soon as I could in order to keep the mortgage payments going. I intended to go right on doing the other things that I had been doing, too—baking pies, caring for children, serving dinners, and renting rooms, all with the thought that as soon as I could I would buy another house.

I kept going through this routine until I was able to buy another house and then another. It meant I had to make a lot of sacrifices. I didn't go places but stayed home. I stopped buying clothes. I didn't even buy those hats I was so fond of having to wear to church. In fact, I had to give up my church going, which was not easy for me. Surely, God was always with me, that I knew. I just cut out all the frills in my life and put everything I could get into my business. Nine years later, I had thirty-three apartments.

My first big crisis as a landlord was getting the woman evicted from that first house I bought on my own. The people from whom I bought the house had let me know that she wouldn't pay her rent, that she hadn't paid them in a long time. I tried to catch her at home, but I never could. She just dipped and dodged me so much that I had to go to the constable to take action against her. Reflecting back, if I had the landlord who I bought the property from evict all of the undesirable tenants, I wouldn't have inherited this problem.

I was very shaky when I had to go down to court for her eviction proceedings. I didn't know anything about going to court and dealing with difficult tenants. I was truly afraid as to how it would all work out. Bernie gave me no support in the matter. Would you believe it, he talked and acted as if he was on that woman's side? Well, he did go down to court with me, but he wasn't any comfort at all. A cousin of mine who lived in Pittsburgh, and my mother, who had come to visit me, went with me.

Bernie had been dead set against my buying the house in the first place. He was jealous of what I was trying to do and acted disgusted with me. I knew he didn't want me to make it on my own. He had tried to discourage me about buying the house. *"If I was you, I wouldn't bother with that house,"* he had said. *"I wouldn't do this and I wouldn't do that."*

Well, I had come to the conclusion that whatever Bernie was against was the thing for me to do. And I told him, *"I'm going to go on and buy that house, because I can't afford anything better. There's one thing you have to remember. I don't have a whole lot of money. So, the best thing I can do is to buy something old and ragged and try to fix it up and go along with it. That's all I can do."*

The eviction proceedings, as I recall, were not held before a regular judge but before an alderman. My tenant was already there when I arrived, and she acted as if she'd been through this kind of thing many times.

"Your Honor," she said, *"I protest this . . . ,"* and *"I protest that . . ."* and *"This isn't right . . . ,"* and *"That woman can't make me . . . ,"* and *"I have my rights,"* and on and on! I hadn't ever seen anything quite like it.

Then I told my side of the story, which was pretty simple and direct compared to what that woman had to say. I knew it was right and fair to have her evicted, because she certainly revealed she had no intentions of paying any rent to me, but I wasn't so sure how it would turn out. Maybe all her talk had impressed the alderman in her favor. When we were all finished telling our side of things, he gave me the judgment and told the lady to get out of my house.

The woman left the alderman's office without a word to anybody. My cousin, my mother, and I—after I had thanked the alderman—started walking out to go and catch the streetcar home. Bernie, I noticed, stayed behind, bent over the table talking earnestly to the alderman. When he came out to join us, I asked him what he was talking to the man about.

"If that alderman had just done a couple of things, that woman would have won the case. I was telling him about it," he said.

"What are you talking about?" I asked. *"Are you speaking up for her? Did you want that woman to win the case, when she hasn't paid her rent to me or to the past landlord even before I bought the house? I can't stand this kind of stuff from you! I haven't got any money to spare in the first place, certainly no money that I can just let a tenant owe me. So, what are you talking about?"*

My mother and my cousin could hardly believe their ears either. My cousin said to me, *"You know, Eula, it looks to me like Bernie's glad that woman didn't pay you and is sorry you got her evicted."*

"I know it," I said. *"Instead of him being glad I got her out, he was showing the alderman how he could have worked some kind of crooked trick so she could stay."*

Well, even though the Voice had told me what to do and to do it myself, with every passing year and day I realized that the only way I would move on up would be on my own. My husband was definitely not going to stand by me. I was learning that I would have to scramble around and do a lot of things I might not want to do in order to make my dream come true.

By the time I got the house fixed up, I was able to rent out four apartments. Most of the houses in Pittsburgh at that time were single-family houses and usually had three floors, with three or four rooms on each floor. My house had three rooms on the first floor, three on the second and two on the third—including a large alcove. I had a carpenter close off the alcove, and that made a third room which would hold a twin bed. Since the house was on a hill, the basement was at ground level in the back. A porch was on the first floor at the back of the house and it extended out far enough that you could walk under it while standing up, with room to spare. The former owners had kept their garbage and trash cans in that area under the porch. As I studied it, I was inspired to make a fourth apartment out of that basement. We put up some partitions and rearranged the plumbing so that the former basement area now had a small bedroom, a kitchen with a window, and a small bathroom. Now, I had another apartment to rent, for which I charged thirty-five dollars a month. Those four apartments worked for me for a long time.

About 1956 or 1957, I was well into my career of owning and managing rental properties, which included thirty-three rental units. In 1955, I was able to buy myself my first, big luxury car—an *"El Dorado"* Cadillac. Before that, in 1953, I had purchased the Ira Lewis estate in Pittsburgh and taken up residence there.

Now, this could have been the end of my story. The point where the little black girl from Orion, Alabama, with her sixth-grade education had gone North and made a success of herself. But, it was far from the end. There were all kinds of challenges and troubles yet to come, and perhaps another twenty years of real struggle before I could truly say *"Well, Father, I have made it."*

One thing I need to point out, because I've never really kept track of it in any detail, is that I have always had many friends and members of my family living with me, in additon to my husband and children. That has always been my way and it still is. I cannot recall a time when I have lived alone or lived so that only two or three people made up my household. I wasn't really conscious of this until I began to think back over my life and to become aware of certain patterns and habits of mine. I grew up with my sister, brothers, grandparents, friends and relatives close about me, and I have lived that way ever since. So, whenever I talk about living in a certain place at a certain time, you may be sure that my house sheltered others besides my immediate family. If there's one thing about myself I know, it is that I love having people around me.

The Ira Lewis estate was a beautiful piece of property in a very private, hilly area of Pittsburgh. Mr. Lewis had been president of the *Pittsburgh Courier* newspaper corporation up until the time of his death. I believe that Mrs. Lewis had come to find it difficult to maintain the estate and the style of living she had always known. After all, it took a good, steady income to maintain the house and grounds, and the Lewises had always lived very well. Mrs. Lewis didn't know how to make money, nor manage it, and that put her in a bad situation. Because, if you don't have any money coming in and you keep digging into the till, you find yourself in a very precarious position.

Mrs. Lewis informed me that the estate was for sale and that it would be a nice place for my girls and me, and that it could be bought for a very good price. I went to Bernie and told him that the property could be bought for a very reasonable down payment. *"Will you come on and be with me?"* I asked him. *"We can buy the Lewis Estate. We'll rent out this twelve-room house we're living in and go into something better."*

"No," said Bernie.

"I'll have some trouble pulling together the down payment," I said, *"but I'll be able to do it."*

"No," said Bernie.

There wasn't any point in talking further with him about it. No matter what opportunity came our way, I saw clearly that he would always be against it. With him it would always be no, no, no. I knew I couldn't let that opportunity go by. So, I went out and arranged to borrow enough money to add to what I already had of my own, and I was able to meet the down payment.

After I had bought the Lewis Estate, Bernie told me that he would not move into it. He insisted that he would never leave the twelve-room house we had been living in. *"I'm not going to move in there,"* he kept telling me. *"I'm not going into that house."* To the contrary, he did move and that is where he and his present wife are living to this day.

I enjoyed living in the Lewis house. The estate was made up of four large lots with big lawns, a garden, and plantings of lovely spruce trees. The house itself was a wooden frame house. It was well-designed and made with the finest woods and had beautiful shingles on the roof. I made a number of changes in it after we moved in. I replaced the smallish front windows on the first and second floors with large picture windows.

The house gave us much more room. It had a large living room, a large dining room, a den, a breakfast room, a large kitchen, sun room and powder room, four bedrooms on the second floor with two bathrooms. There was also such a large attic across the top of the entire house that I was able to have more sleeping quarters constructed, so that I had more room than ever for guests. What a contrast it all was to that shack of my Alabama childhood.

By 1957, I was ready for a vacation. My parents had come to live with me in Pittsburgh at about the time I bought the Lewis Estate. I had continued buying more properties and looking after them, and I was tired.

By 1957 the instructions I had received so miraculously several years earlier from the Voice had made me an affluent lady. I had saved every penny I got and I had gone into real estate. The results were wonderful by any way you want to measure it. In the process, I had learned who I was and that with God I could succeed. I won't say that I was always aware of God's presence as I had been at special moments in my life, like the time I received the gift of tongues, or that day when the Voice first spoke to me. But, I never turned away from God either, and I always knew that without Him I could accomplish nothing of value that would last.

Imagine, then, my dismay—no, my grief, my very real grief—when at this point of my success I began to find my friends pulling away from me. I could name names, but I won't, because most of those friends have come back to me. But, there was a time when it seemed like various persons just stopped calling me. I cried and tried to understand it, but I just went on. It seemed like somehow they were upset when they saw me getting ahead, even though I had to work hard and make sacrifices.

Finally, I began to pray about it. *"Lord,"* I prayed, *"I didn't ask to get where I'm going—and it seems like I'm heading somewhere—just to lose my friends! I really don't want to lose my friends. I'm getting to where my friends mean an awful lot to me, and I don't want to lose them."*

Then there came to me, in plain English, words of understanding. They came into my mind, plain and clear. I had been constantly praying, *"God, dear God, don't let me lose my friends, even though I'm thankful for the way You open doors for me, and I'm kind of seeing my way now. But, I don't want to lose my friends!"*

These are the words that came to me!

YOU GO AHEAD WITH WHAT YOU'RE DOING. JUST GO ON! KEEP ON GOING. THE SAME PEOPLE THAT ARE TURNING THEIR BACKS ON YOU, THAT ARE ACTING FUNNY ABOUT YOU, ARE ONE DAY GOING TO COME BACK. THEY ARE GOING TO SAY TO OTHERS, 'OH SHE'S MY FRIEND. I CAME UP WITH HER. I KNOW HER FROM WAY BACK. OH, SHE'S BEEN MY FRIEND ALL THE TIME.' THEY ARE GOING TO BE SO PROUD OF YOU!

Honest to goodness, that day has certainly come. It's here right now.

3.

"My Mind Was Opening Up"

Anyone who knows me knows I often use the word *"ignorance"* when talking about something troublesome or the devious and foolish things people do. I like to use that word this way. I got it from my daughter La-Doris. As I see it, when people do things to trick and hurt others, they are being pretty ignorant. They just don't seem to know you can't really succeed by being dishonest and hurtful. Oh, they may get themselves a lot of money or some fame, but they have to live with themselves knowing they didn't get what they got in a rightful way. And, from what I have seen in this world, they don't get away with it in the long run. I call that ignorance. There's a lot of it going around— always has been.

What I want to talk about now is some of the ignorance I had to put up with while I was learning how to get somewhere in real estate and how to better my life. I could say that all the ignorance I came up against just taught me to be smarter and wiser. But, I am not going to detail every bit of ignorant stuff that I can remember, because that would be very depressing. I believe in letting go of the ignorance that's behind you, because you need both hands to deal with the ignorance that's before you. Now, when I say this, I'm smiling. I don't want this to be a lot of heaviness. I only want to show that I didn't just go hopping and skipping my way out of poverty into places like the Lewis Estate and my present surroundings. I did it by putting one foot before the other, just as we all have to do. When it got hard, I just kept on stepping anyway. I hope that anyone reading these words and having a hard time in life will really take it to heart when I say to keep on stepping. Remember, while you keep on keeping on, expect to get to a better place. *You've got to expect the best!*

Most of the things having to do with my real estate ventures or with other ways I found to earn money, I had to take care of on my own. Bernie rarely ever helped me with them. He continued to work at the steel mill, working different shifts, but mostly working the swing shift. By working from four in the afternoon until midnight, he was able to take on extra jobs during the day. Bernie had a knack for working and he liked to work. He was a first-class painter. He didn't just paint houses, but he painted churches and steeples, for instance. He was also a good plumber, and he could plaster, and he knew carpentry.

It must seem like I keep on bad-mouthing Bernie, but I am trying to tell what happened without overdoing it. So, whatever I do say here, I have already soft-pedalled it to a great degree. There is no way to avoid saying that I had this problem of having to handle my own business on my own without much help from my husband. I could hardly get Bernie to work on places without a confrontation, but he would readily go work for anyone else who sent for him.

I remember that I had one house in which the tenants needed some plumbing work done in their apartment. I asked Bernie if he would take care of it, since he was a very fine plumber.

"No, I'm not going to fix it," he said. *"I'm not going down there."*

I knew he meant what he said. I was going to have to hire a plumber to do the work.

That day, while Bernie was off on some job, his cousin called and said, *"I have a terrible problem over here with my plumbing. Please tell Bernie to come and fix it."*

Well, I knew he would go and fix it for her, and I was glad for her sake. I knew very well what it was like when you had a problem with the plumbing and had to hire someone, while having a hard time just to pay for the house.

"Your cousin called," I told Bernie when he came in. *"She wants you to come over to her house and fix her plumbing."*

Well, Bernie got right into his truck and drove over to his cousin's house. It was just that morning he had told me he wasn't going to fix anything for me! *"I ain't going to fix nothing for you,"* is how he had put it. However, I got in the truck with him, and while he worked on the plumbing, he kept looking at me with the most peculiar expression. It seemed then that he just wanted me to walk off and leave him. In fact, as I look back at incidents like that now, I think that he was really wanting me to leave him. It was one of God's blessings to me that even though Bernie would not help me, I could always find someone in Pittsburgh who would. I had always believed in helping folks out, and I was fortunate to find other people who believed in that, too.

Bernie would sometimes say, *"People see I won't help you, so they go and help you. That makes me mad."*

Of course, I see now that Bernie, without knowing or intending it, was teaching me to be self-reliant. I learned to keep my trust placed in God and to do things that needed to be done and not to lean on anybody. I now wish Bernie well and good fortune, even though he knew better than to do what he did to me.

One of my most embarrassing and trying moments in Pittsburgh concerned one of the old houses I had bought. It was an old house on Lenora Street that was fixed to have five apartments. One of the apartments on the top floor had a leak in the ceiling that came from a leak in the roof. I was worried about getting somebody to go up there and put some tar on the roof and to at least cover the leak with tar paper, because I really couldn't afford to have any expensive work done just then. Bernie, naturally, knew how to do it.

"Will you go and fix the leak?" I asked him. *"You can take a ladder and Billy will go along and help you."* Billy was Bernie's sister's child, who we were raising.

"I'll go and help," Billy said. *"I'm not afraid, Aunt Eula."* Billy would often feel sorry for me, because he had seen Bernie refuse to help out. *"If you get the ladder down to the house, I'll go there and put the tar on the roof and fix it for you."*

So, I asked Bernie, *"Will you take the ladder in your truck to the Lenora Street house?"*

"Naw, I ain't going to take no ladder nowhere," was his answer.

So, Bernie went off, and I didn't quite know what to do next. But, my nephew and my daughters said, *"Well, we'll just take it ourselves."*

I was trying to take care of a lot of other things at that moment. Before I realized it, those kids had taken the ladder and set off for the Lenora Street house. I just had time to tell them, *"Try not to bump into anybody—that ladder's so long. Maybe you can pick up a friend or two to help carry it."*

Sure enough, a man came along and helped those youngsters carry that ladder. In the meantime, I found someone to fix the leak in the roof. I was so proud that those kids had just set off and carried the ladder for me. But, I was embarrassed and upset to see how my husband would just let us fend for ourselves, when it would have been no trouble at all for him to have taken care of the job.

It probably seems like an insignificant incident, but it wasn't insignificant to me. It was just a humiliating revelation of the sad state of my marriage. It was like the whole world was saying, *"Look, her own husband won't help her."* In a way, it wasn't much different from being a child in the cotton fields and knowing nobody would take me out of them but myself. Only in this case, my husband didn't even want me to help myself.

Even in the matter of filing our income tax, Bernie wanted to go it alone. The tax man would say, *"Mr. and Mrs. McClaney, you will save more money by filing together than by filing separately."*

"I'm going to file alone," was all Bernie would say. *"And, I'm taking these children as deductions, 'cause I'm the one supporting them."*

I would beg, fight and do everything I could to get him to let us file together. He would not give in, not until I had worn myself out trying to get him to help us save some money. He wanted me to give Uncle Sam as much money as I could. Even in the matter of taxes it's much easier for me these days. Today, I'm filing alone after all, but from a position that is not nearly as worrisome as it was with him back in Pittsburgh. I don't know how I managed to think straight being bothered with all that ignorance. God has truly been kind with me.

Now, aside from having to step lively to avoid the traps Bernie set for me and the obstacles he put in my path, I kept very busy looking after my houses and my tenants. Keeping tenants happy took a lot of energy and time. I was busy, too, collecting rents (or trying to at times), paying for furnishings, doing repairs and general upkeep and paying on my notes. There was always something to be done on somebody's apartment. Mr. So-and-So needed this done, or had a such-and-such leaking, or had something-or-other doing this or doing that. It took more and more lively stepping to keep up with it.

My daughters got to be more and more help to me. It was they who collected the rents. I guess you could say we had a unique system for collecting them. Burnie and La-Doris were teenagers, and they would get several of their friends—sometimes a regular bunch of them—to go with them on the day rents were due. I always insisted they not go alone, since you never knew if someone might try to give them trouble, although I tried to rent only to tenants I felt were reliable. But, people can fool you. I've been fooled more than once, and I didn't want to take risks. When it comes to money, you never know how people are going to act.

La-Doris can tell it best in her own words:

On rent-collecting day, my girlfriends and I, seven or eight of us, would pile into the car and drive around collecting rents for my mom.

*We would all go to the person's door—which probably looked a little strange to our **new** tenants. The regular ones were used to it.*

The tenants would count out the money, and I knew exactly how much each one was supposed to pay. When the people gave me the money, I'd go out into the hallway and my friends would gather around me, while I pinned the money on the inside of my coat.

I learned from those rent-collecting excursions how people will come up with different stories for not having the money: a washing machine or some other vital appliance had to be fixed, or a friend owed them money and hadn't paid as promised, or there had been an emergency of some sort. I suppose some of the stories were true, but mostly they weren't. I would just stand there and listen. Then I would tell them I had come for the rent and that is what I had to take back to my mom.

It gave me an early sense for dealing with people in a landlord-tenant situation.

Fortunately, nothing violent ever happened. But, I did learn how to be firm, because people could be very difficult.

It was a great help to have my daughters perform this task for me. I had so much else to take care of, and you just couldn't rely on people to send or bring you the money. There were numerous times when people refused to pay their rent. They sometimes tried to hide from me and many times forced me to take legal action—which I never liked to do. It's one thing to be generous and quite another thing to have people take advantage of you.

There's one case I remember that's typical of the kind of thing I suffered from certain tenants. Right across the hall from the lady gambler whom I had to evict, lived a woman who, I first thought, had two or three of her daughters living with her—very pretty young women. The time came when they, too, stopped paying their rent. Had they continued paying it, I don't suppose I would have discovered that those girls were *not* that women's daughters. They were her girls all right, because she was running a prostitution operation. It was no wonder I had seen her pretty *"daughters,"* and no wonder that reports got back to me about all the young ladies coming and going into that apartment with their gentlemen callers. La-Doris wasn't able to get the rent money from them, and whenever I went to collect it myself they always managed to take cover. So, I finally had a lien put on their possessions and notified the police department about what I thought was going on, and that settled that.

Another time I had trouble with tenants because of rent control, which was in effect in Pittsburgh. I had furnished an apartment with furniture that was old but adequate. Because of rent control, about the only way I could come out ahead was to rent apartments as furnished. Some people who came to rent the apartment from me said they wanted to use their own furniture. I said they could do that, if they pleased, but that I was renting the apartment as furnished all the same and that the furniture was theirs to use. So, they moved in and replaced my furniture with their own, and I stored mine away.

In the meantime, we had recently bought a car, our first Buick. This was in 1948. That car was my one luxury, after years of working hard at everything I could do, saving every penny and going without anything in the way of clothes or extras. So, I was quite happy to have it, and it was a good investment.

One of my friends said to me when we bought the Buick, *"Look, Eula, you're going to get into trouble buying that car."*

"How do you mean?" I asked him. *"I can pay for it."*

"Well," he said, *"your tenants are going to resent having to pay you their rents, which they probably think are too high, because that's how people like to think."*

"Listen," I said, *"I have always charged a fair rent and never tried to take advantage of anybody."*

"Sure, I know that," he said. *"But when your tenants see that car, they're going to get mad and jealous, because that Buick is fabulous to look at."*

What he said shocked me. I knew he was probably right, but it was hard for me to realize that people were going to get mad at me because I had finally managed to make some money. After all, they didn't know what I had sacrificed to make it.

Sure enough, it wasn't long after our conversation before the Housing Authority in Pittsburgh got in touch with me. One of my tenants, they said, had put in a complaint against me, and had said, *"She's charged me sixty dollars for my apartment and it isn't even furnished."* Wouldn't you know, it was the husband of the family that wanted to rent my furnished apartment and use his own furniture who had made the complaint.

So, there I was, being misrepresented again, being painted as some horrible person and as some money-grabbing landlord. It was hard on my patience and on my faith in people. Now, I had always been what I would call a very progressive person, because I believed in doing everything I could to make my own life better. I was also a person willing to make sacrifices in order to progress. I sacrificed for what I wanted most and I wanted a good car. I didn't buy clothes and other things. First, I had wanted a house, and then the furnishings for it. I always figured that other things beyond that would come second. Just let me have a good place to sit down and rest my feet. That is what I had wanted most, sacrificed for, and got. Now, it was my car. And, for this I was having to feel other people's jealousy.

The Housing Authority asked me to come down to answer the man's complaint. I went by myself. Again, I was trembling in my boots! When I got there, I was introduced to a Mr. Anon, a great big, well-dressed man—one of those people you would call pretty. He sat behind his desk, looking very important, as he shuffled the papers that contained the complaint against me.

"What do you have to say about this, Mrs. McClaney?" he asked me, smiling and friendly.

I began to feel relaxed. His friendliness was very real, and I knew that I had done nothing wrong. For once I stopped shaking in my boots pretty quickly and began to feel that I could handle this alone.

I said, *"Mr. Anon, let me be absolutely honest with you. You know, as well as I know, that a lot of folks don't want to see anybody get ahead. Now, I have been struggling and going without, trying to get ahead for my kids, to achieve a little something for them."*

Mr. Anon just nodded in agreement with me, and I began to get my courage.

"I'm going to tell you the honest truth," I said. *"I'm going to lay this on the line. Under rent control a landlord cannot raise the rents. But, unless I get higher rents, I just can't make a go of it. Well, I have a lot of good furniture— not expensive or fancy, but good. I had put some of it in this one apartment which I put up for rent as a furnished apartment.*

"These people, who have brought this complaint against me, knew I was renting the apartment as furnished, and they were willing to pay that rent. They needed a place that was good, because of their children. But, they said their own furniture was better than my furniture. They said to me, 'We would rather use our furniture, and if you let us use our furniture, you can rent it to us as a furnished apartment.' And, I agreed to that. But, I made it clear that they were renting a furnished apartment."

When I was through explaining, Mr. Anon said, *"Well, Mrs. McClaney, do you really have furniture you could put in there?"*

I said, *"I sure do!"*

"Where is it?" he asked.

"It's up on Frankstown Avenue," I said, and gave him the exact address.

"I'll take your word for it," he said, *"because I don't want to go up there just to look at it."*

"It may seem like a bunch of junk to some people, although it isn't," I told him. *"I believe if I put something good in that apartment, they would just destroy it. But, I do have some furniture, I'm ready and willing to put in that apartment."*

Mr. Anon chuckled. I think those people had exasperated him too. *"If that's what you have, Mrs. McClaney, then I think we'll just say to them, 'It's a furnished apartment you folks rented, and Mrs. McClaney offered you the furniture when she rented it to you.'"*

I was certainly pleased with Mr. Anon's attitude. It was obvious that he had had his fill, too, of having to deal with difficult people who didn't tell the truth or live up to their agreements. *"I'll just write this case as settled,"* Mr. Anon said.

I may also add that shortly after the couple made the first complaint against me, other tenants proceeded to file false complaints to Mr. Anon. But, I won all of the cases against me. Afterwards, the couple who made the first false complaint came back to me and apologized and asked if they could stay in the apartment. I refused them.

One final incident I want to tell about, as an example of the way people tried to pull something on me, concerned a little woman who rented an apartment from me. She and her husband were both young, and she was always very friendly and sweet towards me. Being one who likes to help people, I felt I would like to help the young couple, because I knew how hard it was for me when I was their age.

The young woman said to me one day, *"Oh, Miz McClaney, I don't know how you got this house, but it **sure** is nice. I hope someday I can get such a home for my children."*

I said, *"Honey, you can. All you have to do is save your money a little at a time. You will have to make sacrifices to do it. But, one day you'll have enough to make the down payment on a house."*

She seemed to follow what I was telling her. One day she came to me and said, *"Miz McClaney, I got a little money that I'm saving for my brother-in-law. I want to know what bank you would take it to."*

"Well, I have a little account at the East End Federal Savings and Loan," I told her, *"which is a good place to go."* And, I gave her directions how to get there, who to see, and how to open an account.

Sometime after that, that young woman decided she wasn't going to pay me a month's rent. She and her husband just up and moved out one night. I had no idea that she would do that to me, seeing how she had asked my advice and I had been helpful to her.

I got to thinking, *"How can I find out where that girl's gone to?"* I also got to thinking about the account I had told her to open.

I called my attorney and explained to him that I wanted to find out if the young woman's account was still active at the East End Federal Savings and Loan.

"Mrs. McClaney, go to the Savings and Loan and see if you can get a loan officer to look at her files and tell you," he said.

So, I went to the East End Federal Savings and Loan and asked to see the president of the savings and loan, since I knew him pretty well. I explained to him what had happened and why I was there.

"Okay," he said, *"as long as the account is in her name, even if she was saving the money for her brother-in-law as she said, we can put a hold on it, if it is still active."*

"Well, I want to make them pay me the rent they owe," I said, *"because they did not deal honestly with me."*

"I'm not supposed to do this, Mrs. McClaney," said the president, *"but I'm going to."* And, then he opened her file and let me see it, because she still had an active account there. I was able to find out where she was living and to put a lien on her account and to send the sheriff after her.

And, then I heard from her—BOOM! *"Miz McClaney,"* she said on the telephone, *"this is Mrs. So-and-So. That money in that savings account isn't none of my money. That's my brother-in-law's money!"*

I said to her, *"You see, that's what you get for trying to be slick. You tried not to pay me, but you intend to use your brother-in-law's money and the rent money you owe me to follow the good advice I gave you. I hope your brother-in-law makes you pay him, if that is his money. And, you are going to pay me. I will see that you don't get a dime out of that account until you do."*

She began to protest and talk back to me.

"Listen," I said, *"you needn't say anything to me. Learn to treat people right, because you are not that slick. The best way to get through this world and this*

life is to treat people right and do unto others as you would have them do unto you. You didn't think you would ever see me again. You thought all you had to do was to find out some secret from me and then to break off. But, honey, when you try to break it off with someone else, you only end up breaking it off with yourself. I've been through the mill with people doing the kind of thing you have done. And, I'm glad you are making me go over this, because I don't ever want to forget to treat people fairly."

Again, I had to learn and grow through having difficult times and suffering a lot from people's ignorance and low tricks. I don't want the effect of my telling some of these things to be negative, because one of my aims in writing my life story is to show how a person can move on up by moving around and past the negative things and negative people and by not letting them make you resentful and bitter. For all of the negative experiences have been my stepping-stones and have deepened my faith in God's guidance.

I am reminded of a song that Oscar Brown, Jr. used to sing about a lady who came along and picked up a snake that was cold and dying. She put it in her bosom and nursed it back to health. And, when it got warm and well, it bit her. It bit her and said, *"You knew I was a snake when you picked me up."*

My advice to anyone is to watch the snakes. Everyone who seems wrapped up in church and holiness and is saying, *"Oh, Lord, I've got religion, and I'm holy and sanctified,"* may not be so good and loving as they claim. I have dealt with real *"saints"* who were supposedly saved when I helped them, and then they turned on me. I couldn't have gotten worse treatment from any atheist.

Now that I am in a position to really help others, I am sometimes afraid to when I think of how easily you can be fooled. If you're like me, you want to believe the best in others. You want to see people achieve something, and it makes you happy to see them getting along well, getting free of poverty and poverty attitudes. Even nowadays I still find that the snakes are there, sometimes slithering into your life and heart and looking oh, so pretty, and talking oh, so nice, and seeming oh, so sincerely good. But that's the way it is, and you have to be wise and alert, as well as loving and helpful. Even in Holmby Hills, I have to keep an eye out for snakes who, I must say, have sometimes come right through my own front door!

I have watched what happens to snakes, however, and to people who are greedy and ungrateful and only out to get things for themselves at others' expense. Sooner or later it all gets balanced out. So, I do what I can to help people and make sure I do no harm. Then, I just forget about it and wait for the outcome. When you've treated people the best you can, it gives you a good feeling. You will know one thing for sure, God will take care of the situation, whatever the situation may be. He will bless you and bless your kind deeds.

I have known so many lovely people in my life, people who were celebrities and people who were plain, ordinary people like me. I love them all and my way has been made bright and happy by them. One such person was Mr. Gilbert, a very fine man who owned a beautiful furniture store called Gilbert's Fine Furniture, in downtown Pittsburgh. In the early days, I used to go down to his store just to look at all the beautiful furniture.

A few years later, after I had bought two or three old houses, I needed a bedroom suite. I asked Mr. Gilbert to have one made to order. It surprised and pleased me when he said he would do so without my having to pay anything on it in advance. After the suite was made and delivered, I began making payments on it, and in time it was paid for.

A long time later, when I had come to know Mr. Gilbert better, I said to him one day, "*Mr. Gilbert, you were so nice to trust me and have that furniture made without asking me to pay anything down on it. I was so glad you did it. But, I never did understand why you would do that or why you would trust me.*"

He said, "*Mrs. McClaney, I'm the kind of man who, when I see you have confidence in yourself, I have confidence in you, too. When I see someone who has no confidence in themselves, then I don't have any confidence in them either. But, I saw that you came down here by yourself, without your husband. I asked you if you were married and you said you were. And, I knew there was some reason why your husband never showed up here with you.*

"*Now, I knew the folks that lived in your home before you. The man would call from his office and order furniture and his wife would come in and select it. In your case, for some reason, I just knew that you were more or less on your own, even though you were married. I saw, too, that you were a good buyer.*

So, I trusted you. Something in you made it easy for me to trust you. And, you have lived up to my trust and been one of my best customers."

That was good for me to hear. Considering all the untrustworthy people I had to deal with many times, it was wonderful to have the support of people like Mr. Gilbert, Mr. Anon, and the president of the savings and loan company. They were businessmen, men who had to be sharp and good judges of character. Their attitudes and actions toward me let me know that I was becoming a good business woman myself. If I only had the kind of help from Bernie that I wanted and thought I needed, I might never have had to test myself and find out what I could really do. I only went through the sixth grade in Orion, but I was getting on in the college of practical business learning in Pittsburgh, and everybody I dealt with was teaching me more than they knew.

As a side note, I must say that nowadays I do a lot of buying of fine furniture at auctions. It gives me great pleasure. I would love to have Mr. Gilbert here and take him with me to one of the really wonderful auctions that occur when the furnishings and holdings of large estates or private art collections are sold. Also, I still have much of the furniture I bought in Pittsburgh, reupholstered and refinished, a reminder of earlier days when I knew less and was just getting into the knack of daring to reach past what seemed my limits.

During my last years in Pittsburgh, after I had moved to the Lewis Estate, I began to have more in the way of good times and party-giving (which is something I love best to do). After my first trip to California, in the early 1950's, I introduced something new to Pittsburgh—floodlights. I had noticed in Los Angeles the lovely effect that floodlights could make on a house and shrubbery and plantings. As soon as I returned to Pittsburgh, I had an electrician come and install floodlights on my property. At that time, no one in Pittsburgh had seemed to hear of such a thing. I even had to describe what I wanted in great detail to the electrician so that he could make them up for me.

"Just tell me how they look and what you want, Mrs. McClaney," he said, *"and I will see that you have them."*

Well, he did a beautiful job. People came to see them, because the word got around. There were all kinds of comments, most of them favorable, although I didn't much care, because I knew they looked good. Needless to say, it added to my growing reputation as being a person who didn't stand still or just go along with the old ways. Those floodlights in Pittsburgh were sort of like my porch set in Alabama, a little daring for the time and place. They are things that set me apart and probably caused some people to take a negative attitude toward me.

I sort of pushed and pulled on my daughters, Burnie and La-Doris, to be progressive, to step out and make something of themselves. I certainly didn't want them just to rest on my success. When they finished high school, they both went to college—Burnie to Morgan State College in Baltimore and La-Doris to Tennessee Agricultural and Industrial State University in Nashville. Neither went straight through, but they did finish their undergraduate and graduate work later in California. I must say that they somewhat fooled around in between times. I let it go because I knew they would have to see for themselves what I had always been talking about—going on to make the best use of your abilities. So, now they have their undergraduate degrees in the field of Behavioral Science. Burnie has a Master's Degree in Urban Planning and Development while La-Doris has her Master's Degree in Public Administration, plus an Honorary Doctorate of Humanities from Shorter College, Little Rock, Arkansas.

I am grateful that my children are grown and doing well. One thing that always kept me going was my desire to make a cushion for them so that they would have something to fall on, sit on, or stand on—something to make it easier for them than it had been for me. I thank God that has now been done. I taught them to the best of my ability, and I tried to get over to them the notion that you are better off doing your best than not doing your best. If they were to decide to go in some way that was not my way, or was against what I taught them, then it was their business.

I wanted my daughters to be happy with their mother, and I think they have been. It was always important to me, when they were growing up, to be the kind of mother they would like their friends to know. What happened was that they did bring their friends home. Even after they were grown and traveled to other parts of the world and made new friends—they brought them home, too! There are friends of my daughters all over the world who call me *"Mom"* or *"Momma,"* and I love them all.

While we still lived in Pittsburgh, a good friend of my girls' was Maurice Stokes. He was an outstanding basketball player. Maurice was from Pittsburgh, and I remember having a party for him just before he was to become a professional basketball player. La-Doris was still in high school and Burnie had gone off to college that year. But, La-Doris wanted to have the party for Maurice and for his good friends, Ed Flemings and Sy Green, both famous former players now. We asked Bill Powell, a radio newscaster in Pittsburgh, to bring his recording equipment so that he could put some of the party out on the air the next day, because that is what he wanted to do. The party was a great success. I have always been glad we had that party for Maurice. We loved him very much and thought so highly of him. It was a tragedy when he became ill. His teammates and other ball-playing friends in Cincinnati raised money to take care of him and to get him to the best doctors. They were devoted to him. We all were. I came from California to see him, and thank God that I did before he died.

Every summer, we would have Bermuda shorts parties since the weather was always very warm. We would have things set up so that people could dance outside on the grass in the back, the lawn being very large. After one such party, my neighbor across the street, Dr. Holland, remarked on how there were so many people at the party that cars were parked all the way down the hill and beyond. Parties that size were seldom given. However, the Lewis Estate was never more enjoyable than when we could entertain our growing number of friends.

People loved coming to our house for parties. I would tell Burnie and La-Doris to invite all their friends, whether they were people who had status or were on welfare. The only kind of kids I didn't want coming were those who enjoyed wrecking property and being rowdy. Many of the girls' friends had parents who were in high social and economic positions, but I didn't want them to limit their friends only to people who were well-off. I wanted them to ask friends whose parents were not able to give them much or let them have parties in return.

"I don't want you ever to feel that you are better than anybody else," I told them. *"I know what it's like to be left out. I don't want you to leave someone out just because they are poor or in a lower position. I want you to always feel that you are as good as anybody else, but you are no better than anybody*

else. God loves all of us or we wouldn't be here."

We owned two Cadillacs by the time we were living on the Lewis Estate and giving parties. I owned one, and Bernie and I owned one jointly that he drove. Burnie and La-Doris often drove both cars, because their father had a truck he used most of the time and I often didn't go anywhere. They would each, then, have a car to drive.

"Look," I would say to them, *"I know when we didn't have a wagon nor a home. When you're driving down this hill or going somewhere to see somebody, don't step on the gas and go flying past kids you know, like you don't know them and don't see them. Pick them up and give them a ride. Let them go with you, if it's okay with them and they want to. If there's anything I can't stand, it's somebody acting silly. So, don't do it, because it's much easier to fall down than it is to stand up."*

I feel that these principles I taught have become the way my daughters and I live. We love our many friends and we like finding new ones. They come from all walks of life, and they are welcome to our house always. Most of our good times are ten times better than they might be, because we share them. You can do without lots of this world's goods, but you can't do for long without people to love and be loved by.

Now, I'm going to end this chapter with another of my small sermons. (I just have to give these little sermons, because they come naturally to me, and I live by them.) You could call it good advice from a lady who learned it for herself. There is a great blessing in giving your best. God is with you when you do. He's always with you. Where there is one parent in a family, which is fifty percent of the usual family leadership, if that parent is a good parent and gives his or her best, you can come up with a decent family. It doesn't take a hundred percent of anything to come out okay. If you can just give fifty percent, you can make a success of a situation. But, always give your best.

God has proven to me that I could do whatever it was my job to do. I went ahead and obeyed Him, and that is why this book is called, *GOD, I LISTENED.* I want every reader to know my life, to know that each one of us can accomplish more than we ever dreamed. If you consult God, you will find your way. I consulted Him, and here I stand in a way that I never thought would happen.

One day, I had to go to the nursery to get things for the garden, such as soil, lemon trees and fertilizer. Since my van was in the garage for repairs, I had my driver take the Mercedes and I followed in the Rolls-Royce with La-Doris driving. We pulled up to a stop light, both cars, and as I sat in the Rolls, looking at my Mercedes, I thought, *"What a pretty, shining car that is!"*

I said to La-Doris, *"Isn't that car beautiful? I would feel that way even if it wasn't my own. It's just a beautiful car, sitting there, waiting for the light to change. And, here we are, following in a Rolls-Royce. And, both cars belong to me! At one time I didn't have a wagon to ride in. How far God has brought me!"*

I don't have the words or the know-how to give Him the thanks I want to give Him. God has truly been good to me. He has opened up His eyes and smiled upon me. He is no respecter of persons. He loves *you* as much as He loves me. Learn to trust Him. That is what I want to get across. Don't look to find my faults, because they're there, but try to find what I've done that is right and good. Try to look at the same God and trust Him as I have trusted Him.

That's all you have to do.

EULA McCLANEY

MY FAMILY

Mom

Dad

Me, Joe Frank, Jr., Georgia Mae, Jimmy Lee and Tommy Louis

Georgia Mae and I (center)

My favorite dress

Georgia Mae

MY BROTHERS

Tommy Louis   Jimmy Lee

Burnie

La-Doris

Linda Hopkins, my "adopted" daughter

With "my babies"

With mother, La-Doris and Burnie

Burnie and Attorney James E. Morgan

Betty Lewis

Flagstone

Some of the McClaney properties.

With President Ford

Commissioner Hudson, Gordon "Twig" Baker, Jr., and Commissioner Ferraro.

With "Twig" and his mother, Marion Baker.

With Supervisor Kenneth Hahn and Rosa Parks.

ON VACATION IN HAWAII

With Jimmy Lee, La-Doris and Tommy Parker, Jr.

4.
The Voice Again

In 1957, I felt the time had come for me to take a vacation, and I had hopes that Bernie would take it with me. I had asked him to go to California with me. I had been there by myself several years earlier and wanted him to see what a beautiful place it was. *"It seemed to me,"* I said, *"that in California one could do more things and do them more easily than in Pennsylvania, and there seemed to be so much opportunity for anyone who wanted to get ahead."* Bernie said, *"Yes, I'll go with you."* Later when the time drew near, he began to change his mind, until one day he said to my daughters, *"I'm not going."*

Burnie said, *"Don't let it worry you, mother, if daddy won't go with us. He just doesn't know how to relax."*

I was upset. I had really counted on him coming with us. I just never could get completely use to him being so changeable and I never really knew where he stood.

"We'll just go on by ourselves," said La-Doris. *"We'll go to the Auto Club and get what maps we'll need, and we'll go on out there."*

I guess there comes a time in your life, every now and then, when you've suffered enough and have been through enough, that you go ahead and please yourself and give up trying to get anybody to do anything. The girls persuaded me to go ahead with our plans. So, we got our maps, climbed in the car, and in three or four days found ourselves in Los Angeles for a six-week vacation. My father also came along. My parents had come to live with me in Pittsburgh a few years earlier.

Shortly before leaving for my vacation in Los Angeles, I had purchased a building in Braddock, Pennsylvania. It contained five apartment units and needed lots of renovation. I knew that the government was going to take over property in that area for some projects, so I bought the building because I wanted to have some real estate there, even though I knew the building would soon be torn down. So, I bought it, fixed it up, and rented out the apartments. And, that just about tied up all of my money, that and my other properties and expenses. It was time to get away for a while.

When we came to California, I was tired, feeling worn out and weary of facing everything always on my own and always having to do all the thinking, studying, and planning.

On the way to California we stopped in Anderson, Indiana to visit my brother, Jimmy. He said to me, *"Something tells me you are going to buy some real estate when you get to California."*

"No, indeed!" I said. *"I just bought a five-family building and had to have it rewired. I knew what I was getting into, and I bought it cheap. But, I had to have it rewired and new fixtures put in. Then, there was the plumbing to take care of, and a lot of plastering had to be done. I had to do all that to bring it up to standard so it could pass inspection. And, I paid cash every step of the way. So, I've spent all my money, and I'm tired, and I'm just going to California to rest. I don't intend to buy anything."*

"Well, be that as it may," Jimmy replied. *"I know a man from here who went out to Los Angeles and he got into real estate out there. I want you to take his address, 'cause something tells me that you're going out there to buy real estate."*

"I don't know what's telling you that," I said, *"but I'll take his address, if you like. However, I am **not** going to buy any real estate."*

Once we were in Los Angeles, we decided to stay in a motel. We did not have motels back in the Pittsburgh area, so I thought a motel was unusual. But, I liked the idea of them. They seemed to have a mixture of people—no problem about segregation—and I liked that. I was tired of seeing how white people would go running if they saw a black person coming their way. I just liked to see people live together the way we were all born to live together.

The motel we stayed in was in an area of Los Angeles where there were many motels. It was owned and operated by a black lady from Texas. I talked to her about the motel business, and what she told me was truly food for thought. I knew I couldn't run any highly specialized kind of business, because I didn't have much training or background. But, I allowed myself to think that running a motel was something Bernie and I might do together. I made up my mind to tell him about it when I got back to Pittsburgh.

"Let me get some real estate people to show you around, show you some of the other motels," the woman said to me one day. *"That way you'll have a better idea of what it may cost you to buy one."*

"All right," I said. *"I wouldn't mind finding out more about it—as long as I'm here."*

So, I began to go around looking at motels and getting a clearer idea of what they cost, how they were set up, and what it took to run them. It was all out of curiosity. To my thinking, I was just checking out possibilities for the future. I had no idea at the time that my future was closer than I thought.

I have mentioned earlier that an enterprising aunt of mine used to go to California part of the year and work for John Barrymore, Jr. Knowing that I was going to Los Angeles, she wrote me from Alabama to be sure to look them up, because they had always been so nice to her and they all felt very close to one another. As soon as I had the time, I called Mrs. Barrymore, and she told me to come over.

I went over to meet the Barrymores and we got along very well. While we were visiting, I told them that I had been interested in the idea of owning and managing motels and had been looking around at some.

"I think someday I may want to get into the motel business," I said.

"If you want to do that, be sure and let me know," Mrs. Barrymore replied, *"I will give you all the references you need. And, if you want to do it now, while you're here on this trip, I'll be happy to speak on your behalf."*

"Thank you," I said, *"but I don't intend to do it now. I'm not ready for it. I appreciate your offer, and in time I may take you up on it."*

Then one day, soon after my visit with the Barrymores, a friend of mine, Dr. Climie Dorsey, came to me and said, *"I want you to move out of this motel and come stay at my house. I've got plenty of room."*

We had known each other in Pittsburgh, so I accepted her offer, and my father and my daughters and I went to stay with my friend. While we were there, my Aunt Marvelle Holt, who was living in Los Angeles, sent a real estate agent over to see me. He was a black man and seemed very eager to show me some property. I told him that I had already looked at a number of motels and had seen everything I wanted to see. (My Aunt Marvelle, by the way, was married to my mother's kid brother.)

"I have a lot of food for thought concerning motels," I told him, *"so, I'm not going to bother about it anymore right now. I just want to go home and take my time thinking about the future."*

However, the agent insisted that he had one particular motel he wanted to show me. He also wanted to show me the house where Rochester (that's Eddy Anderson), from the Jack Benny radio and television programs, lived. Well, I really wanted to see Rochester's house, so I agreed to let the man show it to me—and the motel.

After seeing Rochester's house, we went to look at two motels the agent had in mind that I might buy. There was something about one of them that I really liked. We were doing a lot of sightseeing, however, so I didn't really think too much about it during the day. But that night— well, it seemed like I was awake all night thinking about that motel.

Then the Voice began talking to me. During the day, as I recall, the motel wasn't too much on my mind. But, at night I would hear the Voice insistently telling me, *"Get that motel. Get that one."* The name of the motel in question was the Flagstone.

I hadn't heard the Voice since It had said to me so long ago in Pittsburgh, *"You do it yourself."* Now here It was speaking to me over and over, saying, *"Get it. Get it. Get it."*

I would get up in the morning and say to Burnestine, *"You know, this Voice, or something, bothers me in the night. It keeps telling me to get that motel, keeps saying, 'Get it, get it, get it.' And I keep shooing It off, because I know I'm not prepared to buy a motel. I spent all the cash I had just buying and fixing up that building back in Braddock. I didn't come out here prepared to buy any building. But this Voice keeps telling me to go ahead and get the Flagstone. I don't know why this is bothering me so. But that Voice keeps telling me, 'You get it, you get it.' It keeps telling me that every night."*

Burnie didn't know what to say about it. She could give me no answer. So, I kept on trying to ignore the Voice. The weather was very hot at the time, and I would often get out of bed and get my pillow and lie on the rug on the floor. But, it made no difference to the Voice.

"Get it. You get it. Get it." The Voice would not stop. I figured that the Voice must be inside my head, because It was not out in the room disturbing Burnie or La-Doris. Every night it was the same thing, the Voice just insisting I buy that motel, and I was getting very little sleep. So, I began to pray.

"Lord," I prayed, *"Why should I get that motel? I have my home in Pittsburgh and my little business—thirty-three apartments. I'm so much better off now than I ever have been before. Why should I get into this? I've spent my money. Where will I get the money to buy a motel? The people want $15,000 down on it."*

"You get it. You get it," the Voice kept on saying.

I went back to praying. *"Show me where to get it. How will I get it? Where will I get the money? Dear God, show me what to do in this case."*

I prayed, just prayed and prayed. I asked God to give me the answers. It must be something He wanted me to do, so I felt He must have the answers for me.

How soon the answer came I don't exactly remember. But, after a while it came into my mind in words that went, *"You remember you bought some stock, and the last time you checked on it that stock was worth close to $10,000. It has just about doubled over what you paid for it. And then, you bought some Ford stock. Now, you're going to lose a little on it, but you sell it. Sell all your stock and you'll just about have the money you need. Also, you have money at home coming in regularly from your rents. It will take ninety days for the property to clear escrow, so you'll have the money in time."*

"Lord," I said, *"I'll go ahead and get it."*

Well, it didn't turn out to be quite so easy to follow that plan. For one thing, when the people who owned the Flagstone discovered that I wanted to buy it, they refused to sell it to me. The main reason they gave was that I didn't live in Los Angeles, and that by living so far away in Pittsburgh posed a problem in case my credit was no good. I also am pretty sure they didn't want to sell to a black person, because at that time the entire neighborhood was White.

I tried to work out a deal with the real estate agent. Had we been in Pittsburgh, I could have used my property to do whatever maneuvering needed to be done. The agent wasn't at all cooperative when I asked if he would forgo his commission for a month or two and let me give him a note against my brand new El Dorado Cadillac. That way I would be able to put down a security deposit of one or two thousand dollars which might make the owners of the motel change their mind and do business with me. Then, I would have a month or two to raise the $15,000 down payment while the property was in escrow. But, the agent refused to go along with this.

I knew I had to buy that motel, but how? I never doubted for a moment that I should do what the Voice had told me to do. Well, I have always been able to find a way to deal with people who didn't want to deal with me. I was determined I would find a way to buy the Flagstone. It was Betty Lewis who provided the way. Betty was a woman who lived in Los Angeles. I had first met her when she and her sister-in-law had come to Pittsburgh for a convention. A minister in Pittsburgh had asked me if I would take them into my home while they were there. Betty and her sister-in-law were great girls, and we got to be good friends. Faced with this obstacle to buying the Flagstone, I called up Betty and explained what was going on.

"You are California material, Mrs. McClaney!" Betty said at once. *"When I visited you in Pittsburgh, I loved the way you lived. Anybody who can make a showing in Pittsburgh, like you made, belongs here. I'm going to see to it that you get that motel."*

Betty also happened to be so light-skinned that people thought she was White. Now, I began to have a demonstration of the wonderful way God works! It turned out that He had moved Betty into my life long before I had any idea I might want to buy property in California. She became His instrument on my behalf! And, it was funny the way it all worked out.

I also believe that God was speaking to me through my brother Jimmy, when Jimmy had said he had the feeling I would be buying property during my vacation in Los Angeles. And, I believe He stirred something in my Aunt Marvelle so that she sent the real estate agent to me. Of all things, then, imagine me even trying to resist what the Voice had been telling me! But, I was still having my faith tested and purified.

Pure and simple, what Betty did was to buy the Flagstone in her own name and then to make a quitclaim deed of it to me! Then, Betty gave me a quitclaim deed with the understanding that I would put up one thousand dollars then and there. She wanted me to send her another $4,000 in thirty days and get the remainder $10,000 to her within sixty days.

I never heard of a quitclaim deed before this. Betty explained it to me. *"If anything happens to me, you can show my family, this quitclaim deed which makes you the owner of the property as of now, because my financial records will show that I paid $15,000 for the Flagstone as down payment. This way you can go back to Pittsburgh and not lose one night's sleep over the deal."*

So, it was settled! I was the owner of the Flagstone Motel! Betty just reached out and made it all possible, because she was not a selfish person and she believed in me. It is the Bettys in this world who make it a better place.

Everything had been completed, I called Bernie to tell him what had happened. I told him about the Voice and said I would explain all the details when I got home. In the meantime, I said, I was going to find someone to run the motel, because I couldn't ask him just to jump up and leave his business in Pittsburgh and move to Los Angeles. I wouldn't even expect that. But, I would find somebody to run the motel, and we could get together later on what we should do.

As soon as I had received the quitclaim from Betty and called Bernie in Pittsburgh, my girls, my father and I went back home. There was a lot to be done. I had to raise the money while the Flagstone was in escrow, make plans for finding someone to manage the motel, and see about helping La-Doris go off to college. As I mentioned earlier, she was going to be a freshman at Tennessee Agricultural and Industrial State University in Nashville. We just scurried around to get it all done.

When I got back to Pittsburgh, I found that Bernie was very agreeable about things. He seemed to go right along with my buying the motel. It was one of the few times he didn't oppose me. Shortly before the property in Los Angeles was to come out of escrow, Bernie and I agreed that it would be best for me to return to Los Angeles so that I could handle things myself and look for someone to run the motel in the way I would want it run. I could have sent the money from Pittsburgh and let Betty find a manager for the Flagstone, but that didn't seem too good an idea. Something inside me urged me to go and deal with it in person.

Bernie and I decided, too, that Burnistine would come with me. She was a pre-med student at Morgan State University, but she had begun to get exhausted from her studies. We thought she should change her major from medicine to something less demanding, but she didn't want to do that. She did agree that if she took time off and came to California with me, the change in environment for a few weeks would make it easier for her to go back to school. And, I really felt good about having her with me to help meet a new challenge.

Late in September, we drove La-Doris down to Nashville. I wanted to check out her rooming set-up and see for myself the kind of place she would be living in and what the university itself was like. Then, we returned to Pittsburgh and were very busy packing, since we planned to be in Los Angeles for maybe three or four months. I also had to make sure that my rentals would be looked after and the rents collected, although Bernie said he would see to them. Still, I didn't want to impose on him too much since his own affairs kept him very busy.

When Georgia Mae heard about the Flagstone and that I was going back to Los Angeles for a while, she wrote and asked if she could come with me. *"If you come by here,"* she said on the telephone, *"I will go with you. I'll help make the beds and do the best I can to help you all out."*

So, a week before Thanksgiving, November, 1957, Burnistine and I got in the car and drove to Detroit where we picked up Georgia Mae. Then, we stopped over in Indiana for a few days to visit with my brother, Jimmie, and then to St. Louis to visit my Aunt Lillian Holt. After that we drove straight across the country—Burnie did all the driving—and arrived in Los Angeles a few days before Thanksgiving, and just a few days before the Flagstone was due to come out of escrow.

I didn't know it then, but when I arrived in Los Angeles in November of 1957, I had arrived in the city I was to call home from then on. The Voice had led me to my promised land, but I would walk through a long valley before I would reach the higher heights. None of this was clear to me then. I was only doing what the Voice had told me to do.

I had listened. I had followed. Now, with joy in my heart, I can tell you the best part of my story.

PART III
Los Angeles, California

1.
Starting Over

Before the end of the year 1957, I was living at the Flagstone and learning the ins and outs of running a motel. It was truly a good thing that Burnie had come with me, because she was able to deal with the former owners, whom I'll call the Smiths.

Burnie told the Smiths that she and her mother (who they did not know was me) were going to operate the motel for Betty (who they thought was White). The Smiths had told Betty that a deal with me would have been a good one, but they were prejudiced all the same about doing business with black folks. It would have been a bad shock to them to learn that a black woman had purchased the motel and would be running it herself.

However, the Smiths were moving to Florida just as soon as they could turn it over to Betty and whomever she was going to have manage it. They were not too upset, then, when Burnie informed them that she and her mother would look after it for Betty. So, they gave Burnie an inventory of all the linens, furniture, and various items that were written up on the sale agreement. After a few days, Burnie had a pretty good idea of how to manage the motel, and the Smiths left for Florida.

Burnie, Georgia Mae, and I moved into the Flagstone and began a way of life that we were to know for the next ten years. It was all pretty exciting in the beginning, because you never knew when somebody was going to show up wanting a room. We were all caught up in it, making sure the rooms were clean, the linens fresh and the beds made. A client would come in and ring the bell, and then there would be a flurry as we tried to remember the details of checking people in, checking people out, making the correct charges and giving receipts. We had to keep records of our expenditures and our income to make sure our accounting was correct for paying our taxes. We had to deal with plumbing, lighting and various other repairs. It went on and on, one thing after the other, something new to learn every day, trying not to forget important things, learning how to deal with all kinds of people and getting use to being up at all hours of the night. During those first weeks the days just flew by!

When I first took over the Flagstone, our clientele was White. People who stayed there regularly were often surprised to see us black folks running the motel, and they would ask about the Smiths. We would say, *"Oh, we're running the place for them while they are on a long trip to Florida. No, we don't really know when they plan to come back."*

We had decided that we would not let anyone know that we owned the motel. We just said that we were working for the Smiths. And, when we figured they had been in Florida long enough, we put them in the Bahamas, then the Virgin Islands. We just worked as if we were working for someone else, because we needed the money and did not want to turn any clients away because they might think the money would be coming to us.

The Smiths being on vacation was our private joke, and we had a good time with it. To hear us tell it, the Smiths were doing a lot of traveling and having the time of their lives! The truth is, not only were all the motel's clients White, but that whole part of Los Angeles was White, and black people were not welcome there. So, we were really pioneers to be coming into that area and having to do it under pretense of working for white owners. That part of Los Angeles now has a mixed population. But, as things have developed, it turned out that the Voice had picked the perfect location for me for more than one reason. If I had not bought the Flagstone, I might never have come to know Los Angeles' Mayor Tom Bradley as one of my very good friends, or others who are now prominent politicians, sports figures, and entertainers. And, I might never have gotten into the board-and-care project which is one of my most rewarding concerns.

After staying with me about four months, Georgia Mae went back to Detroit in the Spring of 1958. By that time, Burnie and I had gotten the hang of things. Rather than hire chambermaids, we maintained the rooms ourselves. At the end of her college freshman year in June, La-Doris came to Los Angeles to be with us. In the meanwhile, Bernie took care of things in Pittsburgh. My mother and father were still living with Bernie in our house in Pittsburgh, although sometimes they would go and stay with Georgia Mae, after she returned to Detroit.

Although I hadn't intended to stay in Los Angeles more than a few months, the idea began to develop in my conversations with Bernie that he might want to move out here himself. In that case, we would just transfer our life together to California.

So, Bernie flew to Los Angeles in the summer of 1958. He seemed very pleased with the motel and said I had made a very good buy. Since he was a good painter and the office needed new paint, he stayed long enough to paint it for me.

Before Bernie went back to Pittsburgh, he told me that he would move to Los Angeles. It would take a while, because he would have to settle his own business affairs. In the meantime, he would continue to take care of my property. We agreed that I would come back to Pittsburgh later on to deal with my property and get everything settled there.

In October of 1958, after Bernie had left, I was told by a doctor in Los Angeles that I had to have surgery at once for a fibroid tumor. I hadn't been feeling too well, but I thought maybe I was having kidney problems. I had gone to Dr. LeRoy Weeks, one of the finest obstetricians and gynecologists in Los Angeles, and a black man.

*"Mrs. McClaney, I know that **you** know you have this thing that needs to be taken care of,"* Dr. Weeks said to me.

"What are you talking about?" I said.

"This tumor," he said. *"You surely know, Mrs. McClaney, that you have a tumor!"*

I said, *"Well, I was told I had one years ago. But, my doctor said . . ."*

"When was that?" asked Dr. Weeks.

"About seven years ago," I said.

*And **what** did your doctor tell you?"* asked Dr. Weeks.

"He told me that if it didn't bother me, don't bother it," I said.

"Seven years ago!" exclaimed Dr. Weeks. *"Well, you have had it checked and have been taking care of it, haven't you?"*

"Well, I'll tell you the truth," I said. *"This tumor frightened me, so I just stayed away."*

Dr. Weeks laughed, but he was serious, too. *"I don't want to frighten you,"* he said, *"but you have got to get this thing out of you."*

I didn't argue with Dr. Weeks. In October, I entered Cedars of Lebanon Hospital in Hollywood to have surgery. When I went into the hospital, I was told I would need some blood. It was then that something just fantastic happened. La-Doris and Burnie contacted some of the friends we had made and told them about my situation, and it seemed that people just came from everywhere to donate blood! I hadn't realized until then how many wonderful friends we had made in California in less than a year. People would call daily and ask La-Doris or Burnie, *"How much more blood does your Momma need?"* (It seems everybody calls me Momma or Mother.) And, they ended up by donating far more blood to the hospital than what I needed.

Then, there were the candy and the flowers and the visitors! My daughters and I would just marvel at all the attention and concern our new friends were showing for me. I didn't see how I could have received any more showing of love if I had been home in Pittsburgh.

It also made a big difference that Dr. Weeks was my surgeon. He was on the staff at Cedars of Lebanon during a time when black doctors were rarely on the staffs of first-rate hospitals. It was obvious from the attitude of the nurses and other doctors that he was very well-respected. So, other patients in the hospital, including the two white ladies who were in my room, as well as the nurses, began to get the idea that I must be somebody very special. Even now, the thought of it amazes me, because it was the last thing I ever expected.

Burnie and La-Doris were pretty upset that I was in the hospital. I was their foundation, and there I was having very serious surgery. They were young and they were scared. But, my Aunt Lillian Holt, who had come out to Los Angeles on a vacation, went and stayed with them at the Flagstone. Aunt Lillian was my mother's brother's wife, and she was just like a mother to my girls.

Aunt Lillian is very fair skinned and is often mistaken for White. She would come to the hospital with Burnie and La-Doris to visit with me. She was there with them on the day I had my surgery . It turned out that my case was more serious than we thought it would be, and I was in surgery six hours. La-Doris and Burnie were very worried, but Aunt Lillian, who was a very sweet and sensitive woman, was a pillar of strength.

While I was in surgery, La-Doris and Burnie were turning into nervous wrecks, and they made several trips to the hospital cafeteria with Aunt Lillian. On one of their trips there, a white woman came up to Aunt Lillian and said, *"Is your maid sick?"* She had noticed how worried the two girls looked.

"What do you mean—my 'maid?' ", said Aunt Lillian.

*"It's my **niece** who is having surgery, and these two girls are her daughters."* She was very agitated and annoyed that the lady had made that assumption. But, it was the kind of thing that was always happening.

When it turned out that my surgery had been successful and I was going to be all right, La-Doris and Burnie began to enjoy all the attention I was getting. I have never been much of a candy eater, so they had a great time eating the candy people kept sending to me. And, it was lots of fun for them to sit and order things from the menu that the hospital gave each patient. I wasn't very hungry for a few days, but, La-Doris and Burnie managed to sample most of the things the menu had to offer!

One night when I was feeling a little like walking, I got out of bed and walked to the little day-room, a kind of lounge, that was down the corridor from my room. Another lady who was also a patient on my floor was there. She came over to me and said, *"The two ladies in your room are wondering who you **really** are, and I am wondering the same thing."*

"What do you mean?" I said.

*"Well, I don't think you are registered here under your **real** name,"* she said to me. *"You are getting **so much** attention! There's just something about you. So much attention from so many people! Are you in show business?"*

I just had to laugh. *"No, I'm just an ordinary person,"* I told her.

But, a day or so later one of the private duty nurses came up to me and said, *"Did you know there's something really remarkable about you? A lot of people are talking about it."*

"What is that?" I asked.

"You came in here," she said. *"and you did something that's not done very often. You came in here, a black woman, and you brought your own black doctor in here with you. And Dr. Weeks is one of the best doctors, Black or White, that you can put your hand on anywhere. You showed that you think as much of your black doctor and his know-how as any Jewish doctor or any other doctor here.*

"What's more," she said, *"the talk that's going on here! One woman over there in your room is giving her doctor a fit. She says to him, 'Now that woman over there has Dr. Weeks, and she's up and walking around. I had my surgery before she came in here. She's doing just fine, and I'm laying up here just hurting, hurting, hurting. It makes me think that something is not right about my surgery. This lady—you see how she walks up and down the hall and how well she's getting along?' "*

Again somebody was telling me I just *had* to be somebody special. But, I wanted it understood that I wasn't special, I wasn't above other people. So I said to the nurse, *"Well, the truth is that I'm from Pittsburgh, Pennsylvania. I have not been here in Los Angeles even an entire year. I knew nothing about Dr. Weeks, but I have some good friends here that will just die by Dr. Weeks. They think he is such a good doctor. And he is! Because I have such confidence in my friends, it gave me confidence in Dr. Weeks. That's why I have him."*

I got a lot of encouragement from that great show of friendship and respect I received while I was at Cedars of Lebanon. It was good for the girls and me to know there were people who really thought well of me. Even though we were expecting Bernie to come and join us, before the year was out or sometime in early 1959, it was still hard on us to be so far away from the place that had been our home for years. Fortunately, the girls were young enough that they made friends very readily and loved having a good time. So, even though they worried about me in the hospital, at the same time they were having a ball running the motel and proving they could do it like professionals.

After I recovered from my surgery and the motel was doing well, I took a trip back to Pittsburgh. Soon after I returned to Los Angeles, Burnie and La-Doris were in an automobile accident and had to be hospitalized. While they were in the hospital, we were informed by the hospital business office that they could not be discharged unless their bill was paid in full! At that time, I was just not able to pay such a bill all at once. So, the girls called their father in Pittsburgh to explain the situation and to ask him to help pay the hospital bill.

Bernie was always *"funny"* about his own money, and in response to the girls' request he said, *"No, I didn't put you in the hospital and I'm not going to get you out."*

That was devastating to Burnie and La-Doris. While Burnie had been talking on the phone to their father, La-Doris had been listening on her own bedside telephone, because she planned to talk to him, too. But, her father's words were so harsh and hurting that she knew there was nothing she could say to him. She just eased the telephone down, while Burnie hung up shortly afterwards.

I managed to get the girls out of the hospital, but it took all my ingenuity to pay their bill. Here we were, far away from home, with a newly bought motel on our hands and not much ready cash available. At least we had the motel to live in, but I wasn't certain we were going to make a go of it. Those first months, as exciting as they were, were also quite often scary. I had to leave all my property and business in Pittsburgh in Bernie's care, and that was a risky thing at best. Well, the Voice had told me to go through with this. Once again It had showed me the direction to go, but again It left the hard stepping up to me. By this time in my life, I was beginning to realize that my days in the cotton fields were paying off, because they had taught me to endure what was hard and get above it.

Bernie had one final surprise for me. But, when he sprung it on me, I wasn't really ready for it. One day, I got a registered letter from an attorney in Pittsburgh. It was from Bernie. Without any warning, he was asking me for a divorce.

When I could think about it calmly, I thought, *"Well, this is really something! The last time I heard Bernie say anything to me, he said he was coming to California. But, I have always known his word was not too good, not at any time. He said he would take care of the property and then he would come. But, what he did was send this registered letter saying he wanted a divorce."*

Not only had Bernie got himself an attorney to send the letter and handle the divorce for him, it was my attorney that he hired! The way people can turn on you was no longer news to me. The next day I called Attorney James Edward Morgan that I knew in Los Angeles and told him about Bernie's action and said that I was going to go ahead and give him the divorce. My new attorney answered Bernie's letter, and we went ahead with the divorce as fast as possible.

Bernie and I agreed, before the divorce proceedings, that he would buy my Pittsburgh properties from me. He would also let me have all the furniture and things that I had bought on my own. This was *promised.* As it actually turned out, however, the property arrangement was so messed up that I only received a check from Bernie for less than $5,000 after expenses. Not only that, he had removed some of my furniture and other belongings so that I got only part of what was rightfully mine. The little I finally ended up with financially was ridiculous. I might as well have given it all away. But, I just took what was left for me, let Bernie go, and trusted in God. (By the way, I took the little money that Bernie sent to me and put it into stocks and a mutual fund, and I still have it today.) I was going to have to start all over again and now be both mother and father to my two daughters, who were young ladies now but still in need of a lot of support. Come what may, I was determined to keep on stepping. If I could start all over I could succeed all over, with God's help.

One of us would have to go back to Pittsburgh to sort out and pack up the furniture, clothes and other things, and have them shipped to California. I was ready to go and do it, as painful as I knew it would be. But, La-Doris and Burnie weren't about to let me suffer that ordeal.

"Mother, don't you go," La-Doris said, *"because I don't want you to get into an argument with him. I'll go and take care of everything."*

It was winter by then, the very worst weather you could get in Pittsburgh. Fortunately, on my last trip *"home,"* I had made arrangements for getting things moved to Los Angeles. La-Doris hired the largest van she could get. But, the weather was so bad in Pittsburgh, and the streets were so icy, that the van couldn't get up the hill to our house. They had to wait for two days until the streets were passable. After the van arrived at the house, it took two days just to pack and load everything. Somehow La-Doris, who is very good at organizing and managing things, saw that everything was done. Two or three weeks later the van arrived in Los Angeles.

My immediate problem was where to put everything. Living in the motel, I just didn't have the necessary room for so many things. No one can really tell you beforehand what it's like to move the contents of a big house over two thousand miles across the country and then find room for it in your own personal apartment in a motel! I filled my storage room, filled every square inch of it, and still there were more things to store. I took a motel room or two and filled them with stuff. Still there was more left over. So, I put my remaining things wherever I could find space to squeeze them in.

Another more important problem was seeing to it that La-Doris and Burnie managed to keep their lives and education on track. It was just a blessing to me that they weren't into drugs or drinking as so many young people of their age were at that time. We had our differences now and then, because they were still too young to always understand why I had certain ideas and certain ways. I realized that they could have been one hundred percent worse. I just trusted God to help them where I couldn't.

Now, I would like to say something about marriage. After looking back on my own marriage and just reflecting on what I have observed of other marriages, a couple should go into a marriage considering every angle they can. I believe in pre-nuptial agreements, especially when one of the partners has independently and previously made a lot of money, has many possessions and is financially involved with others. Husbands and wives should put their own joint money in bank accounts that have both names. Business is business, because love can be awfully sweet until it comes down to getting divorced. I think wives and husbands should look into the record of the person they are going to marry to see how much they already own and how they pay their bills. You really have to watch what is going on. Lord knows, you can't live or love by being suspicious of everybody, but there are things people need to know about each other and agree on *before* marriage. Lies and secrets will work their damage.

My new situation in Los Angeles was practically like beginning my life all over. Only this time, I did have some advantages. I had experience in dealing in real estate and managing rental properties. And, I was free of a husband who almost always opposed me on every issue. It's true that I had taken a bad financial loss and was in a new business that I didn't know too well. I was stepping into the unknown. Yet, I had done it before, so I knew I could do it again, even though I was forty-three at the time and no longer a young woman.

The Voice had led me into this place.

God knew what I didn't know, and I had the faith in Him which helped me let go of the old and open myself to the new. Time would show what He had in mind for me, and He answered in his own way those deep prayers from my earliest years that I could make something good and wonderful of my life.

It took ten years before I knew why the Voice had insisted that I buy that one particular motel, the Flagstone. By 1967, it turned out that I was in the right zone to turn the Flagstone into what it is today: a residential care facility for developmentally disabled adults. This has become one of the most important projects in my life. At the time, I was pushed by the Voice into buying it, I didn't have the least idea that it would one day help me serve others in a very special way and provide a home for those who would desperately need it.

Many times in life it may look like you are going to lose everything you have. And, sometimes you may indeed lose everything. You may come way down from where you were. But, if you trust God, He's able to bring you back all the way, far past where you were before. I *know*. It happened to me, and I *know*.

2.
The Flagstone

I spent my first ten years in Los Angeles living in and managing the Flagstone Motel. What can I say about those years? They were busy ones. They were filled with all the little details and requirements you have to handle when you serve the public. In the motel business, I saw an awful lot of people come and go, people of every kind and character and description. But, those Flagstone years were wonderful. Friends just poured into my life! Flagstone was not only home for me, my girls and later my mother, but it was home for many, many others.

We all pitched in and ran the motel. Even though Burnie and La-Doris got more and more involved with their own lives, we stayed together. La-Doris and Burnie had a variety of different jobs in Los Angeles, but the Flagstone was our mainstay of business. It was our home. I can't begin to tell of all the people, friends and relatives who came and lived with us at different times. I have always liked to have a lot of people around me, and at the Flagstone I was Mother, or Mom, or Big Momma to a lot of folks. My mother and father also came to live in Los Angeles. My mother stayed with me, but since our space at the Flagstone was limited, my father lived with my brother, Louis.

I am grateful for all the friends I made in Los Angeles. They came from all walks of life, high and low. I still love to be with them and have them visit me and party with me. Some of my friends are people who are famous and others are plain people just like me. To tell the truth, whether high or low, famous or not famous, most of the people I know work hard for what they get. They are into politics, government, entertainment, education, sports, and all kinds of everyday things. I still marvel at how I've come to know them and been able to welcome them to my home.

La-Doris likes to say that the Flagstone was a *"fun place to live."* Certainly, one advantage it had was that it was located on the west side of Los

Angeles, not far at all from downtown Los Angeles, Hollywood, and Beverly Hills. Even if you didn't have a car, you could easily get to nearby places. Another advantage of Flagstone was that we always had people coming and going. Some of our guests would stay with us for weeks, sometimes months or years. La-Doris and Burnie's friends were often impressed and intrigued that they lived in a motel in a busy part of town.

We never got bored. Even when La-Doris and Burnie had their own jobs, they would come home, have dinner and help clean rooms. And, since guests might want to check in at any hour of the night, we were all pretty used to getting up several times a night to rent out a room. Many a night, the girls would be up four or five times and still have to be up early in the morning and go to work.

The Flagstone was our means of survival. It was a real help to me that Burnie and La-Doris were grown and working. They would go to school part-time and work part-time. When they weren't in school working, they were helping me with the Flagstone. A few years later, they each had earned their Bachelor's Degrees and Master's Degrees, for which I am very proud of them.

As it has turned out, La-Doris and Burnie are the backbone of the McClaney Enterprises. Burnie's special gift is to be able to come up with new ideas for new things to try and new ways to do it. La-Doris has a great talent for organizing things and running them. Together they have brought me love and support. They are two of my greatest blessings.

Sometimes, we would have good business, lots of guests during the week and on the weekends. Other times, business would be slow, oh, so slow. But during the slow times, the girls would give me some of their money, so I was able to keep things going. I never believed in throwing money away. If I was doing pretty good, I'd put the money to good use. If I was doing poorly, I'd put it to good use, too. So, the good days made up for the bad days.

A lady who owned the motel next door to mine said to me, *"Mrs. McClaney, you have a lot of slow days in this business, and it sometimes seems like you're not doing anything. But, my experience is that when the year is up and you total all your records, you'll find that you kept your head above water.*

*It will definitely carry you through. There's one thing you've got going for you—
you don't have to pay any rent. When you pay your mortgage, your rent is
paid. So, everything is taken care of under one note, and that's a blessing in
itself. And, your lights and gas are all paid under one payment, too."*

I was satisfied staying there, grateful to God just to have that place.
I made the best of it that I could, year in and year out, working with
my children the best that I could. Sometimes, they would see things
wisely, very wisely, and a lot of times they would see things very
unwisely, as children will. I was being both a mother and father, talking
to them regularly and trying to steer them in the right direction. I'd
sometimes pray to God that they would listen to something I felt I
had to tell them or advise them on. And, with God's help, we made
it through.

My mother, who was living with us at the Flagstone, was the kind
of person who would seldom say anything to her grandchildren, even
if she knew they were wrong. She always wanted them to love her,
not dislike her. She was completely different from me in that way. I
can't help who doesn't like me, if I'm right. I believe in putting what's
right above getting people to like you. If my nephew or niece doesn't
like me for saying something to him or her, that's fine, as long as I
know I've told them what is right. Now, if they love me after I teach
them what is right, that is beautiful! If they can only love me when
I allow them to do what's wrong, because it's what they want to hear
at the time, then they will eventually hate me. I will always tell a person
what I think is right and let God take care of the rest of it.

Some of our guests stayed with us at the Flagstone for four or five
years. They really became part of the family. Some of them were so
close to us that instead of going and having to clean their rooms once
a week we just let them do it themselves.

"Momma, I need my sheets and towels," they'd come and say. And, they
would also have their meals with us quite often. I guess the Flagstone
was part motel and part boarding house.

La-Doris and Burnie were very active young women, and with their
jobs and their interest in people, we kept making new friends all the
time, such as Wilt Chamberlain and his mother. Archie Moore was another
good friend, as were Roosevelt Grier and Bill Russell. Many black athletes
and their friends became our friends during that Flagstone period.

The Harlem Magicians would always stay with us when they came to play exhibitions in Los Angeles. It was great fun to have them all check in and then see them practicing all day in the courtyard. Their visits were something we really looked forward to for several years.

It was always a treat, too, when Archie Moore would stay with us. Archie lived in San Diego. He owned a dairy chain called Archie Moore Milk. Whenever he was with us and the Archie Moore Milk truck made deliveries at the liquor store across the street, Archie would go over and bring back gallons and gallons of milk! He also loved to go to the store and bring home watermelons. Archie came to be just like a father to La-Doris and Burnie, and we all loved him.

Because we knew several athletes, we were introduced to many other athletes. Many of the players you read about in the papers now and see on television were friends of ours in the early days of their careers. I couldn't begin to name them all, but it seems there's hardly a baseball, basketball or football team that doesn't have *someone* I know who belongs to it.

One very good friend I made during my years at Flagstone is Tom Bradley who, as I write this, is the distinguished mayor of Los Angeles and an important political figure. In the 1960's, Tom Bradley was a Los Angeles City Councilman, and the Flagstone was in his district. I first met him at some local meetings he attended, and we got to liking each other. Over the years, we became very close friends, and when La-Doris was married in 1976, Mayor Bradley did the honors of giving away the bride.

So, that is how it went during my ten years at the Flagstone Motel. In terms of friends and activities, life just kept opening up and getting better. Financially I was holding my own, but I still hadn't got back to the level I had achieved in Pittsburgh. I was buying the motel, saving my money, and slowly pulling out of the slump Bernie had left me in, but I wasn't back into real estate in any big way.

I've indicated that nothing earthshaking ever went on at the Flagstone. It's true, except for one awful event that I will never forget. We had a murder. I knew such things as murders and suicides happened in motels and hotels, but I was not ready for something like that in *my* motel. How could a person ever be *"ready"* for such a terrible thing?

Before getting into the details of that dark day, I had better set up the background. Since some people stayed at the motel for months or years, they more or less spent a lot of time with us. One young woman who lived with us for three or four years was Marion Baker. Marion had gone to college with Burnistine and had become a school teacher.

When Marion came to live at the Flagstone, she had left her husband and moved to California with her mother and her little boy, Twig. They lived in their own rooms at the motel but took their meals with us. Twig was about six years old when they first came to us. Marion didn't teach at that time. She had just grown tired of teaching and preferred doing other kinds of work. Twig was the *"baby"* of our household, and he was a very bright child. He loved to look in the newspaper and read the stock reports! He was just fascinated by business, business of any kind. He loved to hear people talk about it, and he would just look at you with his great big eyes and listen. He also liked to go to the bank with me. I used to tell Marion that he was brighter than her, even if she did have a college degree. She would laugh at that. She was so proud of Twig. We all were.

It was during a summer holiday that the murder occurred at the Flagstone. La-Doris, Burnie, Marion, and some of their friends had all driven to San Francisco for a little vacation. While they were gone, the motel just filled up with guests. People came one after the other, and Twig and I were as busy as we could be registering guests, handing out keys, making beds, and cleaning rooms.

A man and woman came one afternoon and registered as a married couple. I remember that I rented them our last available room. It didn't seem to bother them that they couldn't have a choice of rooms. In fact, they said they would rent the room for a week, sight unseen, and they paid for it in advance. That was a little unusual, but at the time it didn't arouse any suspicions in me.

The next day, my daughters and Marion returned home and wanted to know how things had gone with us over the holiday. Twig and I told them how busy we had been and that we'd been filled up every night. And, I was pleased with how Twig had been such good help to me, since he was only about eight years old at the time.

During the following week, as guests left, we were busy changing the linens and cleaning the rooms. When the week was up on the room I had rented to that one particular couple, I began to wonder about them. I had not seen them since the time they checked in. When another day had passed and they had not showed up, I figured they were not coming back, so I decided to clean the room.

When I went into the room, the bed was made, and it looked as if nobody had stayed there. But, I cleaned the room anyway, and I made the bed up with fresh linens, and we went on to other rooms. It was all part of our regular routine. We left the door of the room open to air it out, because it hadn't smelled quite right. When I went into it later, I was certain something was wrong, because the smell seemed much worse, so bad that I thought it might be a dead rat.

I noticed that the closet was closed and that the smell seemed to come from there. Then, I noticed that the knob was off the closet door and the door was locked. I grew very frightened and suspected something was truly wrong, and I began to feel very shaky. I supposed I already knew what we might find in that closet, but I just didn't let the thought come to my mind. Twig was with me, and he said, *"I'll stick something in the keyhole and unlock the door, Aunt Eula."* So, he got a hairpin and managed to unlock the door and open it.

When Twig opened the closet door, the smell was much worse. We saw that a dress was hanging in the closet, too. Now, there was a dresser in the closet, and right away both Twig and I knew that something was behind it. The odor was terrible by now, and Twig bent down and said, *"I see somebody or something back in there behind the dresser!"*

I was really frightened to hear what Twig said. La-Doris and Burnie were both at work. Even though I knew I would have to call the police, I didn't want to deal with the situation without at least a friend there with me. I didn't really know what had happened in that room, and I was afraid that once the police got there we would have all kinds of excitement and complications that wouldn't look too good in a motel. So, I called a good friend of mine, Jim Morgan, who was an attorney and had his office nearby.

"Jim, I'm afraid there's been some foul play here at the motel," I told him. And, I explained about the closet and the terrible smell and the people

who had rented the room. *"I know I should call the police, but I'm frightened, and I want you to come over here first. I don't want to handle this alone."*

Jim said, *"That scares me, too, Eula. There's no telling what you're dealing with. Look, I have a friend, a probation officer, who is studying to be an attorney. He's coming over here in a few minutes. I'll come right over and bring him with me. Then, we can do whatever calling needs to be done. I know this is just shattering you, but you won't be alone."*

Soon Jim and his friend, the probation officer, arrived at the motel. The probation officer was a very calm man who just went into the room and checked it out. When he came out, he said to me, *"Do you keep some kind of big doll in that closet?"*

"A doll?", I said. *"No."*

"Well, I didn't think so," the man said. *"That is a dead woman there in the closet. She has been shoved—standing on her head—shoved behind the dresser. They have pushed this dresser in front of her to keep her from falling down."*

"Oh, Lord, are you serious?", I cried.

"Yes, I am," said the man. *"And, we don't want to touch a thing in that room, because the police will want to examine it."*

"Jim, call the police," I said. *"Call everybody that needs to be called about this, while I look for the card those people signed when they registered for the room."*

I was so nervous, that when I began to look through our registration file I just managed to get the cards all tumbled up and couldn't find the card that the man had registered on. In the meantime, the police arrived. Then, the coroner came. Before long, the place was swarming and buzzing with people.

The police asked all kinds of questions. If Jim hadn't been there, I'm sure I would not have made much sense. I did my best to explain how a man and woman had rented that room for a week. The police wanted to know how come I hadn't noticed anything unusual or discovered the body until a week later. I explained to them that at the Flagstone our patrons made up their own beds and kept their rooms straightened themselves, if they were staying more than one night. We changed the linens and cleaned the rooms when our guests checked out, or once a week if they were staying longer. That way we could take care of the rooms ourselves, and by not hiring chambermaids we could keep our rates low. That explains why I had only just then found a dead woman in the room.

By this time, La-Doris had come home. I had called her when I was trying to check the registration file and told her what was happening. She was working for the Sheriff's Department then and was able to answer the police officers' questions and back up what I had said. Marion also came home about that time from her job, since it was now late afternoon. So, there was all kinds of coming and going, the police, people from the coroner's office, friends, and those who were guests in the motel. It was just the kind of thing that made a person like me very upset. It was so terrible and frightening.

Later on, after the body had been taken away and the police and others had finished their questioning and were gone, we sat around the dining table trying to make sense of what had happened and to pull ourselves together. Jim Morgan had stayed with me throughout all of it, and if anybody could get you to stop thinking of trouble and put a little humor into life, it was Jim.

Jim said, *"I'm going across the street and get me a bottle of liquor, because I've just got to live. There's no sense in my dying, too, over this."*

That sort of broke the fear and gloom we were all feeling. I do not drink, and neither does La-Doris or Burnie, but we were in sympathy with Jim. After he had a drink or two, he got to talking and being funny and got us to laughing a little bit.

Now, one of the men in our group said that the only way we were going to get the stench out of that motel room would be to put some coffee grounds directly over the fire in an old pan or skillet and let it burn. This was the only thing, he said, that would take the odor of a dead body out of the room. So, Jim volunteered to do it.

"I was too upset to go into that room earlier," he said, *"but now that I've had a drink I feel like going into the room, now that I can talk and now that I can see. Give me a hot plate and a can of coffee."*

We gave Jim the coffee and the hot plate and he went to the room and fixed it so that the coffee would burn all night. By this time it was late, and we were all worn out. At least we were tired enough and had talked enough that we could go to sleep.

As for Twig, who had been witness to all the excitement, he had been strangely quiet. The next day, however, Marion told me that Twig had talked to her that night and told her something he had seen earlier in the week.

"Mother, I saw the lady who rented the room from Aunt Eula," he told Marion. *"She went out in her car one day and brought two ladies back with her. One of them was an old lady like Aunt Eula's mother. She and the other lady took the old lady into the room. That was at the time Aunt Eula was fixing up her bathroom—putting up some curtains and decorating it. She sent me to the store to get some things for her.*

"When I went past that room on my way to the store, I heard that old lady hollering, and I thought something bad was going on in there. And, when I came back from the store, she was still hollering. Aunt Eula didn't hear it because she was so busy redecorating her bathroom."

"Why didn't you tell Aunt Eula about it?" Marion had asked Twig.

"I thought those people might hurt Aunt Eula, too," Twig had replied. *"If they were doing something bad to that old lady, they might grab Aunt Eula and shoot her or kill her if she ran out and tried to stop them."*

Marion kept questioning Twig about what he had seen and heard. It turned out that when the woman brought the old lady to the motel, the old lady had seen Twig and asked if he was one of the woman's little boys. The woman had said he wasn't. Then, after Twig had got back from the store and given me the things, I sent him to buy, he had gone outdoors and pretended to be playing. What he was really doing was listening to find out what was going on. He also wrote down the number of the license plate on the car that belonged to the man and woman who had rented the room. He put the paper on which he wrote it on the table in Marion's room, and Marion had just thrown it in the wastepaper basket along with some other things.

Marion found the piece of paper on which Twig had written the license plate number and brought it to me. That was the first real clue we had to give to the police, but it was enough. They were able to trace the couple and arrest them.

The man claimed he didn't know anything about the murder. Nonetheless he, his girlfriend and the other woman Twig had seen were all put on trial. It came out that the man was telling the truth. The two women confessed that they had killed the old lady in order to keep her from turning them in for having stolen her charge account card and using it to buy clothes and wigs and other things. The department store had been writing to the old lady to pay the bill. When she checked it out, she realized what the two women had done. It so happened that the old woman lived in a retirement home and that the two young women worked there. In an effort to avoid being reported by the old lady, the two women had managed to get her to go with them. They had rented the room at the Flagstone, planning to get the old lady there and to kill her. Somehow they thought they would not be found out, but Twig's good thinking was something they hadn't counted on.

The aftermath of that terrible day was that Twig and I were subpoenaed to court. Before that, however, we had to go to police headquarters and identify the man and women in the police lineup. They had them put on wigs, too, because the woman who had originally rented the room had been wearing a long, red wig that day. She had a gap in her teeth, however, so that I could recognize her very well with or without a wig. I had never seen the other woman, but Twig had, and he was able to identify her with the wig and without it. There was just no mistaking who they were, so Twig and I had our first (and our last, I hope) experience with a police lineup.

When Twig appeared in court to testify against the people who had murdered the old lady, he did a beautiful and bright job of answering questions. They set him up on the stand, and he just replied to the questions the attorneys put to him in a clear and intelligent way. He told them how he thought something bad was going on when he heard the old lady hollering and how he was fearful that those people would harm me if I tried to interfere. He explained very clearly why he didn't tell me what he had seen and heard and how he had thought to get the license number by pretending just to be a little boy at play. That was typical of Twig. He was always bright and clever.

Evell Younger was the district attorney at the time, and he invited Twig to his office. After all, Twig had done a pretty remarkable thing for a boy his age. It was his presence of mind and his writing down of that license plate number that enabled the police to catch those people. Mr. Younger presented Twig with a plaque to honor what he had done. Then he took a cap, which he had worn as an officer in World War II, and gave that to Twig. He said he had been trying for years to figure out who it would be fitting for him to give the cap to and that it seemed to him that little Twig Baker would grow up to be the kind of man who could wear that cap. That was such a proud moment for us all. I am also pleased to say that today Twig has grown up, completed college, served in the U.S. Army and is no longer Twig, but Captain Gordon Baker, Jr.

I will always be proud of Twig, and I shall always be grateful for Marion and Twig staying with us through that dreadful time. We lived just as if we were one family. A few years later, Marion decided she would go back East and start teaching school again. She went to Philadelphia to teach school, and later she became a reading specialist working with children. And, just two or three years before the time of this writing, Twig came to visit me in Los Angeles. He had become very knowledgeable about the world of business and how to invest money. Marion told me that had she listened to him, followed his advice, she could have done very well in the stock market. I am not surprised, because I sensed all this in Twig when he was a little boy who liked to ask me about business and accompany me to the bank.

After things settled down following the murder and the trial, I found that I was having a hard time trusting people who came to the motel. I learned that many motels had similar things happen. It wasn't all that unusual for people to murder someone and then register in a motel and dump off dead bodies in the room, or there were others who came and registered and then killed themselves. Even though I had been in the motel business for several years, I had not experienced such terrible things. Now, following the murder at Flagstone, I was very apprehensive about the bad things that could happen. If you have never been in the motel business, you just don't expect to walk into a room and find someone hanging or shot. I had to pray hard to get hold of my fears and to maintain my trust in people. However, I think it was the experience of that murder that made me ready to give up the motel business a few years later and to turn the Flagstone into a new kind of venture. When I did, the changes for the better really began.

3.
The Turning Point

The year was 1965. As a business, the motel was running along smoothly, but I was beginning to get tired of it and felt that I really wasn't getting anywhere. Burnie was working for a government program in Watts. In the course of her work, she met a woman who ran a board-and-care home for handicapped and mentally retarded adults. She was really turned on by the idea, because it was a way to guarantee yourself a reliable income while helping people who really needed it. So, she came home and told me about it and said she thought I ought to investigate it as something I might want to do.

I was interested in the idea as soon as Burnie told me about it. I had a strong feeling that I would rather do something for physically and mentally handicapped people, who might need what I could offer, than to be bothered with motel patrons. I was really tired of so much coming and going and having to deal with people trying to be slick. In spite of all the good patrons and tenants we had over the years, I was ready for a change. It seemed to me that people in a board-and-care situation would need me more than my motel folks who could look after themselves. I began to pray over it.

I learned that I could get the Flagstone Motel licensed to be a board-and-care home, but I felt I should try to set up in another facility. The more I talked it over with Burnie and La-Doris, the more we all thought it was something I should go after. Since I had kept foster children in Pittsburgh, I had confidence that I could successfully run a residence for mentally deficient adults.

It was then I began to be anxious. I prayed over this. *"Oh, Lord,"* I thought, *"am I doing the right thing? I only have my two daughters to help me, and they are trying to get settled in their own lives. Besides, neither they nor I am strong enough to deal with mentally retarded adults if they should get unruly. What if they should try to hurt one of us? What if they should hurt each other? Should I go ahead with this?"*

I didn't get any help from the Voice. I prayed. Not a word. But my bottom thought was, try it. Whatever may happen or not happen, try it. And that made sense. After all, every time in my life that I had tried something new, it had worked out well. I had been looking only at the negative side of things, and I knew better than to do that. I began to believe that Burnie had been given that idea because it was something I needed to hear about and do.

It makes me laugh now to look back and remember the many conversations my daughters and I had about the pros and cons of board-and-care. No sooner did we decide to get into it than we started to worry about what might go wrong. We had a a lot of stereotyped notions about the mentally ill. We had heard that some of them were so brain damaged or mentally deficient that they would urinate in the front yard or go outdoors and disrobe, as well as wander away and get lost. We not only worried ourselves about those things, but we talked about how we would never let ourselves be alone with one of the men, in case one of them might do something crazy. We promised ourselves that we would always be together, all three of us, whenever we were around the men! We would never be in a room by ourselves. We would never drive by ourselves in the car, if one of the men was to be with us.

As it turned out, we didn't know what we were talking about. Most people with mental deficiencies are completely honest with their feelings, and they are trusting and ready to be trusted. They have the good and lovely qualities of children. We found out that all our fears were silly. My most rewarding work has been with these men, many of whom we are able to help learn to live by themselves or with one of their friends. I think they can teach us a lot about how to be better human beings.

Putting my fears and doubts in back of me, I began to do what I could to get ready to take in men only, if possible, as soon as I could get my license. A lady of foreign extraction at the licensing bureau came out to talk to us. I have never heard anyone talk so discouragingly as that woman. For a while I thought it might be her way of testing us to see if we were sincere about going into the board-and-care business.

She showed us one reason after the other why we shouldn't go into it. She never gave us one reason why we should.

The lady from the bureau said that I would have to put twin beds in each of the ten rooms that we would be using, which meant twenty beds in all. At the time I had only double beds in each room, and to change to twenty twin beds would be expensive! This was something I was totally unprepared for. Not only was there the matter of beds, and all kinds of other big and little details, but the woman insisted that I would have to move myself out of Flagstone, if I made it into a board-and-care facility. Every time she opened her mouth, it was to tell me one expensive thing after the other that I would have to do. She was obviously just against my doing what I had decided to do, although I could never understand why.

Nearly two years went by while we tried to achieve our new goal for the Flagstone! The woman from the bureau was just one of several stumbling blocks that I kept falling over. But, my mind was made up. I knew in my heart that I was going to go into board-and-care and that I was going to find the way to do it. I learned that it's awfully hard to find the right person who will steer you in the right direction in a matter like this. We found ourselves dealing with officials who just didn't seem to care if they gave us the right information or not. Here and there were a few people who did give us correct answers, but they were only a few.

After the woman from the licensing bureau had come out to talk to us and lay on me a load of discouragement, I called her up and talked with her as best I could. I just couldn't get any satisfactory answers from her, still. She kept dragging her feet. Then, we heard about some people who were in the board-and-care business, and we got in touch with them. A man came and gave us some pointers on it, pointers which turned out to be no help at all. And, he was as dry and glum and discouraging as the lady from the bureau!

We were becoming totally exasperated! The time was going by, month after month, and we were getting nowhere.

*"I **know** we can use the Flagstone for a care home,"* Burnie said. *"And, I'm just not going to give up."*

"Well, these people who know about it," I said, *"seem very well-educated, and I'm beginning to think they may be right."*

"They know what they're talking about, Mother," said Burnie, *"but they are not trying to help you."*

"And why not?" I asked her. *"Why not?"*

That was a question we couldn't answer. I have always been so ready to help others get started, to get their foot in the door, that I find it difficult when people won't help me. We were not asking for handouts and special favors. We just wanted to get properly licensed and meet the requirements to go into the board-and-care business. But, everything was just going haywire. Burnie was very busy with her job, so she couldn't give a lot of attention or time to this licensing problem. And, it was the same for La-Doris. We knew we had a good idea, but, we were just trying to maintain our lives and put up with the frustration and run-arounds we were getting.

Then, one day, about two years after we first met with the woman from the licensing bureau, I got a letter from her saying, *"Mrs. McClaney . . . we've closed out your application."*

When I told Burnie and showed her the letter, she was furious. She said, *"I will not accept this treatment from that bureaucrat! She's over there holding down a job that I wouldn't be allowed to get, if I wanted it. I don't care how qualified I am, I couldn't get that job."*

I had been up against this sort of thing before. In this case, I felt I knew very little about what it took to be licensed to operate a board-and-care facility. I thought to myself, *"Well, Lord, maybe we can't get into this after all."*

But, Burnie kept telling us, *"We're going to do it. I'm going to get us into it."*

It so happened that a friend of ours, Ondra Lewis, knew about the delays and frustrations we were having. Ondra worked for the Board of Education, and she said to me one day, *"Eula, I know a man who is really sharp. He would know how to get your application reopened. I'm going to talk to him and see what he can do."*

A day or so later, Ondra called me. *"I talked to the man, and he says he can help you get the license. I'm bringing him over to see you."*

The man came with Ondra and we told him our story. To this day, I cannot recall his name. As a matter of fact, we only saw him the one time Ondra brought him to the Flagstone. However, he seemed to know what to do.

"I'll talk to the people in Sacramento," he said. *"I will walk your application through myself and get this thing on the road for you."*

More time passed and there was no word from the man. Everything just lingered, you might say. But, finally the man telephoned me and said, *"I'm at the airport, Mrs. McClaney—on my way to Sacramento. I called the licensing bureau downtown and talked to the lady who closed out your application and gave you such a hard time. I told her I'm taking this thing over for you and gave her my name. She'll be out to see you this afternoon."*

I was glad to hear he was getting some action started, but I wished he'd given me a little warning! I didn't really feel ready to deal with that woman just then. It just so happened that when the man called me from the airport, I had just finished having a new fence put around the yard. I rushed outside and picked up the pieces of trash and left-over lumber the workmen hadn't taken away and hurried to get the front area cleaned up as good as possible.

When the woman from the licensing bureau arrived, she gushed, *"Oh, how beautiful this looks! It's so much nicer . . ."*

You would have thought I had turned water to wine. I explained to her that I was fixing the property and improving it as much as I could. I told her that I would do whatever had to be done for the licensing, if she would only put on paper whatever requirements I had to do. But, I quickly saw that nothing I could say would do any good.

"Who is that man that called me?" she asked. It was obvious she had felt forced to come and talk to me. *"Does this place belong to him? I didn't like the way he talked to me."*

I told her his name and said that he was trying to get things moving for me.

"Well . . . well . . . well, all right," she sort of sputtered. *"I'm going back to my office. I promise you, Mrs. McClaney, I'll send the fire department out here and the health department, too."* It was like a threat.

But, nothing happened! I don't know what the man had said to her, but whatever it was, it made her pay him some attention. As for us, she paid us no mind whatsoever. It looked to me as though she was just going to road-block us until doomsday. As for the man, he just drifted off somewhere, because we never saw or heard from him again. Ondra was furious about it. He had told her that he didn't think Burnie or I knew what we were doing.

"Well, if he thinks I'm a straight fool," I said to Ondra, *"he can go right on and think it. I'll take whatever he wants to think about me, just as long as he does something to help me get set up in the board-and-care business. The bottom line for me is to get this place open so I can start taking in the mentally retarded and handicapped. That's what I want to do. He can call me stupid. He can have them put me in Sing-Sing. I don't care, because he doesn't know anything about me and my intelligence. So, let him just say whatever he wants to say. You just take it easy, Ondra, and don't make him mad as long as we need his help. That's the way I feel about it."*

"But, Eula, I just can't stand the way he's talking," said Ondra. *"He keeps saying, 'If I get that place open for Mrs. McClaney, then for every dollar she makes I'm going to get twenty-five cents.' "*

"Listen to me, Ondra," I said. *"What you're failing to understand is that this man doesn't know Mrs. McClaney. He doesn't know I'm not as dumb as he's figured me out to be. But, let him keep thinking I'm dumb. Let him think he's going to get a pay-off for this. Whatever he thinks is his business. Now, I will pay him for his time, for a day, for whatever time it takes him to do what needs to be done to get things moving. He can think he's going to get my whole place, if he wants to. But, when he tries to collect that twenty-five cents on the dollar, that's when he has a rude awakening coming."*

As it turned out, the man just faded out of the picture. The woman from the licensing bureau was true to her word and sent out the people from the fire department and the health department. The man from the health department was the nicest man you ever wanted to see. He told me that he himself ran a board-and-care home.

"The woman who sent you," I informed him, *"told me I would have to get another place to live in. But, I don't have the money to buy another place right now."*

"Oh, she's got to be crazy!" said the health department officer. *"My wife and I live in our place. We live in one part of the house, and the people we take care of live in another part. You don't want to pay any mind to what that woman told you. You don't have to move out of your home here. You just stay here and go ahead with your plans."*

That was the best news I had heard yet. Besides, when I had been looking around earlier for a house to buy, in case I had to move out of the Flagstone, I had run across a woman who was bootlegging people into her place, calling it a sanitarium and getting State money to run it. It turned out that the authorities put her out of business soon after, because everything she was doing was illegal. Also, her neighborhood was not zoned for that kind of business. But, the Flagstone was in the best kind of neighborhood for board-and-care operations, as I've already stated.

Anyhow, the roadblock was removed! After the man from the health department encouraged me to stick with my idea, everything began to work out beautifully. I got the board-and-care license and made the changes that the fire department required. However, there were still a lot of mickey-mouse details to work out, some of them just silly. There were changes made for the building and safety authorities, with papers signed that said everything was in order, only to be followed up by a letter saying the changes weren't right after all. We just put up with it as best we could, and when it got to be too much red tape and nonsense, I went to Councilman Tom Bradley and he helped us make headway. In spite of all the troubles with paperwork and permits and clerks and bureaucrats, however, it was all worthwhile. But, whoever said anything worthwhile was easy?

Then there was the matter of beds. I have forgotten a lot of things that were troublesome about getting started, but the problem with beds still stays in my memory. It was all worked out that I could have twenty men in my home, but I would have to have twin beds for each of them. That would be no problem now, but then it was a big one because I didn't have much money left. Then, my friends came to the rescue. One friend was Blanche Bradshaw, a woman who had had a big rooming house near the campus of the University of Southern California. They had bought her home, because they were buying up property all around in order to expand the campus. So, she had five or six beds she just gave me. And, then Marion Baker gave me a bed or two, as well as some other pieces of furniture to put in the rooms. So, the bed problem just solved itself.

Although I was licensed to take in twenty men, I didn't want to do it all at once and put out some of the people who had been living at Flagstone on a steady basis. I wanted to give them time to find other places, and I wanted to be careful about who I took in for board-and-care. In fact, I didn't even know where I was going to find the men to take in.

The Flagstone went on being a motel. After all the troubles and delays and *push*, I was now ready to go and didn't have a single board-and-care client. A friend of mine, a man who had turned his own large motel into a board-and-care facility, came over to see me. I'll call him Swear, because he would swear his way through whatever he said.

Swear looked over my place and said, *"Yes, Mrs. McClaney you can go ahead and get started. You've got a nice place to get going."*

That was encouraging, but still no clients. Another month went by. Swear called me one day and asked, *"Mrs. McClaney are you underway now? Did you get started?"*

"No, baby," I said, *"I'm still stalled. I'm okayed to start, but I don't have anyone yet."*

"Aw hell, Mrs. McClaney," said Swear, *"you ain't gonna never be ready! I've got some men around here. They ain't worth so and so, but I've got some down here and I'll give you three of them. They don't do nothing but lay up here and drink liquor, and I've got too many people down here that will keep them supplied with it. You ain't got nobody up there to give it to them and they ain't got no money, so your place will be a good place to put them in.*

*"One of them is a good carpenter-man, and you said you need somebody to fix your screened windows and do some work around there. Well, I've got another one here, too, that can do some of your work. And, I'm gonna send all three of them up there. I've got a driver, and I'm gonna send all three of them up there in one of my cars—with their bags. I'm gonna start you **today**, with three people."*

Those three men were the first men I got. Swear sent them over, and that's actually the way I got started at last. After so much delay and having to put up with rules and regulations that never seemed to have an end, there I was with the actual beginning of a board-and-care facility! It seemed like you sometimes have to go through so much effort to realize an idea, then all at once it just happens, and everything falls into place and begins to seem like a dream, and the worrisome details that kept you awake at night and anxious by day slip away in your memory like so much smoke.

Ondra and Swear were the two who really made the difference. Burnie had the idea and the determination that it would work. I in turn came to the conviction that going into board-and-care was something I *must* do, and La-Doris supported us in it. I must say that Ondra was the one who got the wheels turning. She found the man, difficult as he might have been, who was able to get those bureaucrats to give me a license. And, Swear was the one who just saw to it that I had some men to take care of to begin my business. It's a wonderful thing how friends come by and do what needs to be done, just when you feel you've hit a total dead-end.

I'm really proud of Ondra. She has gone back to school, gotten her degrees, became an insurance broker and is now studying to be a lawyer. When I first knew her, she was a school dropout. I used to kid her about that, and she and my daughters would always answer back by saying, *"Well, Eula, look what you've done, and you didn't go to college—not even high school."* I would say, *"Yes, and see what a hard time I had."*

Burnie and La-Doris really got the message about an education, too, once we were running the Flagstone as a board-and-care place. It really helped them make up their minds to go on and finish their college degrees. We came up against so many things trying to run our new project. The authorities wanted you to have a college degree in order to take care of the mentally disadvantaged and disturbed. So, the girls returned to college and completed their Bachelor's Degrees in the behavioral sciences, which gave them many of the qualifications that social workers must have.

Speaking of social workers . . . Some of them I had to deal with would talk to me as if my own everyday experiences had not a thing to do with what they had learned or read in the book. They came out with some of the most unreal ideas I had ever heard! More than once they would tell me what working with my men was supposed to be like, how it was supposed to be done-according to the book. I would tell them what it *was* like, and what I *knew* needed to be done-according to Eula McClaney and experience. Books are wonderful, but they can't substitute for experience. However, not too many of those who had studied the book were interested in what my experience had taught me. They were a little like Dr. Spock, the author of the baby books. He had a lot to tell you about having a baby, but he never did have one. Some of those social workers were the type who thought that even though you might have had twelve children, Dr. Spock knew more than you on how to birth a baby.

Social workers and state rules and regulations were all news to Burnie and La-Doris. When they learned that their home experience and job experience, gathered day by day, would be kicked down the drain, they got the message. They picked up their books and went back to school. I was really grateful for it. If it took bureaucrats and social workers to provoke them in going back to school, thank God for it. I knew they had enough real experience that they weren't going to forget it or think that books had all the answers. Moreover, I knew that having an education would help them deal better with all the big shots, experts and authorities who would try to be coming down on us. The world has always been full of people who are just waiting for the chance to tell you what to do and how to do it, and it pays to be ready for them.

Once we got the Flagstone Guest Haven going, previously called the Flagstone Motel, it soon became filled with men to look after. Those three men that Swear sent to me brought a change in the climate, and my board-and-care enterprise just went smoothly ahead. I had really expected to have men and women residents in the beginning. Since I preferred to work with handicapped and mentally retarded men, and since there were more than enough of them needing a home like the Flagstone, it just turned out that I had only men and have had only men ever since. Soon all of my twenty twin beds were filled.

La-Doris and Burnie who both had their own jobs, also helped out with the board-and-care operation. Burnie was still working in Watts for the anti-poverty program called Opportunity Industrialization Center. La-Doris was now with a stock brokerage firm in Beverly Hills, working as a teletype operator. Burnie still lived at the Flagstone with me and my mother, but La-Doris had her own apartment.

In the first months of managing board-and-care, I took the responsibility for cooking all the meals for the men. I was so concerned about feeding them well that I practically prepared a banquet for every meal! We did have the employees that the State required, but the girls and I were very involved with the daily operation. I was so involved, and I loved it so, that I was paying attention to every detail, big and little that is, when I wasn't cooking a huge breakfast, lunch or dinner.

Everything about board-and-care has worked out well. Even in the first days of it, I found that I liked it better than running a motel. In fact, I loved it. I am no longer involved in the day-to-day activities of managing the facility because La-Doris supervises that along with administering McClaney Properties. But in the first years, I managed it and went on living in my own apartment, just as I had when the Flagstone was a motel.

There are slack times in the motel business, but in board-and-care you are busy all the time. You get used to your men, and you know exactly what you have to do each day. I preferred to have men, because I felt I could work with them more easily.

We have mentally retarded young men who can go to school every day. Some of them go to school that is in walking distance of the Flagstone. The others are taken by bus to a special school in another part of the city. Some of the men we have, maybe four of five at any one time, do not talk. They can understand what is said to them and they can take care of themselves pretty well. We have a speech therapist who is hired to work with them. Some of them have a more serious problem talking, a bit more than others; however, the therapist never gives up. Those who can handle themselves pretty well are able to go out on their own. We also take them in our van for outings, and sometimes bring them to my place to use the pool. On those occasions, we have to make sure we have an expert swimmer who comes along and helps us keep an eye on them. So, we do all we can to help them to enjoy life.

On Sundays, we hold church services for the men at the Flagstone. I love being with our men on Sunday mornings. We have a minister come in and conduct our service. And, we welcome friends and others to come and join with us. I believe in putting God in everything I do— just to have God around.

Throughout the year, we also give many special events for the men, such as birthday parties and big barbecues. At holiday times, especially Christmas and Thanksgiving, we give our men parties. So many of them don't have anyone to come and see them. They are as good as abandoned. It is not unusual for them to start thinking of me as somebody who belongs to them, and they call me Big Momma. Well, I am a big woman and I love to mother them. We just have a great time.

Of course, we are required by law to have an administrative staff, a complete medical staff that includes a doctor, dentist, psychiatrist, speech therapist, and a full staff that works around the clock. We are a family, people who love one another, and that is what the Flagstone is all about. That's what it was all about when I ran it as a motel. That's what it is all about now—but even more so. It is home and family for men who otherwise wouldn't have such blessing.

Sometimes, we do have vacancies. And, sometimes we do have men that can't get along with the others. If we find that we have some bad apple about to ruin the whole barrel, we call someone who has a board-and-care home to see if they can handle such a person. We tell them what he's like and ask if they can take him. If no one will take him, then we do take him back to the hospital. It's sad when that happens, but it doesn't happen too often.

Our men are of all kinds of backgrounds and nationalities. They are just a mixture of people: Irish, Japanese, Mexican, Jewish and Black. They get along as well or better than most folks. Some are veterans of the Second World War. The man who plays the piano for our church services was hurt in the war. He was going to the Berkeley School to be a concert pianist, I've been told, but something happened to him while he was in the service. Anyhow, he hasn't forgotten how to play the piano. Another of the men loves to play the harmonica, so he plays at the services, too. And, all the men learn a Bible verse which they say, and everybody also has a chance to stand up on Sunday morning and say their verse or whatever they want to express.

It is fascinating for me to see how the board-and-care idea blossomed and bloomed. I think I was being put to a test during those two years of set-backs and all the exasperations. It was as if everything negative was trying to get in my way, to keep me in the motel business for the rest of my life. Yes, I am sure I was being tested and just didn't know it. But, I kept on keeping on. And, when I had worked my way past all the ignorance of bureaucrats who didn't want to be helpful, other people who tried to discourage me, and all the questions and fears I had about being able to carry through with things, then all at once the way just opened—thanks to Ondra and Swear. Without realizing it at the time, I went around a corner and I turned directions! I had passed the test. I see it plainly now.

What was the test? I'm not sure I can put it into the best words. It was a test, in part, to see if I had learned my lessons about perservering and letting God guide me. It was a test, too, to see if I was just going to play it safe, take care of Eula, and let the world go its own way. Because by this time in my life I had experienced enough ups and downs that I might be easily tempted to settle into something comfortable and let it go at that. But, I didn't want to play it safe or just take care of myself. I wanted to reach out and help others while I kept on improving my own life. I didn't see it that way at the time, but I do think that's what it was all about. When I had shown my determination to go into board-and-care by putting up with all the ignorance, and when I just *let go and let God*—it happened! I went around a corner and never knew how big a corner it was until a long time later. That was my turning point. I hope that anyone reading this book will keep on stepping, because you never know when that turning point will come.

Mark, a friend of mine who assisted me in writing this book, says it's like taking off in a rocket. It takes a lot of energy to lift off the ground and fight all that gravity to keep moving skyward. And, for a while you think you won't be able to take the pressure. Then, all at once you're free of gravity and the pull of the earth, and there you are—floating, seeing farther than you ever saw before and existing in a whole new space. That's a little what it's like. Only I wasn't dealing with rocket engines and gravity. I was dealing with bureaucrats, regulations, dollars and cents, and a lot of negativity. The turning point was when I just turned away from that and went with God.

There's one more thing I think best belongs here. Soon after I had the Flagstone turned into a full-time board-and-care facility, my father passed away—on December 28, 1967. We took his body back to Alabama, because that's where he wanted to be buried. While we were at the cemetery, I looked around through the weeds and grass and found a broken gravestone with the name Johnann Rayford—my grandmother's niece. While the services were taking place in the cemetery, I thought about my grandmother, and Johnann Rayford who had lent her dresses for my sister and me to go to a concert at Corner Flat. Afterwards, I gave some money to a friend who promised to have her grave restored.

Later on, in Montgomery, following my father's funeral, we stayed with some cousins who fixed a big dinner for us and the many other guests who had come to pay their respects. Later, I had my cousins take me to a place in Montgomery where I made arrangements to have my father's grave covered with onyx, a gemstone, with directions of what to write on the onyx pillow. (A year later, I went back and saw what a fine job they had done.) I wanted to do this for my father, because out there in the country the cemeteries get overgrown with weeds these days. So many people have left and gone to the cities that there's no one to take care of the cemeteries. I felt better knowing that my father's grave would be kept intact. It was the last thing I could do for him.

The following year, I moved from Flagstone. Having turned that corner, many swift changes reshaped my whole life. Like the little cemetery down at Orion, my past was behind me. The country was far behind me in time and distance. As the words go in the song for the television series, THE JEFFERSONS, I was *"movin' on up."* The Eula who received the gift of tongues as a little girl in the backwoods of Alabama was Big Momma now and getting ready to go live in Beverly Hills, then Holmby Hills, the world of mansions, famous friends, good addresses and lots more. But, I'll tell you this one thing, no matter how good my address may be, I still like to plant my bare feet in the earth and to thank God daily for what He's done for me.

4.
The Widening Stream

By the end of our first year of actually being in operation, I was very pleased with the board-and-care business. It had turned out to be just as challenging and rewarding as I had expected. However, it was a strain living at the Flagstone and managing things as well. The strain was more than I liked. We had a little family conference and decided that the time had come for us to look for another home for ourselves, so that we could still run the business and come back and forth.

We started looking around for another place. La-Doris thought she would get things rolling by calling a real estate company and trying to get a feel on what duplexes or four-unit apartment buildings might be selling for. When we moved, we wanted to live together, my mother and me in one apartment, Burnie and La-Doris in another.

When La-Doris talked to Phyllis, a real estate agent at the company she called, she gave Phyllis her name and her Beverly Hills telephone number. She didn't tell her that she worked at the brokerage office, just gave her that number to call. She also told Phyllis that she didn't have time to go running all over town looking at properties. She asked Phyllis just to give her the address and asking price of any property she would recommend so that she could go and look it over from the outside and know if she wanted to see the inside or not. La-Doris told her to look for something in the Beverly Hills area. But, she was truly careful not to let Phyllis meet her or know that she was Black, because very few Blacks lived in that area in 1969.

After La-Doris and Phyllis had the ground rules set, Phyllis began to call and tell her about certain pieces of property that might suit her. Then, we would go and look at them on our own. Finally, Phyllis called one day and told La-Doris about an apartment building on Beverly Drive—a four-unit building.

When we saw the Beverly Drive property, we loved it. It was a very fine looking building that looked more like a home than an apartment building. We knew right away that we could make improvements in its appearance and have a very handsome place to live in a very good neighborhood. At that time, the neighborhood was mostly Jewish. In fact, we found out later, there was a statement in the deed that said Blacks, Mexicans, and other minority people could not buy property there. Of course, that was outrageous and illegal, but we knew that Blacks would hardly be welcomed.

La-Doris called Phyllis and said, *"Now, I think you have found a winner and I'd like to see it."*

"That's wonderful!" said Phyllis. *"So, we're going to meet at last?"*

"Yes," said La-Doris. *"We have communicated back and forth on the phone for some time, and now we need to know what each other looks like."*

The thing that La-Doris was not going to do was to tell Phyllis that she was Black. Instead, she said, *"I'm five-feet-five and weigh one hundred and twenty pounds. And, I'll be wearing a gold dress."*

"Well, I'm driving a dark blue Pontiac," said Phyllis. *"I'll be wearing a light blue dress. I'm short and very heavy."*

"Fine," said La-Doris. *"I'll meet you at the building."*

La-Doris, Burnie, and I made sure we arrived at the Beverly Drive building fifteen minutes early. As we pulled up in the car and parked at the curb, a woman was coming down the steps from the second floor of the building next to the one we had come to see. When she saw us pull up, park, and not get out, she turned around and hurried back to her apartment.

"I wonder what she thinks we're going to do?" said La-Doris. *"I don't imagine she's prepared for black folks showing up like this,"* I laughed. *"You know how we scare some people."*

We all laughed. To tell the truth, it was more amusing than anything else. When you're Black, you don't let such things get you down. I just feel sorry for people like that lady who seem to imagine the worst.

The time we were supposed to meet Phyllis came and went. After about ten minutes, we started saying amongst ourselves, *"Phyllis switched* cars. *She rode by and saw us here and didn't stop."* And, while we were going through all those speculations, a blue Pontiac drove up across the street from us with Phyllis in it.

Phyllis took a look at us and after taking a few moments to compose herself, got out of her car and walked across the street and over to our car.

La-Doris got out of the car and said, *"Hi! I'm La-Doris."* Phyllis said, *"Well, I am Phyllis."*

After La-Doris introduced Burnie and me, we all walked up to the front door of the owner's apartment. I recall that the door was slightly ajar, not open. As we came up the walk, an older teen-age girl looked out and saw La-Doris who was ahead of us. She screamed *"Aaagh!"* I'm telling the exact truth. She just took one look at La-Doris and screamed as if she had seen a monster. She turned out to be the owner's granddaughter.

We were quickly introduced to the lady who owned the building. The situation, you might say, was somewhat strained. As La-Doris remarked later, *"It was funnier than hell to see those white people squirm, 'cause we knew where they were coming from."* I didn't think it was all that funny. I thought it was just ignorance. I will admit, though, that we have had many a laugh remembering it.

The owner and Phyllis quickly showed us around the downstairs of what was a two-story apartment. When we all went upstairs to have a look, Phyllis and the lady disappeared very quickly. It was conference time for them, and we knew it. While we were in one of the bedrooms, La-Doris told Burnie and me to keep on talking while she slipped away down the hall. She came back and reported to us what she had heard.

"Phyllis and the owner are in a back room," La-Doris chuckled, *"and they don't know how to handle this. When I came upon them, Phyllis was saying, 'I didn't know what they were. This shocked the hell out of me!' "*

We three were in the bedroom that belonged to the owner's granddaughter. Now, I must say a word about that room. Considering how startled that girl was when she saw us and how she just cleared out of sight as if she was afraid of us, we were amazed to see a huge painting on the bedroom wall.

"Good Lord, what is this?" La-Doris said when she first saw it.

What it was, was a huge poster of Jimi Hendrix with a natural, as Black and beautiful as could be! I guess that girl could relate to Jimi as a black man who made records and appeared on stage, but to have flesh-and-blood black people come up her walk was something she couldn't handle.

We all went back downstairs and stood around in the living room. La-Doris, Burnie, and I stood on one side, Phyllis and the owner stood on the other. The owner said she didn't want to disturb the other tenants just then by showing their apartments, and we said that was fine, we had seen enough. I knew it was a place I would love to live in. The front apartment was big enough to accommodate my furniture and my mother and me. And, I knew that there was another two-story apartment with two bedrooms and two baths in the back of the building, plus two, one-story apartments. It was perfect.

When we left and went to our car, Phyllis came along and talked to us.

"I think we should all go home and think this over," Phyllis advised.

"I intend to do just that," I said.

"The owner will want thirty-thousand down," said Phyllis, looking as if she hoped that would finish us off. After all, it was a thirty percent down payment she was asking. But, this was one game I knew how to play.

"I will give you right now a check for five thousand, pending inspection of the other apartments," I said. *"And, I will pay her what she's asking. Is there any way she can wiggle out?"*

"Oh, no, no!" stammered Phyllis. *"You don't have to pay her what she's asking. You can counteroffer."*

I knew better than to do that. It would provide the loophole by which the owner could call off the deal. So, I told Phyllis that I wasn't interested in a counteroffer. I liked the building and what I had seen, and I would be willing to pay the price and the large down payment. But, first we scheduled a time to come back and see the other apartments.

The very next day, I turned the matter over to a real good friend of mine, an attorney by the name of Jerry Rosen. Jerry was a hell-raiser when it was for a good cause, and he enjoyed it when people came up and tried to play all their funny little games with other people and the law.

A few days later, we went back to see the rest of the building. The atmosphere was no friendlier than the first time. If we walked on one side of the room, Phyllis and the owner walked on the other side, as if something might rub off us onto them. I didn't care. Besides, I liked the building and I wanted it.

Jerry Rosen wrote the owners a letter, asking them to let us know whether or not they would sell. But, the situation got a little shaky, because they were supposed to let us know in three days and didn't. After the fourth day of waiting for a reply, Jerry got right on it. The gist of his message was that they must sell it as agreed, or we would sue them. Things began to move and the property went into escrow.

When I went down to the escrow office, I was wearing the white uniform I wore at the Flagstone. Burnie and La-Doris were dressed in what you might call a flappy-flip style. I don't think anyone was favorably impressed by our appearance. The escrow people were further amazed when I asked if I could put up my stock certificates instead of liquid cash. They couldn't seem to understand. Not only could they not understand why I wanted to put up stock certificates instead of money, but they could not understand why I, a black lady, wanted to live on Beverly Drive.

"I don't know about stock certificates in place of cash," said the woman we were dealing with. "I just don't know . . ."

"Listen, Honey," said La-Doris, sweetly but firmly, "all you have to do is to call the stock brokerage house and ask them to quote you the current price." It was really helpful that La-Doris worked in a brokerage house and could talk like she knew stocks and the market backwards and forwards and all other directions.

In the meantime, Jerry was reading some of the papers that pertained to the property. "Isn't this a goddamn shame!" he said.

"What is it?"

He was furious. "These papers!", he said. "In these papers it's stipulated *that the neighborhood where you want to live—it's stipulated that the property isn't to be sold to Blacks, Mexicans, or anyone of a minority group! Well, they're all Jewish over there. What the hell is a Jew? We're a minority, too. This is illegal."*

That was just the ammunition Jerry needed to load his gun. We just weren't given any more trouble about buying the Beverly Drive property. The escrow company accepted the stock certificates, Phyllis got her commission and found out it was no disaster to deal with black folks, and I bought the first real *"house"* I had lived in for years. I could feel I was on my way up—feel it in my bones, my heart and mind.

When it came time to move, all our friends came and helped. We rented a big U-haul truck and put everything in it. And La-Doris rented one, too, for the things in her apartment. We had a grand time! Wilt Chamberlain's brother, Wilbert, and brother-in-law, Elzie Lewis, gave us a hand, also many very close and dear friends. It was nice, too, not to have to pay the heavy cost of being moved professionally.

I had chosen the front apartment for myself and my mother. The other two-story apartment was for Burnie and La-Doris, since we had asked the tenants to move. For the time being, we let the other tenants stay on. Later I found out that there had been a lot of concern amongst the neighbors as to whether I was going to make all the tenants in my building move and fill it up with Blacks. I don't think the Klu Klux Klan itself would have been more worried about it.

I also found out later on that at the community meeting, during the period when I was moving in, the very first thing on the agenda was the question of me and what I was up to. *"Those Blacks are taking over the whole building! They've asked the other Whites to move out. What are they going to do?"* You might say they were convinced that the whole neighborhood was *"going to turn Black."*

The truth is that I had no intention of kicking out white tenants in order to bring in black tenants. I planned to have the two big apartments for my mother, my girls and myself. I planned later to hire someone as a live-in housekeeper, Black or White, to live in one of the other apartments and to have two or three of the men from the Flagstone, who could look after themselves, to live in the remaining unit. However, I didn't do that right away. When I did find a housekeeper, it turned out to be a couple, a Spanish-speaking man and wife. I had given the remaining tenants three-month notices to move, which in those days gave them plenty of time to find something else that they would like. The three fellows that I moved in from Flagstone were White. So, I did not fill up my building with Blacks, and the neighborhood did not *"go."* However, for approximately the first three months that we lived on Beverly Drive, a police car sat across the street from our building. I don't know what they were expecting. I do know that I at least gave them a lesson on how to improve property.

Yes, the neighborhood did not *"go,"* and the police who were keeping an eye on us had a wonderful opportunity to see how Blacks can do up things right. Because I saw to it that the building was turned into a showplace. I had the place completely repainted inside and out. In came sheets of mirrors for the walls, custom-made draperies for all the units, tiles, carpeting and fixtures of all kinds. There was remodeling, painting, cleaning and new planting. The garage had a flat roof, and I had it turned into a patio, complete with astro-turf and garden furniture. The garage was converted into an *"outside"* den with tiled floors. I still had parking space under the building for our cars.

I spent a lot of money on fixing up what was already a fine piece of property. And when I was done, the neighbors had to admit to themselves, if not to me, that the Blacks in their neighborhood had pulled its quality *up*. So much for color. The building was truly transformed. When we would go out in the evening, I would leave my draperies open, because I kept everything in the apartment spotless, like something you might see at the Los Angeles Design Center. When we would return, after an evening out, we would find people walking past the building looking at it and going up the lawn to peer through my front windows. We all found that very amusing, considering our initial reception.

Then, we began to give big, fancy parties. We would have red carpeting down the drive and valet parking service for our guests. The neighbors got so they would stand out in the street to catch a glimpse of celebrities who came to my house.

"Look! There's Tom Bradley!" they'd say. Or, *"Isn't that Congressman Tom Rees?"*

They would actually stand out in the street and watch my guests arrive. People would be passing by, if the weather was warm and the party was outdoors, to see what might be the theme of the party and what kind of entertainment we might be having. I recall one wonderful party when we had a Polynesian theme with Polynesian food catered for us. Three of La-Doris' friends, who had been studying the hula, came and danced up and down the driveway in their grass skirts to Hawaiian music. One of the girls was Japanese and two were Jewish. How they enjoyed shimmying down the driveway for all of our guests and for the people out on the sidewalk! Those parties were the big occasions of Beverly Drive.

I am going into details about the first days on Beverly Drive, because once we were living there the neighbors realized we were human beings and not something to be feared. We even found ourselves introducing our neighbors to one another, because hardly any of them knew each other, although they may have lived there for years. We began to invite many of them to our parties. When we finally left Beverly Drive, many of our neighbors told us how sorry they were to see us go.

There was one funny incident that happened during our first weeks in our building on Beverly Drive that really tickled us. La-Doris is not what you would call a shy person. She is very capable and very sure of herself—and very, very able to speak her mind. And, she is a master at being outrageous. Now, we used to put our trash cans out once a week to be taken care of by a professional service. In Los Angeles and Beverly Hills, trash pickup is a very important issue. Many a politician has been judged by the way he or she deals with the trash pickup problem. When La-Doris went out to bring in the emptied cans one morning, one was missing. The lady next door was out in front of her house, and La-Doris said to her, *"I told my mother I didn't want to move here in the beginning. I told her, let's sell it and go back to Watts where we came from. Up here, any time you put trash cans out front they're stolen. This is not the kind of neighborhood I want to live in. They didn't ever steal my trash cans in Watts!"*

La-Doris came in, laughing, and told us what she had said to the lady. In about an hour, I looked out, and there was the trash can.

Life on Beverly Drive, on the whole, was very pleasant. My sister, Georgia Mae, came to live with my mother and me. La-Doris and Burnie referred to my apartment as *"the old folks home."* But, we were all happy, and our financial situation kept improving in a wonderful way. Flagstone was turning out to be a very successful board-and-care home. When I moved to Beverly Drive, I owned eight other pieces of property besides Flagstone. I think a lot of people thought at that time, and still do, that I was using board-and-care as a way to feather my nest and get ahead financially, but that just isn't so.

Many a time, I've heard people saying, *"Look at that Mrs. McClaney and how well she's doing! That woman's getting rich! How does she do it? Her board-and-care facility isn't as big or any bigger than mine, but she's getting rich and I'm not. What's that woman up to?"*

What I was up to was real estate enterprising. La-Doris met a very fine man, Richard Baum, a broker who knew a great deal about real estate, and he kept us abreast of new deals. With his help, I began to buy apartment buildings. I set up the McClaney Properties and, since the real estate market was growing in the late sixties and early seventies, I did very well. La-Doris also continued working for the brokerage firm, and she became very knowledgeable about the stock market in which we had already had some success.

One day my accountant came to me and said, *"Burnie and La-Doris are going to have to stop working."*

"Stop working?", I said.

"Yes," he said. *"The money they are making on their jobs, plus the money your enterprises are making, is putting you in such a high tax bracket that they are actually working for free. In fact, La-Doris and Burnie have actually worked one year for nothing."*

What a change in our fortune that was! Burnie and La-Doris gave up their jobs and came into the business with me. Burnie was full of ideas as usual. Many of them were fabulous, but we just couldn't always follow through on them. Burnie was the one, even before Richard Baum, to tell me that we should diversify our activities. And, La-Doris pointed out that we needed to buy real estate in some of the better parts of town.

"We have those buildings in the southwest part of Los Angeles," she said, *"and we could have twenty-million dollars worth of property there and, the way it is, we couldn't get a quarter out of it because of the location."*

I agreed completely with the girls. We started buying apartment buildings two at a time. We would fix them up, get them really going well, then buy two more. We just went on doing that and we began to grow fast. In fact, we grew so fast that the accountant I had, a very fine Jewish man, came to me and said, *"I can't handle it."* But, Richard Baum was right there, helping me and encouraging me to pick up speed.

So I did *not*, as some people wish to believe, *"take them poor little people in the board-and-care home and get rich off them."* It was the real estate that did it, with the help of Richard Baum and his father, DeWald Baum, and the three of us, La-Doris, Burnie, and me, working together to go forward. I must say we went forward so fast that I could almost sympathize with the accountant who couldn't keep up.

By 1974, I knew the time had come that I must step up even higher. That step was a big one, but the Lord was with me all the way. It just seemed natural and almost easy to move to where I am now, on the McClaney Estate in Holmby Hills, living in a mansion designed by the late distinquished black architect, Paul Williams.

Buying my present home took a lot of ingenuity and powerful prayer and thought. The day I was shown the estate was the day I also had the agreement to buy it written up and signed. The first thing I learned was that moving into an area as exclusive as Holmby Hills was an entirely new ball game. If a prospective buyer could not pay for over half the cost of a home in cash, the person was advised by the agents and banks not to attempt to buy it. Of course, it made sense.

The next thing was to see if I could really afford the estate and could readily raise the large amount of cash it would require. I saw where I could raise a good bit of money, but this was rougher than I thought. If I were to refinance some of my holdings, I would be able to do it. La-Doris and I talked it over, since she is the *"book lady"* in our business. She does all the dealing with banks, brokers, accountants, agents, and tax people, while I stay mostly in the background and advise—like chairman of the board.

"Mother," said La-Doris, *"I'm not willing to refinance some of our property to buy that estate. We are in excellent financial shape just as we are. We have never refinanced anything in order to buy more property, because you have always known how to come up with the extra money. I wouldn't mind our refinancing*

our building on Beverly Drive in order to buy something that was a sound investment. But, I don't feel we should refinance several of our properties."

La-Doris was right. Still, she was willing to give it all she had to buy the mansion. As she said, "I feel like someone going into the ring to fight Muhammad Ali. I know I am not going to win, but I will give it all I have. And, if I do lose, well, I have my home on Beverly Drive and will go on living there. Without trying to go for it, as the saying goes, how will I ever know whether I could make it or not?"

La-Doris, Burnie, and I talked the matter over that evening. The bank wanted fifty-thousand dollars more than we could raise. I listened to the girls and didn't say much, but just went along with them in deciding to let any thought of buying the estate go. We agreed that we would not refinance our properites in order to buy it. On that note, we all went to bed.

I couldn't go to sleep, however. Something was moving and stirring inside me, keeping my mind on the Holmby Hills property. I began to ask God to show me how to turn the deal, show me how to get the extra cash without refinancing anything. "You brought me all the way from Alabama," I told Him, "and You have taken care of my family and me right up to this time. You have blessed me with all these fine apartment buildings, including the building once owned by Bing Crosby, and all these buildings which amount to more money than the estate I want to buy. I know, Lord, that You own all the buildings—everything in the world belongs to You. Now, I know You are able to show me what to do." I kept on talking to Him just as I would talk to another person.

Suddenly, during the night, a kind of revelation came to me. I thought to myself, "Eula, it's time to pay your property taxes next month. Don't pay them. Instead, take the twenty-five thousand you owe on your taxes and go to the bank and ask them to add to that amount by raising the mortgage another twenty-five thousand. That way, you'll have the fifty thousand you need without refinancing any properties."

When I finished reasoning this way, I knew I had the answer. It was as if the Lord said, "They will let you buy that estate and you will not have to refinance anything." God had given me the answer.

"Thank you, Jesus!" I cried. I got up out of bed and woke up Georgia Mae. She had been living with me for some time and was ailing more and more, but I just had to talk to her. I didn't want to wake up my mother, so I went over to Georgia Mae's room and whispered and called her. She didn't sleep very well anyway.

"Georgia, Georgia," I called in a loud whisper.

"Huh?", she said.

"Come over to my room," I said. *"I've got something to tell you."*

She came over to my room. Now, she had seen the Holmby Hills mansion, and she loved it on first sight and wanted very much for me to have it. So, I said, *"Georgia Mae, I think I have the answer as to how to get that estate!"*

"What happened?", she said. *"What do you know?"*

I told her about my answer not to pay the property taxes and all the things I could do to raise the cash I needed. I said I was going to have La-Doris start taking care of things early in the morning.

"Bie," said Georgia Mae, *"I believe it's going to work! I've just got the best feeling that it's going to work."*

"I have that same feeling," I said. *"I'm going to call Burnie on the phone right now and tell her."*

I telephoned Burnie in the next apartment. *"Now wake up, wake up good, and let me explain this to you. I've been dealing with the Lord again on what I want. He is my source of information. That's where I really go, and I've been going to Him for years. I think I've got the answer on how to get the house."* I explained to her what I had explained to Georgia Mae.

"Mother, you know, I believe you've got something," said Burnie. *"I feel good about it."* She was excited.

"Go wake up La-Doris," I said, *"and tell her to pick up her phone, because I want to tell her about this now. I know she doesn't like to be awakened at night. You and I will always wake up any time and talk. But, tell La-Doris to wake up. It's no foolishness. I've got to talk business with her."*

La-Doris woke up and picked up her phone. I explained to her what had happened. She said, *"Mother, that sounds real good. It will be about ten o'clock before I can get the man at the bank, but I will call his office first thing in the morning. I believe it's going to work!"*

The next morning, when La-Doris explained my plan to the bankers, they said, *"Yes! If your mother can arrange things the way you say, we will work this out for her. She's got a deal."*

Praise the Lord, I did have a deal! By June of 1975, I moved to Holmby Hills. In the years since, property taxes in California have gone down, and land and home values have gone up. I couldn't have bought my home at a better time. When the arrangements for buying the estate were being made final, the real estate people asked La-Doris if she thought I could do certain things in the next year that were part of our agreement.

"Well, anything my mother says can be done, can be done," La-Doris told them. *"If my mother sees where it can be done, then it will be. I'll go into any deal that Mother says can happen, because I've watched Mother. When something looked impossible to me, Mother has looked through it and said it could happen, and it happened. I'll always take her word."*

I don't mind that La-Doris puts such faith in my word, because I feel that I get my word straight from God. He doesn't talk to me every day. But when the Voice speaks, I listen, and I see where that listening has taken me!

The real estate agent who worked with us on buying the property in Holmby Hills was a young woman named Lee Raymond. She was divorced at the time and raising a son and daughter by herself. She came to my house on Beverly Drive to meet me. Now, Burnie doesn't like going to look at property we may want to buy. She leaves all that to La-Doris and me. She says that whatever we decide to buy is all right with her.

I said to Lee, *"I must be very frank with you. I am a busy woman. I have no time nor any intentions of having to take up your time to show me property in areas I already know I do not like. I am strictly up for business. I've been shopping areas on my own time for years. I've got to like the area in the first place, then get a good feeling for the street and the building."*

One day I had Lee to come over. *"Now you get in my car,"* I said, *"and let me take you to see a couple of houses that I have driven by. My oldest daughter saw them first and told me they were in top areas and good-looking houses. And, when I went to see them from the outside, I liked them. I also picked another one that I want to show you."*

The minute Lee saw the house in Holmby Hills, one of the two houses which Burnie had liked, she said, *"Oh, I think that's for sale! Somebody has been trying to get up the money to buy it, but can't. After tomorrow the house is going back on the market. I think I can get you in there tomorrow."*

Lee did get me in to see the house the very next day, because it was going to go back on the market. For that reason, and because I liked it so much, I had the agreement drawn up at once. But, what seemed strange to me was what happened when I went to the escrow company to get the agreement written up. Lee began to cry.

"Why do you cry?" I asked her.

"I get the greatest feelings from you," she said. *"I can't explain it. But, to see the faith that you have, to see you tackle these things, when you are a woman, Black, and on your own without any husband . . . to see how you are already set up in your home on Beverly Drive . . . It's beautiful! It's something I haven't had. You're somebody I need to know, because I am down-hearted. I have two teenage children that I'm trying to raise alone. I see where I need to follow your example and the advice you have given me."*

That made me feel so gratified. I felt so good about Lee. We went on and worked out the deal, just as the answer had come to me. Then a year or so ago, Lee came driving up to this estate in a brand-new Cadillac. She said, *"Look, Eula, look at me!"*

"Now this can't be you!" I shouted.

"Eula, God has blessed me so, since I met you and your family. I don't feel or look or act like the same woman. He has truly blessed me with that same spirit, that same identical source that you get your blessings from. I've stepped on board the ship of faith, through talking to you. I'm doing so well, and my credit goes to you and your daughters. I am so happy!"

Now that was a true gift to me. That is the way I like best of all to help others, by serving as an example of what can be done. If I can do these things, then others can do them, too. No matter what your education or brains or lack of them, ***just listen to the voice of God when He speaks to you in secret.***

When we put the Beverly Drive building up for sale, people began to come and look at it. Many of them were people from the neighborhood who had always wanted to see the interiors of our apartments, and now they had a good excuse to do so. It seemed like all kinds of people took a very great interest in looking at our building and bringing with them—can you believe it?—their interior decorators, just to show them what we had done! People also came up with all kinds of offers to buy the property, but always at much lower figures than what I was asking.

It soon became obvious that a good many people, some of them pretty flaky, were going to try to play every angle they could think of to buy my building at a price way under mine. There seemed to be a feeling among them that I was somehow going to have to move and would have to sell the place and that I could be forced into some deal that would be to the buyer's advantage. It was just something to see how determined people were to maneuver me, take advantage of me if they could, and to tour my building and pick up all kinds of ideas on how to arrange and decorate. I finally told La-Doris and Burnie that when the time was up on selling the building, we were just going to keep it and rent the apartments. That's what we did.

I am telling this in order to let people know that just because I live on an estate in Holmby Hills it does not mean that things are easy all the time. I am in good condition now, financially, but it is still not always easy. No matter where you get to in life, there are always some lessons you have to learn. I thank God for giving me the mind I have and the faith to trust Him, to be willing to stick with it and to be willing to have the patience to go through with whatever I have to do.

It all came out well. It's going all right. And, my life has just opened up to such good things that it seems like the floodgates of Heaven itself have opened up to me.

5.
Home Free!

Praise God!

I'm home free! It would take another book to tell of all the friends and good times and wonderful things that have filled my life since I moved to Holmby Hills in 1975. In a certain sense, I am now retired. However, I am now very busy appearing on television and radio shows, speaking to all kinds of groups who want to hear *"The Eula McClaney Story,"* setting up the McClaney foundation, traveling, and just being the lady of the manor.

In a way I should say it comes as no surprise, because it was foretold to me while I was still living on Beverly Drive. Over the years a number of psychics have predicted events in my life that have come true. The first such prediction I remember happened when I lived in Pittsburgh. Prophet Jones was a very charismatic minister who had a church, senior citizen homes, and child-care centers in Detroit. He was a most flamboyant man. The person who most reminds me of him nowadays is Reverend Ike. Prophet Jones was very articulate and overpowering. He wore long mink coats and had many diamond rings on his fingers. The members of his very large congregation loved to listen to him, and they turned over to him large gifts of money, various possessions, and *perhaps* even their property. They also eagerly hoped to be touched by him, because his touch was considered almost magical, as if it could cause good things to come to you. I went to hear the Prophet at one time, and when he walked through the audience, he touched several people. That was his custom. Well, I was one of the people he touched! When he went back to the pulpit, he declared that all of us he had touched must watch our lives very closely for the next week, because we would receive some gift. Before the week was out, I received a dress from someone—a totally unexpected gift! Needless to say, I was impressed.

During the time my present estate was in escrow, and there was still some question as to how it would work out, I met Reverend Ralph Boyd who had studied under Prophet Jones. A friend introduced us. Reverend Boyd is a very fine, well-respected minister in Detroit.

While we were having lunch, I found out that he was a psychic, and he graciously gave me a *"reading."* Having only just met me and not knowing that I was negotiating to buy a new home, he told me that I was in the middle of some negotiations that were very important and that I should not worry, because they were going to turn out well for me. Then, he said that he saw me in a place of many rooms and every room was filled with money. In fact, he saw me surrounded by such quantities of money that he was truly amazed and said that my present wealth was nothing to what I would have in the future. He also saw me in places where there were many eyes looking at me. At the time, I couldn't imagine what he was talking about.

Everything about my present circumstances is what I would call *"fabulous."* When friends first came to visit me and saw my new surroundings in Holmby Hills, they were filled with awe and joy. It is quite a contrast to have grown up in a shack and now to live in a beautiful mansion. That little shack in Orion would probably have fit into one part of the pool house on my estate, and where that shack was barely big enough to hold six people (with next to no privacy), my home easily holds three-hundred guests with room left over.

The house and estate are so perfectly designed and landscaped that we have numerous requests to let it be used as on-location sets for television commercials and for scenes in television programs. The beautiful *Charlie's Angels* television series made a segment of one of their shows here. It was an exciting day, having the stars, the cast, the director, the crew, and all the equipment here. Much of their filming was done in and around the swimming pool. They served lunch to all of us from long tables set up near the entrance gates and treated us to dinner, too. It was a very nice day here at home with the Angels.

The McClaney Estate is also a popular place for various benefit parties. A party for the premiere of the *Leadbelly* movie was given here, and that was quite a night. I saw and met celebrities I never dreamed I would meet or see. A very large benefit was also held here for the restoration of the Dunbar Hotel. The Dunbar is a hotel on Central Avenue in Los Angeles. For many years it was the only hotel of any quality where black entertainers and celebrities could stay. They might entertain at the Ambassador Hotel's Coconut Grove, but Blacks couldn't stay there. Then, as the situation changed over the years, the Dunbar fell on hard times. Its restoration was very important, because it has a special place in Black History in the city of Los Angeles.

The benefit for the Dunbar was a very big affair. My dear friend, Linda Hopkins (who created the play *"Bessie and Me"*), was the featured entertainer. A large band was installed on the front veranda and while they played, Linda sang and some dancers performed. The guests strolled about the grounds and around the swimming pool area where they were able to hear the music from loudspeakers and to look up at the house which was like a beautiful back drop for the musicians and performers. It couldn't have been more impressive if it had been at Caeser's Palace in Las Vegas. The event was covered by CBS Network News, and some friends of mine in Arkansas called to tell me they had seen it on television.

I guess I am a natural-born party giver. From the time of our little church socials in Orion, I have always loved to have a lot of people around me all having a good time. My parties these days are impressive affairs compared to what we knew in the backwoods of Alabama. I doubt if we could have imagined in our wildest dreams back then parties we give now. And, I get as much of a kick out of watching the caterers do their work as I do out of watching the guests eat and dance and talk.

Many very important people came to the Dunbar benefit. But, the five guests I remember most fondly are the five I asked to come. They were in no position financially to afford to attend such an event, so I bought tickets for them and had them come to dinner first with me. Two of them were very old ladies I knew from Alabama. One was a hundred-and-fourteen years old and the other one was a hundred-and-nine. There was also a woman in her late sixties, and there were my husband's first cousin and his wife.

I should say a word about some of my neighbors, because I still find it a little unbelievable that they are who they are. For instance, often when I walk out on my patio, I hear beautiful music coming from Henry Mancini's house. Mr. Mancini may not know I am his neighbor, and he probably doesn't know that a grown up little girl from the cotton fields of Alabama is sitting here listening and loving the music he plays. Then, not far away, is the Hugh Hefner estate. People are always being impressed and talking about the Playboy Mansion. What I like about Mr. Hefner's place is the small zoo that he keeps on his grounds that I have sometimes visited. Next door to me is the home of Mrs. Dell Webb, a name known around the world. On the properties in back of me are the homes of Neil Diamond and the late Jack Benny. In fact, during one of the high winds we often get in Los Angeles, one of Mr. Diamond's trees fell onto my grounds. Having such neighbors does give me the feeling of being in the middle of things.

Of course, when you live in a place like Holmby Hills, you are more aware of the need for excellent police protection and patrol. There are those people who think you just fell into your wealth and that what's yours is theirs, if they can find a way to take it from you. I would like such persons to know there is a better way to provide for yourself, but until they do, I'm glad to know that the Bel-Air Patrol is on duty. Several times during the day and the evening they will check our gates and the grounds. They will also get out and check my doors to see if they're locked. I confess that sometimes the doors are not locked and the officers will call me and say, *"Look, Mrs. McClaney, lock your door. It wasn't locked."*

I can remember the day when we didn't hardly have what you could call a decent door, let alone having somebody to watch it for you and see that you were tucked in safe. I thank God for bringing me to the place where I am now—respected and looked after even by the police. And, that reminds me of an incident several years ago that was very funny.

My daughters, my mother, and I had all gone away for the afternoon, and there was no one, it so happened, looking after the house. It didn't seem too important, because we didn't plan to be away long. However, when we returned, we found a side door unlocked. Since we were sure we had locked everything before we left, we were very alarmed and thought that someone might be in the house. We summoned the Bel-Air Patrol who came in a few moments and made a thorough inspection of the house. They found that everything was all right. Apparently, we had forgotten to lock that door.

"This is a beautiful place," the officers said to us. *"And, the people who live here must be very pleased with you girls; it is so immaculate."*

We burst out laughing. It was wonderful to see the looks on the officers' faces, when we explained that we *girls* owned the house. Since then, they have become very protective of us and give us the very best patrol service.

I appreciate my luxury. It's wonderful to have bathrooms lined with marble, sunken tubs, and individual steam saunas. I enjoy owning my Rolls-Royce and the Mercedes. It's always a pleasure to take the van and go to the nurseries and buy all sorts of plants and bring them home and supervise their planting around the grounds. I love looking out the windows of my bedroom in one wing of the house at the stone lion fountain and the hillside covered with ivy and set with beautiful "lacey" Eucalyptus trees. At night, everything looks like the scene from a fairy tale, when tiny lights twinkle in the shrubbery and small spotlights cast a soft glow on the exterior of the house.

However, as wonderful as it is to be surrounded by material wealth, my greatest wealth is my friends, the old and the new. It does seem as if new friends are just coming into my life with every passing week. There is the young man I met who deals in exotic plants and has taken an interest in helping me acquire them and helps me keep the house filled with fresh cut flowers. There is Lil Neville, my publicity agent, who has done so much to tell people about me and arrange for me to speak to all kinds of groups who want to hear how I prospered in real estate and how I made something out of my life. And, there is my wonderful advisor, Ron Weisner, who also manages many top Hollywood performers. Ron and Lil believe so deeply in my story that they gave me much of the encouragement to share it with others.

I have mentioned many people in this book, and there are so many others I haven't mentioned. If I could, I would name every person I have known and loved, but it would be such a long list that it would far exceed all the names you find in the Bible of who begat who! I hope, as they read this book, that those I haven't named will understand.

There is one young man who is responsible for bringing two important and lovely people into my life, and that is my hairdresser, Ray Hall. Ray's salon is on the Sunset Strip, and he works with many outstanding people in entertainment and politics. One of Ray's clients is singer Gladys Knight. At the time I was about to be interviewed on a noontime television show in Hollywood, *The Steve Edwards Show* (CBS), Ray did my hair a few days before the show so it would be in good shape. Right after learning I was going to be on the show, Ray was working for Gladys on the set of a show she was taping. Gladys' business manager, Ron Weisner, was also on the set, so Ray told him to watch my interview. Ron watched it, and he was so enthusiastic about the things I told about my life that he called me at once. That was the beginning of a truly fine association with a truly fine young man. I thank Ray Hall for that.

Some years before I met Ron Weisner, Ray's brother, Nate Hall, came to my house on some occasion and brought with him the singer, Linda Hopkins. Linda was already well known for her wonderful performance in *"Bessie and Me."* Something totally magical happened when Linda and I met. We just loved each other from the outset. I felt she was like a daughter and she felt I was like a mother. And, that's how it's been with us ever since. Again, I must thank Ray and his brother Nate for this.

Several years ago, Linda was appearing at Caesar's Palace with Sammy Davis, Jr. This was her first time in Las Vegas and she was tickled to death about it. We were all so pleased that Sammy had given her this opportunity. Linda insisted that I come to see them perform.

We had a glorious trip to Las Vegas riding in my new Rolls Royce, chauffered by Lloyd Pierson, a young man who is like a son to me. Wilt Chamberlain's mother, Mrs. Olivia Chamberlain, went with me, as well as Lil Neville. I had been to Las Vegas several times, once as the guest of Wilt and his mother, but on this occasion Mrs. Chamberlain was my guest. It was a treat to drive in such style through the California desert and to be on the way to see a woman I so loved and admired.

As we drove up the strip in Las Vegas and came near Caesar's Palace, we could see on the big billboard in large red letters—SAMMY. Just SAMMY. No need to add Davis to that famous name. And, there on the billboard, in large black letters were the words—*"Guest Star—Linda Hopkins."* I almost shouted in my car, thinking, *"How beautiful it is! How God takes care of you, whatever you are doing. He makes a way for you and takes care of you."*

One thing that has always made me feel good is to be proud of others when they succeed. When others work and get somewhere, I am happy as can be. When I see others struggling and having a bad time, I feel sad about it, and then I want to stand up and show them, as best I can, that God *will* open doors for you. I know that no matter how dark is the way, He has not forgotten us. We must have faith even when things seems dark. Job went through so much, but he kept his faith in God, and finally he was healed. The important thing is that *"he hung in there."*

As soon as we arrived at Caesar's Palace, Lloyd, I guess, told the doorman to have Linda paged. She came out, saw us in the car, and screamed and did all her beautiful thing of making you feel right at home—being just Linda, as she is wherever she goes. When I got out of the car, she proceeded to hang a gold medallion around my neck, a medallion reading *"Welcome to Caesar's Palace,"* making me feel like a celebrity myself.

While our car was being unloaded and our things taken up to what turned out to be a very plush two-bedroom suite with sitting room, four baths and more comfort than you find in many a home; Linda took me all around Caesar's Palace. She introduced me to all the *"floor people"* in the Casino, including waiters, cooks, and almost everybody who worked there. She is like that. She loves everybody, and she is not one of those untouchables. All you have to do, when you see Linda, is to walk up and make yourself available, and she will make you feel welcome. This is the kind of person I admire.

It was Friday night, and we intended to see the nine o'clock show. After standing in line for a while, people began to get restless, because the place was packed. The people in charge of seating looked upset about something. Finally, they announced that the nine o'clock show was cancelled because of a bomb threat and said we would have to come back at eleven. So, after relaxing in our rooms, we went back down at eleven and found ourselves seated in a very good location close to the stage. Secretly, I had been asking God to look after us all and take care of any bombs. It seems that every now and then there are unhappy people who like to put a stumbling block in your way or threaten to blow you up.

When Linda came on stage, we were sitting close enough to her that I could have reached out and touched her feet. I was pleased to see the orchestra in back of her and to see in person the conductor, George Rhodes, whom I have often seen on television and whom Sammy talks about all the time. It also pleased me to see several young women playing in the orchestra, because I like to know that women, Black or White, are getting more opportunity to hold their own in the professional world.

Linda was beautiful to look at and was dressed fabulously. She was holding the mike in her hand and the spotlight was shining down on her. She sang and it was beautiful and glorifying. She even sang some religious songs, because Linda never forgets God, not even in Caesar's Palace. She just grooved with the music, and the audience was just thrilled and grooving with her. I felt like getting up and testifying or shouting—right in Caesar's Palace. At that moment I knew, because I could feel it, see it, that God is everywhere!

During the show, Linda took a little time to talk to the audience. She began to talk about how happy she was that particular night.

"I'm just so happy tonight," she said. *"Do you all want to know why I'm happy?"*

"Yes, we want to know!" the audience answered back.

"I'm especially happy because my mother is here," she told them. And, then she went on to say all kinds of sweet things about *me.*

"Now, I want you to meet her—my mother!", she said.

And while everyone applauded, Linda had me stand as she introduced me to Caesar's Palace. Could a child, hoeing cotton years ago in Alabama, ever have expected that?

Linda also introduced Mrs. Chamberlain, La-Doris, Lil Neville and Lloyd. There we were, the four of us, making our own kind of debut in Las Vegas. Linda then went on to tell people about some of the things that were yet to be written in this book. She told them, too, what had been said about me in articles in *Ebony*, the *Los Angeles Times* and other newspapers and magazines. With a daughter like that telling the world about me, my heart just overflows with joy and gratitude. It's wonderful to hear, and it could easily swell your head. But as wonderful as it sounds, I always know that I am really plain Eula Hendrick McClaney and must keep my feet on the ground.

When Linda's part of the show was over, Sammy came on. He had been suffering from the flu, but he came on like a genius, full of energy, and like the masterful showman he is. His part of the show opened with the showing of a movie made of him when he was a little boy, singing and dancing *"I'll be glad when you're dead, you rascal you."* Then he tap-danced out on stage and showed everybody what a great performer he is.

After the show, he joined Linda in her dressing room. Then together we all went to Sammy's apartment. Caesar's Palace had built a brand new kitchen for him, his own private kitchen, with beautiful crystal chandeliers. His apartment was dazzling, with a bar built in different sections and beautiful and spacious rooms and furnishings.

When I was introduced to Sammy by Linda, he gave me a great big hug with his outstretched arms, because Linda had told him so much about me beforehand. Now I am quite heavy, and Sammy is a small man, but we just managed to stand in each other's arms. It was the warmest greeting I ever had from anyone. I told him how much I had always loved him, and said, *"Here you are in my arms, Sammy, and this is one of the greatest feelings there is!"*

On this trip to Las Vegas, I had taken one of the very tasty poundcakes that I always keep in my freezer. Whenever I am going on a trip or to visit someone, I take a poundcake along with me. As a matter of fact, I took two poundcakes with me to Las Vegas. I gave one to Linda, the day after I had been to Sammy's apartment, and said, *"Take Sammy this cake."* She took it to Sammy and reported to me that Sammy sliced a piece of the cake and put it in the oven to warm—which is exactly what I do when I have poundcake to eat.

"Sammy ate that cake and raved about how delicious it was," Linda told me. *"I'm not giving anybody any of this cake,"* Sammy said. And, he put the rest in his freezer. Since then, I have been with Sammy in Lake Tahoe, and he still likes my poundcake. So, I know what to do to bring him a little pleasure.

On our last night in Las Vegas, we attended Sammy's show again. When Sammy came out, he had me stand up just as Linda had done the night before. He may have mentioned the poundcake, too, but I was too excited to notice or remember. It seems there were many celebrities in the audience that night, many of whom I met. Several of them came over to shake my hand. By then I was getting ready to believe that I, too, was part of Sammy's show.

It is such a warm feeling I get when I am treated by people the way I was treated in Las Vegas. I hadn't expected it. It makes me feel good when people stroke me once in a while, because I need that just like anyone else. All my life I have always tried to stroke others, especially since I got big enough to get out of the back woods of Alabama and put my cotton sack down. I have always made it my business to stroke people. So, getting stroked back means a lot to me. It means that I'm noticed, because people don't have to notice me and often they haven't. That is why I will never forget the way Sammy chose to stroke me my last night at his show. While he was singing, he came to where I was sitting, reached down, took my hand up to his mouth and kissed it. And then, as he walked away, said, *"That's my girlfriend."*

I've talked about entertainers who are my friends. Now I want also to talk about people who are outstanding in other fields who are also my friends. I am very proud of the black people who have been able to get into government and into law. They are able to speak up and say what must be said, without being afraid, even though a lot of people take offense. They have one big purpose in their lives—to get something done to help *all* people.

I think one of the greatest people to step her foot on the soil of legislation is Little Maxine—Maxine Waters. I knew her when we all used to sit and talk at the Flagstone and wonder how we would get our rent paid. Her children were babies then. This little lady has made me happy since she has become an assemblywoman in California. Everytime I see her we have so much fun, because the minute the chauffeur drives her up to some place where I happen to be, I throw my arms around her and hug her and whisper, *"I'm so proud of you, because I never thought I'd be able to make anything out of you!"* And, Maxine falls right out laughing, because she expects me to say that.

Another woman I am proud of, a black woman, too, is Diane Watson. Diane was on the Los Angeles Board of Education where she fought for busing and integration. I am honored to be her friend and so delighted that she is now a State Senator. And, there is Yvonne Braithwaite Burke who has done such a beautiful job as a California Assemblywoman and a representative in the United States Congress. She was later appointed by Governor Jerry Brown to the Los Angeles County Board of Supervisors, where she, as a liberal, represented for several years a district of people who were largely conservative. All these friends of mine have really struggled and have great courage and drive. My heart and my home are always open to them, and I've enjoyed their company many times over the years and watched them grow and progress as women and lawmakers.

It might seem that all my distinguished friends are Black, but that isn't so. I've enjoyed meeting many white people who are very successful and able in their professions. I consider the Baums very fine people, tops in what they do and close friends. So, whether I am calling Wally Amos, founder of the *"Famous Amos Chocolate Chip Cookies,"* my friend, or Pat Russell, President of Los Angeles City Council, my friend, or Reuben Panis, a top Beverly Hills dress designer from the Philippines, my friend, and numerous other people who are my friends, I am not selecting them by color. The shining of peoples' characters, not the hues of their skin, is what matters to me.

The spirit I look for in my friends is the spirit of something Wally Amos once said to me. He said he always believes that whatever you're doing, you do your best. That's the way he did his cookies. He made the best cookie he could make at all times, and he'd always give away a cookie even when he couldn't afford to give many away. He would always give them away for people to taste, just to try them out. Plus, he always said, *"If you do your best and give your best, people will come back again and again for your product."*

Speaking of spirit, one of the friends I have made since moving to Holmby Hills is the Reverend Ike. Some people think he is famous, and some think he is notorious. I think he is wonderful and spiritually courageous. I had seen and heard him on television years before I met him. He was such a pretty man—his hair, his clothes. He was positive and funny, and how he talked about money. Money, money, money! When I would watch him on television, I would think, *"Oh, if I could just meet that man someday, because a lot of the things he says have so much logic in them. The things that he is teaching are based on the same principles*

I use—that you can get what you want if you have the faith in God and have the know-how to want something. God is able to supply all your needs, instead of your having to go around thinking God wants you to be poor and wants you to have nothing. After all, He gave man dominion over everything on this earth."

What I notice is that so many people go around and spend their time coming up with excuses for poverty. So, I felt that Reverend Ike was teaching *a good lesson*, to have faith in God, to want something and believe you'll get it. Reverend Ike's preaching and my thinking were one and the same. I believe in this teaching so much, because I have *lived* it all my life. I feel it can't be preached enough. People don't have any faith in themselves, because they don't have faith that God stands with them. They don't think they can do anything to amount to much for themselves or anybody else. They are so filled with *can't* that they leave little room for *can*.

I remember Reverend Ike's saying that once he heard some sister praying. He listened and she was saying, *"God, I need some money!"* And he said, *"I really liked the way that sister was praying, because she was getting right to the point."*

Now, I had been wanting for a long time to meet Reverend Ike and I used to say to my family, *"You know, almost everything I say I want doesn't come the minute I say it, but it sure comes to me. Somehow it will come about. Now, I want to meet Reverend Ike, and I wonder how could I get in touch with him? I believe he would visit me, if he could just only know me."* I would say this from time to time.

As I have said earlier, the premiere party for the *Leadbelly* movie was held at my home. It began around eleven o'clock in the evening, with a band on the front terrace, entertainment, and celebrities everywhere! I had had no idea so many famous people would be there. Finally, after so much entertainment and music and meeting exciting people, I was tired and decided to sit inside the house in a room by the kitchen where I could still see and talk to people.

After a while, Burnie came to me and said, *"Mother! Get up, Mother. You've got to come into the kitchen. You can't imagine who's in that kitchen!"*

I said, *"Burnie, what's the matter with you?"*

She said, *"Mother, you just can't imagine . . ."*

Right about then, I heard my mother cry out, *"Oh, Lawd-a mercy, I know you! I could call your name, 'cause I know you!"*

I went into the kitchen, and there stood Reverend Ike right in the front of the refrigerator! I was so happy, I didn't know what to do. And, Reverend Ike looked right snappy—so many folks were coming at him. I hollered out, *"Lord, there's Reverend Ike!"* and walked over to him and put my arms around his neck. For a moment I thought my knees were going to give way, and I know that poor man couldn't carry me if I were to faint. But, I was so outdone that I didn't know what to do.

"This is the happiest moment of my life!" I said to him. *"I've just got to tell you, Reverend Ike, that many times I've said to myself, 'I hope one day I'll be able to meet Reverend Ike and invite him to come to my home.' So, I can't tell you what this is doing to me! Here you are! and look where you are—standing in front of my refrigerator!"*

"And, this is such a beautiful home," he said. *"If the kitchen is this magnificent, what is the rest of it like?"*

La-Doris was there by then and said, *"Well, Reverend Ike, let me show you the place."*

It turned out, as he toured the house with us, that Reverend Ike knew a great deal about antiques and was readily identifying our many pieces of antique furniture and furnishings according to the period and place they came from, and the styles they represented. He seemed truly impressed with my home. He also came upstairs where we showed him Georgia Mae's bed and asked him to pray over it for her. She had previously suffered a stroke and was in the hospital dying of cancer. I knew it would make her happy to know that he was in our house, in her room, and had prayed for her.

I don't recall whether Georgia Mae actually ever got to meet Reverend Ike. He began to visit us often. But, Georgia Mae was back and forth to the hospital quite a bit during her last year with us.

Reverend Ike and I have since become very good friends, and we see each other now and then when he is in Los Angeles. He is a fine, down-to-earth man. Sometimes, I see him at parties at Linda Hopkins' house, because they are good friends, too. When he is in town, often staying at the Beverly Hills Hotel, he will call up and say, *"Are you all going to be home? I'll be around soon. When you see the Rolls-Royces, open the gates, because you know it's Reverend Ike!"*

He always comes with two Rolls-Royces, two—one for himself and one for his bodyguards. Once he drove up with his two cars, he and his chauffeur were in one, and his bodyguards in the other. When I went out to greet him, he said, *"Momma, get in the car."*

I said, *"Let me get in and see this chariot."*

He laughed. *"A chariot?"*

I said, *"This fails to be a car, anymore. This is a chariot."* Because that car was beautiful inside as well as outside. The seats and the floor were covered with real leopard skin.

I got into the car. His beautiful walking cane was lying on the seat with what looked like a real gold knob on the top. Inside, there was an arrangement of a mirror and two pictures on either side, all in beautiful frames.

"Reverend Ike," I said, *"do you actually sit on the leopard skin and put your feet on it?"*

"Oh, yes. Get in, Momma," he said, *"and relax, 'cause this is the world to get used to."*

As I sat there, I said, *"Oh, Lord, this car doesn't feel like any other car. This is the last word!"* Reverend Ike laughed to hear me carry on about it.

When I finally got out of the car and we went back into my house, I said to him, *"Well, Reverend Ike, the only thing I can say is that I want a Rolls-Royce myself. Only one. Now, I have more faith in getting it, because if the Lord blessed you with two, then I know He can give me one."*

He really did laugh then. *"With two?"* he said. *"Momma, this is my nineteenth Rolls-Royce!"*

*"Then I **know** the Lord can give me **one**,"* I said.

He said, *"Let me tell you something, Momma. With a house as fine as this and as fine as you have it furnished—I say it's not even right without a Rolls-Royce. You have just got to have a Rolls-Royce with a home like this."*

He was right, too, to my way of thinking, and now there is a Rolls-Royce sitting in my garage that I was able to go out and buy with cash. But, there's a lot more to Reverend Ike then just owning Rolls-Royces and all kinds of material possessions. He is really a sweet, everyday kind of man, and very down-to-earth. What he is basically telling people is that they deserve to have the good things of life in whatever form they most want them. For some it might be a Rolls-Royce. For others it might be a Ford or Chevrolet, or a small car that doesn't use much gas and lets you go traveling around the country economically. For God is in anything that is good. Everything doesn't come to us overnight. Some people get their blessings real early in life, some people get theirs later. If you just have faith, just hang on, just keep praying, and keep doing what God would have you do, it will come to pass.

When you are around Reverend Ike, however, you must be prepared for the unexpected. That man believes in spontaneity and can catch you completely off your guard. One Sunday, La-Doris and I went to see Reverend Ike at the Sports Arena in Los Angeles, and the place was packed. He had a place roped off for his special guests, and we were made to sit there. I really wasn't ready for it, none of us were, because it was a very hot day and we dressed as coolly and casually as we could. I didn't think anybody would be taking any note of me.

Reverend Ike looked as good as I've ever seen him look, dressed in a beautiful dark blue suit, with a cream-white vest, like something straight out of a magazine ad. No matter how hot the weather, what the situation, that man always looks beautiful. After a while, as he was talking, he said, *"I have just got to tell you about some of the people who are here today. Here's a man who has a great big yacht and great business. A few years ago this man had no faith in doing anything. But, I preached to this man, 'You can get what you want.' Now this man has a yacht, and his business is just going terrifically."*

The man that Reverend Ike was talking about stood up there, together with his wife, and everybody could see who he was. The television cameras were there and showing him to thousands of other people across the country as well. The man and his wife stood there smiling and looking what I call *"progressive."*

Then after a while, Reverend Ike said, *"There's a woman I got to tell you all about . . . Come on up here, Momma!"*

I thought, *"Oh, Lord, he means me!"* I wanted to roll right off my chair and get under it. And, considering the way I looked and was dressed . . . !

There we were, none of us looking too good, up on the platform with Reverend Ike and facing about ten-thousand people in the arena and those television cameras. Oh, Lord! Reverend Ike just began talking, saying, *"I want to tell you all about Momma. Now, Momma, you'll pardon me for calling you Momma, but you know that's what everybody calls you. Now, I'll tell you all, Momma came here from the South, and I want to tell you what God can do, because Momma had so much faith in Him. She works on the same principles that I teach."* And, on and on he went.

Then, he handed me the microphone and said, *"Now, Momma, take the mike and tell them yourself."*

Lord, I don't quite know how I got through all that. La-Doris, knowing she was on national television, was doing her best to carry it off like something perfectly natural. I just wanted to roll off the stage!

In spite of all his good work, a lot of people like to complain about Reverend Ike and say, *"I don't think it's right teaching folks about getting money."* When they say that to me, my reply is, *"People have to have a little confidence in themselves to just make a living. I think it's great that God has somebody out there pushing them so that they can gain more confidence in doing something."*

If I give a lot of space to writing about Reverend Ike, it's because he teaches what I have always tried to live. I think the fact that he finally came into my life and became a good friend at the time when I was able to settle down with the McClaney Estate tells me that I followed the right course.

Having talked at length about my friends and some of the well-known people I have met, now I would like to tell about my meeting with President Gerald Ford. A good attorney friend of mine, who occasionally did some publicity work for me after I moved to Holmby Hills, found out that various magazines and newspapers wanted to do articles about me and how I *"built a million-dollar empire,"* as Reverend Ike once exaggerated. He had some connection with President Ford's people and he sent Mr. Ford an article about me that had appeared in *Ebony*. By this time, Mr. Ford was out of office and living in Palm Springs, California. President Ford was inspired by my story and he invited me to call on him.

I sent word back that I would be honored to visit the President and asked if I might bring some members of my family and a friend or two. I was told I could. So, we drove to Palm Springs in two cars. There were Burnie, La-Doris, Nate Hall, attorney Laurence Labovitz, and myself in the party. I had a great and beautiful feeling, knowing that I was going to see the President and that he was the first President I had the pleasure and privilege of sitting down and talking with. I had seen President Roosevelt in Pittsburgh, and I had also had a glimpse of President Eisenhower at the airport in Los Angeles. However, just to go in and sit down and shake hands with the President was a wonderful event.

The President had his secretary send us a map showing how to get to his place. When we finally came to his residence, we found huge, iron gates that completely closed off the road with guard houses on both sides. The guards, their guns at their sides, came and wanted to know who we were. The attorney said to them, *"I have Mrs. McClaney and her family. She is to see the President this morning."*

The guard said, *"Wait just a minute,"* and picked up a note that was inside the guardhouse. *"Oh, yes, the President is expecting Mrs. McClaney this morning."*

It was strange just to hear those words—*"The President is expecting Mrs. McClaney this morning."*

The guard asked for the names of everyone in our party. He had all our names on the list except Nate Hall's. We explained that Nate was a good friend. The guard said it would be all right for him to go in with us. Soon, the gates were opened; we drove in and parked our cars as we were instructed. Then, we were met by some men who came out of the President's house, who led us into a building and into a room with a huge conference table and twelve chairs around it. At one end of the table was a chair larger than the rest.

The man who had escorted us to the room pointed to a chair over in the corner and said, *"That chair over there was the President's chair when he was Vice-President. They always give them their chair."* Before he left us alone, he said, *"You are a little early, but the President will be here on time. Just look around and make yourselves comfortable."* After he left, I knew I just had to go and sit in that chair, and I did, thinking that maybe some of the good luck that has happened to the President would rub off on me.

My attorney, Laurence Labovitz, told us where we should all sit at the table and on what side I should sit, since I was the guest of the President. We sat down in our correct seats, and before the President came, we asked the attorney how we should address Mr. Ford.

He said, *"Always refer to him as Mr. President."*

Then we asked what we should do when he entered the room. He said, *"When he enters the room, we'll all stand."*

So, we sort of had a rehearsal.

When the President finally entered the room, he caught us not quite ready. I was sitting in such a way in my chair, which swiveled all around, that I was facing the door where the President stepped in.

"Good morning," said the President. *"I'm Gerald Ford."* We quickly stood up. *"Good morning, Mr. President."*

He came around the table and the attorney introduced me to him and introduced each one of us, and we each shook hands with him. Then we all sat down and began to talk. I found him to be a very warm, nice man right from the beginning, and he put us all at ease.

President Ford and I talked about the depression years. He said to me, *"Mrs. McClaney, you know I'm a lawyer, don't you?"*

I said, *"No, I didn't know you were a lawyer. But, I do know that you played football. I thought you played pro-football."*

He said, *"I had to play football so I could go to college. I had to do something to get into college. Back then, we had no money. We had a hard time in Battlecreek, Michigan at that time."*

"Oh, yes, it was tough everywhere," I agreed. *"But, Mr. President, if you think it was hard in Battlecreek, Michigan, what do you think was happening to us in Alabama—and especially being Black, too?"*

We talked about that. We talked about politics. He told me about going to Tuskegee, Alabama where he spoke at Tuskegee Institute, and also about speaking in Montgomery at the University of Alabama. He said he was raised up with black people in Michigan, and that back in the days of the Depression he just never saw such problems as people are having these days.

I asked the President if he was going to run for the presidency again, but being a good politician, he didn't give me a direct answer. And, Burnie, who can be very comical, said, *"Mr. President, we are in this building which is, I guess, for official events and visits. Then there is the building next door where you live—your home. Tell me, are we paying for this building and that building next door, too?"*

President Ford gave a big hearty laugh and said, *"Now you own this building that we are in. But the one next door—unfortunately, I have to pay for that one myself."*

I must say that the room in which we had our conversation was rather plain, because it was being redecorated and all the pictures had been taken off the walls. However, among the pictures that were set on the floor against the walls, I did see Anwar Sadat's picture, Mr. Ford's picture (several of them), Mr. Kruschev's picture, and pictures of a good many dignitaries from all over the world.

We talked about many, many things and just stayed there as if we could stay as long as we wanted to. The President obliged us by letting us have a lot of photographs taken with him. It was no problem for any of us to stand with him and put our arm around him, because he would put his arm around each of us as well. I shall always remember President Ford as being a very lovely and a very human person.

So, you see, moving to Holmby Hills opened an entirely new chapter in my life. Imagine my pleasure when I could show some of this new life to my old friend, little Twig, who is now grown up, but at that time he was pursuing his education. It was a joy to have him stay with me and to drive him around Holmby Hills to see the homes of so many famous people. It was fun, too, to take him to see some of the apartment buildings I own, like the one Bing Crosby once owned and lived in, and to another one where two well known basketball players, Roy Hamilton and Dave Greenwood, were my tenants.

Twig said to me, *"You know, visiting you here and seeing how you live, seeing your beautiful home, hearing you talk about where you came from and how far back you came from, and to watch you now and see what you are doing and how you keep on progressing and moving forward, has given me the shot in the arm that I need. Now, I have the ammunition I need to go back and continue my schooling and do just what I have to do."*

It is for people like Twig that I am telling my story. I want it to encourage young people to see the way, to know that great things can be done if you trust in God. If you want it bad enough, you can get it. When people would say to me, especially my own black people, *"You know white people are not going to allow you to do anything,"* I knew they were wrong. You can talk to God any time, when nobody can hear you, in the morning, at midnight, or just walking along the street, telling Him what you want. Nobody can hinder Him. That's what I knew even in Alabama. I didn't care how mean the people were who kept me and others from riding in the front section of buses or living in integrated neighborhoods. I knew God was above all of this. Now, I thank Him. I am living as well as I ever want to live, and I thank God, too, that money is not all I want, because I want to love my fellow man, trust in God, and love Him above all things. Because everything else is going to pass away, but God will always stand and never fail.

Not long ago, my friends Dr. Mildred Singleton and Les Brown, also known as the *"Motivator"*, introduced me to a very bright and talented young man who would touch my life in a very special way. His name is Anthony Sweeting. La-Doris asked Anthony if he would read my book to me. Because of his career as an actor/director/writer, Anthony read with tremendous vitality, humor and color. I was very moved by my own words. In a later discussion with La-Doris, I discovered that Anthony was working on a Ph.D. in Theatre Arts at UCLA. I've already stated how it delights me to see our young people, Black and White, striving to improve themselves, and I love giving a helping hand when I can. Until a sudden tragedy struck, I thought my book was finished. It wasn't. Life is ever unfolding. And, not one of us knows what is going to happen from one moment to the next. I wasn't prepared when tragedy struck. Some days Anthony's reading would make me laugh and laugh. It was just so natural to ask him to assist me as I wrote the subsequent chapters which included one of the most painful experiences of my life—an experience that would make me cry, and cry.

6.

Death Knocks At My Door

Now, I have come to the part of my story that is the most painful to remember and tell. All my life, I have struggled through adversities and kept on stepping over, through and around troubles. Always knowing that I was never alone, and that God has always been there when I needed Him. Well, I can truly testify that if it wasn't for the Savior, I don't know what would have become of my life. Death came knocking at my door, and asking for my lovely daughter, Burnistine (Burnie) McClaney.

It's been well over a year now, and sometimes my heart is still heavy—even though I've come through the storm. I remember everything as clearly as if it was yesterday. It seemed as if death had come into my house and dug a big, black pit that just opened and swallowed me up. And, although everybody knew that I was inside, nobody could dig me out. They didn't know how.

Down in the bottom of that pit, I felt like a helpless Cinderella in a magical story that took an ironic twist. Suddenly, all the lovely music at the ball had stopped, all the beautiful people had vanished, the clock had struck midnight, and I was lost in the dark searching frantically for my beautiful carriage—which was not waiting. Alone and lost, I found myself groping desperately to find my way home again. Yes, Burnie's death was a sad and terrible time for me—and afterwards it seemed as if life would never be the same again. As I pause to collect my thoughts, I can't help noticing how my words fall like locked up tears now free, splattering on the pages sometimes and then just trickling at others. However, now that I've started, it's a little easier to continue. This is how it happened.

In mid-August of 1985, Burnie, La-Doris and I were very excited while making preparations for our first *"Song Fest."* We wanted people from all walks of life to visit our home, and have it strictly a religious experience. We were busy planning a menu, since we had decided to serve everyone a full course meal. We decided that no alcoholic beverages would be served, and no one would be permitted to smoke. Our affair was simply to be a *"ringing out"* in the name of Jesus. We were scurrying around at the last minute trying to get a variety of things done. Burnie had her hands full with a bunch of last minute details. But, she was happy to do what she could to make the *"Song Fest"* a success.

Even now, when I think of Burnie, it hurts. I love my children more than anything, and Burnie went so fast—telling me *"Mother, I love you."* I'll never forget our last conversation, which was on the telephone. Burnie kept begging me for forgiveness for any wrong she may have done or any hurt she may have caused. She told me that I was the best mother anyone could ever have, and whatever mistakes she had made, they were hers, not mine. I said, *"Burnie, whatever happened in our lives, I'm not holding a thing against you . . . I love you. We all make some mistakes."* Burnie, then, requested I bring La-Doris to the phone. She said she wanted to tell La-Doris how much she loved her, and if she had ever hurt her, she wanted her forgiveness too, because she truly loved us both. She went on like that, and then she started coughing.

As a concerned mother, I said, *"Burnie, you know, you cough, and that will cause you to spit up blood. I understand everything you say."*

My dear reader, I know that I have jumped ahead in my story, and I should provide some additional information, so that you may follow better. However, when I think of Burnie, and I often do, my mind automatically goes to our last conversation. Up to the time that I found out that Burnie had lung cancer, I didn't know immediately about her coughing up blood. La-Doris didn't tell me at first. Later, I was to learn that Burnie's troubles really started the day of the *"Song Fest."* Burnie had shared with La-Doris that she was coughing and spitting up blood. She wanted to be seen by Dr. Madison Richardson, an ear, nose and throat specialist, who was also a family friend. He had delayed a trip to see her. Afterwards, he immediately referred her to another doctor for a prognosis. It was after this doctor's findings, which was lung cancer, that I learned of my child's sickness. So, you see, there was a lot I wanted to get across in that conversation Burnie and I were having. I really had to tell her that if it was forgiveness she wanted, she had to go to God herself, and ask Him to forgive her.

I said, *"Burnie, you ask **Him** to forgive you for any wrong that you've done . . . and own you as His child, and save your soul."*

I continued to reassure her; I added, *"That's what I have to ask Him for, and I want you to do the same. And, everything that I can do, such as medical bills, treatments and all that . . . don't worry because you'll have the best."*

Anyhow, I went on talking to her like that. Then I said, *"Alright, it's time to get off this phone, and get some rest."*

My main concern, at the time, was that further conversation might worsen her spell of coughing and spitting up blood. So, when she got off the phone, in just a few minutes, I told La-Doris what she said.

I said, *"La-Doris", we need to go down there . . . to her apartment,"* and before we could get out the door, the phone rang. One of Burnie's neighbors told us that Burnie was real sick. I told the person to call the paramedics, that I would call, too. I quickly gave them the number, called the paramedics myself, and rushed out of my house. On the way, La-Doris (bless her heart) was driving as fast as she could in the city, cutting corners, finding short-cuts . . . simply trying to get us there as fast as she could. When we arrived, twelve minutes later, I saw this truck in front of the building. *"Oh, good!"* I said, *"The paramedics are here."* Burnie lived in one of the apartment buildings we all owned.

Everything seems to have happened so fast after we got there. La-Doris asked me to stay in the car a minute, then she dashed out. But, Burnie was *my* child and I had to know what was going on. So, even though I was having trouble with my walking, I got out of the car. There was a lot of water running down the street, because somebody had been fooling with the fire hydrant. Nothing was going to hold me back; I had to find a way through those puddles, or around them. I was praying with every step, and while I was on my way, La-Doris was headed back, and was approaching me.

She said, *"Mother, come back to the car. I've got something to tell you. Now, don't get yourself all unnerved . . . because there's nothing you can do, and nothing I can do. Burnie is dead."* I can't find the words to describe the pain I felt at that moment. It hurt so bad, but I knew we had to go on and do the things we had to . . . the best we could.

I really don't know what all happened upstairs in Burnie's apartment. I only know what La-Doris told me. However, since she is still with me, I'll let her tell you in her own words. La-Doris remembers, *"Before I could get upstairs, I found one of the paramedics walking towards me. I identified myself as Burnie's sister. Before I could rush upstairs, he stopped me. 'Wait a minute. Wait a minute. I want to ask you some questions . . . just stand over here so I can say something to you.' He made me identify myself again, then he said, 'Brace yourself. Your sister just expired.' At that time, I wasn't too concerned about La-Doris. I was more concerned about my mom, getting this information to her . . . and getting her stabilized somewhere so I could come back and do what I had to do. That's just my personality."*

I think I need to say something here about how wonderful La-Doris is in a time of crisis. She always keeps a level head, and if La-Doris wasn't with me that evening, I don't know what would have happened. La-Doris was there to make the arrangements and everything. She has always been good in business, and she's always taking the hurtful and disastrous things into her hands and handling them . . . especially with me and Burnie. But, I'll let La-Doris continue herself. La-Doris continues, *"After I told mom what happened, her response was 'Oh, my God!' I led her back to the car. At that time, there was a young girl entering the building, one of the tenants, whom we all knew. I asked her to take my mom to my office and leave her there until I called, and that's when my mom left. When I returned to the scene, I had to give a lot of information to the paramedics. I informed them that Burnie had recently been diagnosed with lung cancer, and she was hemorrhaging internally, and that's what it was. Later, I learned that Burnie was having difficulty breathing so she walked outside her door, thinking the fresh air would help. She took about three big gulps of air, and turned to go back inside. On her way, she collapsed. Friends and neighbors tried to administer CPR before the paramedics arrived . . . but nothing helped. Burnie was gone. The paramedics informed me that they would have to call the police, even though they were assured it wasn't a homicide. The police arrived quickly. They told me that I wouldn't have to release the body to the coroner's office, if I could immediately get a death certificate from a physician. I called our good friend Dr. Madison Richardson who was very shocked and upset upon learning of our tragedy. He informed me that the death certificate would be no problem . . . that he would take care of it, and he did. Mother had reminded me that Burnie had always said that in her transition, she wanted to go to Harrison and Ross, so I called them, and arranged for them to pick up the body. The most difficult thing for me, the most painful, was to walk over my sister's remains, which was lying right in front of the door, to make the many necessary telephone calls. But, I had to do it to make everything move. I know the God my mom talks about, and I knew at the time it was real important for me to stay intact. People prey on you . . . when you're sad, when you're stressful . . . anxieties are high and everything else, and I did not want to make a mistake of some sort that I would regret later."*

I knew that La-Doris was under a lot of strain, and my heart really went out to her, too. People were extremely nice to us. So many people loved Burnie. We got calls from all over the world. People came over and really helped, some handled the house, some handled the phone. They had it set up in shifts so that when one set left, another set came and took over. Things were very hard on us at this time, and I couldn't get my mind off of Burnie. She was a very giving person. I always thought *too* giving. I really don't think we would have anything today if I had let her do it her way. Because she would just take it and give it away . . . everything. But, I didn't always let her have her way. However, she had her own business. She did this thing called excavation, I believe, where she prepared lots and grounds for people to build houses on. She had her license as a contractor and hired the people, and ordered the machinery. I was really impressed. She did excavation on the freeways, too.

Sometimes, she would take me to see the work. I would laugh at her and say, *"Lord, this is so funny to me . . . that you would be excavating, and you can't even run a bulldozer or nothing, don't even know when the ground is right."*

She said, *"Mother, what you do is get your license and hire these men who know how to do it . . . and it's easy that way. When it's done correctly they'll write it off and if it's not right they'll tell you what you have to do."* She was real happy because it was a job that paid a lot of money.

I remember when my sister, Georgia Mae, passed, I was shown two plots that were side by side in Forest Lawn Cemetery. When I informed Burnie that I had bought both plots because I didn't know who would be next, she said, *"Well, one thing for sure, somebody's going to be next. One of us. That's alright, Mother. I'm thankful that you did that."*

228

I guess I'll always feel that Burnie knew that she was going to die quite some time before we all knew she was ill. Even though she died so fast that La-Doris and I had no time to even try to find out what her last wishes were. She was diagnosed with lung cancer on Tuesday, and by Friday she was gone. Yet, Burnie must have known because she had scattered her final wishes among family and friends.

Soon after Burnie passed, our immediate family and some close friends came right over. I was pondering aloud over what Burnie's burial choices might be when one of her cousins said, *"Oh, I can help you there. She told me she wanted a bronze casket with a blanket of yellow flowers over it."* I was glad to hear this.

That same cousin added, *"She showed me the dress she wanted to be buried in, and its hanging right in her closet."* They even knew the kind of shoes and pocketbook she wanted. It was clear to La-Doris and me that she had talked a lot more to others about what to do for her after she was gone. Even near the end she was still trying to spare us what little hurt she could.

She even told one of her friends that she didn't want her chipped fingernails seen like that. I was told that she said, *"Look at my nails where it's chipped and cracked here. I want you to do my nails, and do them up perfect. I don't want no raggedy nails! And I want my gold evening bag, with the rhinestones, the one my sister gave me. Put that in my hands."* La-Doris had given Burnie a beautiful evening bag for Christmas so I knew exactly what bag she meant.

Suddenly, I was reminded of a conversation Burnie and I had just a little before she died. She told me, *"Mother, one night I died and came back too."*

"What do you know about death? And, how do you know that you died?" I questioned.

" 'Cause my throat and nasal passage were clogged with mucus and my breathing was stopped. I know I died for a little while. Even though God did revive me, and later I was able to get to the bathroom and get all cleared up."

She paused for a moment before she said, *"Mother, I'm not afraid to die."*

"You're not?" I asked.

"*No,*" she said.

I thought about things for a moment then I said, "*I do have some fears about death. My thing is that I don't know whether I'm truly going to be saved, but if I'm saved that would cut out a lot of the fear.*"

Her voice softened and took a very serious tone. "*I'm not, I'm really not,*" she whispered.

I was no stranger to death when Burnie passed. I had already lost Georgia Mae, and a brother who had passed years ago. I had just gotten married when Joe Frank, Jr. passed. He was only twenty-one, and I took his death very hard. But nothing had prepared me for this kind of pain. It just knocked all the wind out of me. I was so helpless. It seems that I just wasn't fit to do anything. I thank God for La-Doris. She really took care of all the arrangements. I'll let her tell you what she did. La-Doris recalls: "*Mother and I were very thankful to learn from family and friends the exact things that Burnie wanted for her funeral. So, when I went to view the coffins, I had a very good idea of what I would select. I wanted something beautiful for Burnie—elegant but not gaudy. Because Burnie was plain, but very elegant. She wanted a bronze casket, and she wanted yellow flowers . . . So, that is what we, a couple of friends and I, selected.*

"*A close friend of Burnie's, Mary Waller, laid a Harvest of Wheat over her for the viewing. And, on the day of the burial, that was removed and replaced with a blanket of yellow roses. We knew that we did not want a lot of flowers because Burnie had given so much of her life to people. We knew that she would have preferred the flowers and money to be used for the living who would be able to reap the harvest and benefit from it. So, mother and I decided that in lieu of flowers, we would ask for donations to the United Negro College Fund. And, that's what we did. Through the donations we collected almost six thousand dollars. Later at a telethon for the United Negro College Fund, my mom gave ten thousand dollars more in Burnie's memory. Burnie had joined Founder's Church with Dr. Hornaday and she loved that church. So, I called a friend to make arrangements at Founder's—and I called Dr. Dan Morgan, who has known us since we were very, very young girls, to ask if he would officiate Burnie's funeral— and he graciously complied.*

"*Burnie and I had always said that we would never say goodbye to each other or to mom. That was just something Burnie and I never wanted our mom to do. I wanted my mom to remember Burnie as she had seen her last. My mom never went to Harrison and Ross to view Burnie's remains. I did go the night before the funeral while mom stayed home in prayer . . . knowing that I was there to represent her as well as myself . . . and we agreed that mom would not attend the funeral, but that I would make that last ride for both of us."*

The day of the funeral is deeply carved in my memory. There were many family members and friends gathered at our home. I was very fortunate to have a very dear friend, Dr. Leroy Vaughn with me. He interrupted his European vacation with his family and had left Paris early to be with me. I don't know when La-Doris called him. I was aware of Ken Smith, La-Doris' play brother and cherished friend, looking out for her, and making sure she had the things she needed. We were both quite overcome. I watched family and close friends get into the limousines and drive off. La-Doris rode in my Rolls Royce. She was attended by four of our closest friends: Dr. Madison Richardson, Dr. Leroy Vaughn, Mr. Ken Smith and Dr. Gus Gill. When I saw them drive away, my heart broke, but the pain was too deep for tears. I just watched and prayed.

La-Doris later informed me that the church was overpacked, over 1,700 people attended. And, I felt good knowing that Burnie was that well loved. La-Doris, also, told me that Burnie looked gorgeous.

She said, *"Mama, Burnie looked more beautiful than I ever saw her alive. Because her death was so short, her coloring never changed. How they held her* **up**—*statuesque—in that casket. She looked like somebody who was powerful . . . who had been here, and had contributed something worthwhile."*

I was so proud of La-Doris for being the strong and loving daughter she was. She even spoke at the funeral informing the well wishers that my health impeded my being there. And, I thank God that she was able to do it because I know it wasn't easy. It was both my daughters' wish that I not attend. A dead body was not the last memory they wanted me to have. They tell me that there were so many cars in the procession that it looked like two funerals—over two hundred cars. I really appreciate and thank all those people for the love and respect they showed Burnie.

There were just so many nice people. While La-Doris and the rest of the family were at the funeral, Bill Withers and his children, along with others, came to stay with me and keep me company. When La-

Doris returned she informed the many guests and visitors that we wanted to devote the rest of the day in loving memory of Burnie, and we preferred to be alone. Everyone seemed to understand and quickly respected our wishes. La-Doris wasn't being rude, but our privacy was so very important during this painful experience.

Burnie died on August 30, 1985 and was buried on September 5, 1985, just a short while after our first *"Song Fest"* which was a tremendous success. We were so happy that Burnie had lived to be a part of it. La-Doris and I decided after her death to give the *"Song Fest"* annually, always a religious affair, given in memory of Burnie, and should I go next it would be given in memory of Burnie and me, or La-Doris should she be next, until all of us are gone.

Not long ago, I went to Forest Lawn to visit Burnie's grave for the first time. Even though a year had passed, I still miss her so much. I miss talking with her. After she died, I would get on the phone, and call her number. I thought it would help my heart some, just to call. I knew there would be no answer, but I would still call her number occasionally. I did everything trying to find ease. All the time I was praying and trusting in the Lord. And, he blessed me to accept it, far better than I thought I could. God has taken away a lot of the pain, and he has let me live through it.

Sometimes when I catch La-Doris in a good mood, and I think she wouldn't mind sharing some of our humorous moments with Burnie, I ask her to tell me about a funny conversation she and Burnie once had. La-Doris' face usually lights up when she tells this story.

"Mama, you know, Burnie could always make you laugh," she would say. *"Burnie told me, 'Girl, don't you come to my funeral wearing black—and looking all down and out, and ugly.' You remember she always called me Alexis from Dynasty. 'I want you to always be sharp as I know you can be, honey, and come in there looking good, or I'm going to reach up and slap you.' "*

I really get a good chuckle when La-Doris tells that story. I can see my Burnie so clearly, her big brown eyes bright and shiny, her smiling face—and I hear her jolly laughter spilling over and dancing around my ears. She was such a fun person, so easy going and down-to-earth, just like a ray of sunshine.

Since Burnie's death, La-Doris and I have prayed harder, and we continuously ask God to guide us and direct us. He has answered, and that's why we've been able to carry on. Today, the hurt is not as fresh as it was when it first happened. I prayed hard asking God to allow me to give Burnie up. And, He has blessed me to reach a level of understanding that I thought might be beyond me. I am left mainly with a lot of fond memories of Burnie. My warmest and most treasured remembrance is how much she loved people, and how well they loved her in return. I do still miss the fun we had together, and our little chats. She was always interested in my progress in business. She was always coming up with new ideas. The strangest thing is that she never seemed to run out.

Burnie was always so considerate of others. She often went out of her way to help somebody. Yet, as nice and giving as Burnie was, some people would still do little nasty things to hurt her. This was the case even after she died. I remember this one friend of hers, a very close friend, who did something after Burnie died that La-Doris and I felt was very mean. La-Doris had given this girl Burnie's phone book so she could call other friends and tell them about Burnie's death, give them funeral arrangements and things like that. After she got the book, she never would give it back to us.

When we asked her for it, she said, *"Well, I gave Burnie some money to buy me some cloth, and Burnie never gave me my cloth. So, I'm going to keep this book until you-all pay me my money or give me my cloth."*

This really shocked and angered me. I could hardly believe my ears. She and Burnie had been such good friends that La-Doris and I never imagined she would do something like this. But, I did ask her, *"Do you have the bill? We do need to see what you're talking about."*

She answered, *"I'll get it sometime and show it to you."*

Well she never showed us the bill, and she never returned the telephone book. Even though I was hurt and confused by her actions, I didn't pursue the matter. I decided to just let it go. One thing that I know is that a lot of times when you set out to hurt other people, you wind up hurting yourself. I figured she would find that out.

God has helped me to work through a lot of heartache I felt over Burnie's death. I have more good days than bad ones. Sometimes, I'm still Cinderella, home from the ball, my beautiful memories stored tight inside, securely packed away in my secret place. And, when I need uplifting, I quietly pull them out like a kid who has hidden away a few gumdrops, and I chuckle to myself, feeling good inside. During the times when the old hurt and pain begin to surface and overflow, I just stuff them down deeper, and keep on stepping, leaning on my Jesus. I just keep on reaching up and aiming for higher ground.

7.
And Now. . .

. . . so much keeps happening to me, I can't think of any final place to stop! These days I find myself quite frequently asked to go and speak to different groups of people. I have talked to groups of realtors, children in elementary schools and students in college. I have been interviewed numerous times on television shows, including *Good Morning, America*. There is always some radio station asking me to come and talk, be interviewed, and share my life and my view of things. And, more and more I find myself attending various benefits and openings and receptions. What always pleases me is how people come up and tell me what an outstanding life I have led and how much they have been inspired by what they know of my story, because I never thought I was doing anything all that special, even though I knew I was following where the Lord was leading.

I think that some of the popularity and notoriety I have enjoyed began when the *Los Angeles Times* published an article about my success in business. It turned my life in a new direction, a direction that brings me into contact with people and groups who want to hear from me and learn from me whatever I can give them of practical value. After the article appeared in the *Times*, *Ebony Magazine* did an article about me and a local black-owned newspaper, the *Los Angeles Spirit*, has run several articles about me. As a result, I now receive many letters from people, some from as far away as India. With so much of this going on, I was glad when Lil Neville not only became my publicity agent but my close friend as well.

Being a person who has always stayed in the background, it makes quite a different life for me being asked to go before people as a speaker. I promised God years ago that if He would just show me the way out of poverty, I would be willing to help somebody else find their way out. However, I never expected it to happen this way. I can remember being asked to speak at a meeting at the Hyatt House in Los Angeles, and at a college in Santa Ana, among so many other places. I didn't refuse, I accepted them. I confess that I didn't readily accept them, but I did accept them, because my mind went back to my promise, and I heard, *"You promised, if you could ever see a way, then God would bless you to help somebody. Now, they want your help."* And, I thought, *"Well, I can't renege, especially on a promise I made to God."*

So, I've been doing the best I can. I am a person who never spoke in public, so I can't make notes and speak from them. I find myself, at the last minute, when I walk into a building where I'm to speak, wondering what in the world I'm going to say. At the last minute, just before I step on stage, I still don't know what I will say. Then, my mouth opens up and I start talking, and it seems that's just what the Lord wants me to do—open my mouth and He'll speak through me.

All of this speaking in public, all these articles about me and television shows that I am on, plus having old friends who are now political and educational leaders, have also served to make me more of a public person. For example, I found out that there was going to be a dinner party for me and that I was getting an award from State Senator Nate Holden for my work with mentally retarded men. I expected it would be a nice dinner party with a few of my friends. I couldn't believe it when I found that there were about five-hundred guests at the dinner at my home. Mayor and Mrs. Thomas Bradley were there and they gave me an award from the city. The Honorable Maxine Waters also presented me with an award. Dr. Ruth Harper Creary, Director of South Central Los Angeles Regional Center for the Developmentally Disabled, gave me an award. It was a fantastic evening.

Those weren't the only awards I received. Congresswoman Yvonne Braithwaite Burke gave me one, as did Diane Watson from the Los Angeles City Schools' Board of Education. There was a telegram from Governor Brown and awards and citations from members of the Los Angleles City Council. United States Senator Hayakawa also presented me with a citation. And Joyce Hendrick even gave me flowers, a rose for each one of her family members and for each of the years I had known her—twenty-four red roses.

That was a party I will never forget. Imagine, five-hundred people at what I thought was going to be a simple dinner party! Linda Hopkins was there to sing a couple of songs for me, as well as Dolores Bousqueto, an opera singer. Mr. Joe Dyer from the CBS radio station, KNX, was the master of ceremonies. By the time he had introduced everyone who was making a presentation to me and after we were entertained by people like Linda, I was just in a dazed condition to see so much love and honor poured out for me.

It had all started pretty simply, when La-Doris told me that Senator Holden wanted to present me with a resolution honoring me for my work. *"Mother, he wants to give you one at the house, or wherever you want it done,"* she said.

I said, *"Well, let's do it at the house here."*

So, La-Doris and the others agreed to that and said they would get the cooks together, fix a nice dinner, and invite a few other friends. I thought it was sweet of them to want to host a dinner for me.

"Don't do anything for me to get me excited," I had often told them, *"because I might fall out in your hands and be gone for being overjoyed. You know your mother hasn't been used to much but hard work and sacrifices. But, don't do anything exciting for me directly . . . ever . . . like a surprise party . . . because I'll get excited and maybe go out on you or maybe pass out. So don't surprise me ever."*

I think at first they remembered my words and were afraid to do too much in the way of a surprise. As the time went on, however, they said to each other, *"Let's invite this one and that one."* And, I said to what little they did tell me, *"Well, invite anybody you want to invite, because I love people, and one of the great things in my life is to invite people to my home and to have plenty of food. We'll just go downtown to the produce market and get plenty of vegetables and fruit, because I want you to serve soul-food for the dinner, for the Senator and any guests you invite."*

As the time went on, they decided they should let me know there would be a crowd coming—but they didn't say it would amount to five hundred. So I said, *"Well, I believe in having plenty of food, so we'll buy more than enough at the produce market, because we can always freeze and cook whatever is not used and take it to my boys at the Flagstone."* And, I went to the market and bought, as I recall, at least twelve crates of fruits and vegetables.

It turned out that they had a full-course dinner served to all those guests. The house was filled with fresh flowers. It was overwhelming, and I was truly surprised. It was a good thing that I didn't pass out on them either, although if I had, it would have been a fabulous way to go. With so many awards and nice words of praise being heaped on me, perhaps I could have said to St. Peter, *"Look there! If they're making such a fuss over me, back where I just came from, maybe you'll be favorable to letting me in up here. I've come with some mighty good recommendations!"*

To tell the truth, although I love all the attention I am getting, there is something that thrills me even more, something I cannot say much about as yet, because it is a dream that I am nourishing and praying that God will bring to great fruition. I have established the Eula McClaney Foundation which will serve to help children in need get a good education. I may call myself a *"sixth-grade success,"* but I believe in getting all the education you can get and using it to good advantage. The idea for the foundation came to me because of my encounters with children in the schools in Los Angeles, mostly black children from poor backgrounds.

Some months ago before Burnie passed, I invited all the sixth-grade youngsters from the Loren Miller School in Los Angeles to come to my home. Together with their teachers, there were about one-hundred and fifty people, including student teachers, principals and bus drivers. The children toured the estate, and Channel Two television news filmed the event. I thought such a visit might encourage the children to want to do the most they could with their lives.

One child said, *"If I could just get one of these chandeliers when I grow up, I wonder how long I'd have to work to buy it?"*

Each of the kids seemed to pick one or two things that they would like to have in their own homes one day. While they were looking around, and while my daughters talked to them about learning to work for what they want and to set themselves a goal, the newspeople from Channel 2 filmed what was happening and went around talking to the children. That night I was happy to sit back and watch the report on the evening news.

One beautiful little girl was asked, *"What did you learn today from visiting the McClaney Estate?"*

She said, *"Anything you want to do and anything you want to be, it can be done. You can be anything you want to be and have anything you want to have. I learned that."*

Those kinds of comments made it all worthwhile to me, worth all the time we took and all the chances I took with so many young people walking through this *"museum."*

Both my daughters had spoken seriously to those children. They told them how they felt about me, when they were growing up, when they felt that I worked them too hard and was too mean and such things. But, when they were grown, they saw what came out of the way I raised them. They saw that I was exactly right. And, when they looked at all the kids who had been snatching purses and getting into trouble rather than working for what they wanted, and saw how so many went to jail or what it was like when people let themselves be raised up on a welfare pacifier, they were glad they had learned to work hard. Working for what you want was so much better than just sitting down and doing nothing with your life.

The next day after the visit was shown on television, the niece of Admiral Byrd called me. She had seen the report on the evening news and was moved to tears by it. She told me she had seen me several times on different television shows, that her children were born in Alabama, and that she couldn't for the life of her see how certain things could have happened to me with only a sixth-grade education and being Black in the South. She was so impressed by the story and to see that I was now living in the best area in Los Angeles, that she felt a oneness with me. She said she had some land in the San Fernando Valley and was thinking there was something I might want to do with that land for children.

The Eula McClaney Foundation is still mostly a dream, but it now exists. I don't know exactly what it will turn into, but I intend to build up its funds and to accept big and little donations to get it going strong. And, I really have to thank those children from the Loren Miller School and Admiral Byrd's niece and Channel Two for starting up my dream.

Now it is time to talk a little more about my two daughters, because they are the children I know best, the children God gave me to my everlasting satisfaction and joy. Were it not for Burnie, I might never have gone into the board-and-care business and found my turning point. Burnie was the one in the family with great creative ideas.

One day, not long before she passed, Burnie said to me, *"Mother, you know what? I didn't know you! You raised me, and I lived with you all my life, and I knew you were a good mother. I knew I had a good mother, because my friends would often say to me, 'I wish your mother was my mother. I wish my mother was like yours.' But I didn't really know until recently—and I learned through other people—that you are really the type of person you are. I really didn't have sense to see the real type of person you are and what you really have on the ball.*

"Now I went down with you to see President Ford, and I've gone with you to the studios and watched you talk on television shows, heard you speak to a President and to all kinds of people, and I didn't know you could talk to people like that! Knowing how bashful you were—sitting in the back and not getting up and speaking in public—I didn't know my mother was a star. I didn't know you were a genius. I didn't know this until now. Mother, I have gotten to be this age before I really knew who you were and what you were."

I said, *"Burnie, thank you for the compliment, but I don't feel that I'm a star. I don't think I'm a genius. I am just your mother, a mother who has tried hard, who has worked hard, and who has been led by God to do what I've been doing."*

However, it warms my heart to remember what Burnie said to me. It is a wonderful thing when a parent and child come to see the other in a new light. I feel we each had a new and greater love and respect for one another.

I thank God for those many happy, though sometimes troubled, years with Burnie. I have many fond memories stored away, and I am so grateful for them. Months after Burnie passed I would still catch La-Doris watching me, her eyes filled with love and concern. Sometimes if La-Doris found me sitting alone, she would join me. If something interesting or funny happened at work, she would share it. She got a lot of pleasure out of making me laugh. But most times, we would sit quietly, thinking our private thoughts. We both missed Burnie terribly, and even though we seldom talked about it, we knew that Burnie would want us to be a comfort to one another. La-Doris and I realized how unpredictable life could be, and we wanted to do something special for Burnie while we were still together and in good health.

We could never forget how much Burnie loved people. She believed in helping everyone. Burnie would often sacrifice her own needs to help someone whom she considered less fortunate. We wanted to do something that was befitting in Burnie's memory, something that would make her very proud and happy.

We thought about a lot of the different organizations Burnie had been involved with, and how important that work was to her. La-Doris and I agreed that Burnie would be pleased if we took her portion of the estate, along with some of ours, and joyously gave back to the God that had given to us. Burnie was not a petty person, and we knew that to maintain her spiritual support we would have to do something significant and beneficial to others. Immediately, we began to establish The Charitable Remainder Unitrust, which would be a multi-million dollar gift.

After careful consideration, we decided to give to ten organizations plus the American Lung Association who would act as trustees. The American Lung Association of Los Angeles was chosen as trustees, who would oversee the distribution of percentages alloted to the other organizations, because Burnie had died of lung cancer, and La-Doris and I were sure that she would approve of them as administrators since they were working to save others from this dreaded disease, and were sympathetic to all human suffering.

I had never been able to get either of my girls to stop smoking, so I was really impressed with the work that the American Lung Association was doing to educate people on the hazards of smoking. They were about the business of saving lives, and I felt assured that Burnie would approve of the major role they were assigned in presiding over the trust. The other ten organizations included in the charitable trust had, at some time or other, been very special in all our lives. Even though the trust fund was established in Burnie's honor, we were all contributing. So, we tried to select organizations that reflected all our interests and concerns.

Burnie had given a considerable amount of time to the United Negro College Fund. For years, she had worked on their telethon, and volunteered her services where they were most needed. The United Negro College Fund was a natural selection because their work had been very important to Burnie. Years ago, I had the privilege of meeting Dr. Mary McCloud Bethune. I was impressed by her warmth, intelligence, drive and her commitment to education for black people. Her background and principles were similar to mine; she believed in faith and hope. She was a very positive role model for black youth, and I always loved and admired her for her tireless efforts and tremendous contribution. I have kept a picture of her in my home for many years, and sometimes I feel a sense of friendship and camaraderie when I think she would appreciate something I'm doing. That is why even though our gift was given to the United Negro College Fund, I requested that a certain portion be donated to Bethune Cookman College because I had such love and respect for Dr. Bethune and all the wonderful work she had done.

A lot of people are dying daily of heart disease and diabetes. Unfortunately, I have people in my immediate family who suffer from diabetes. That is why The American Heart Association and The American Diabetes Association were selected for gifts.

World Vision, Trinity Broadcasting Network and Christian Broadcasting Network were quickly added to the list. There really was no decision to make as far as these organizations were concerned. La-Doris and I spontaneously agreed, almost without discussion. As I've said throughout this whole book, I lean and depend totally on God. I felt that, in a small way, if I could help keep the religious television programs going and His word lifted up all over the world, then I would have made a worthwhile contibution to a Christian cause. Also, I would be helping to feed the hungry, the homeless, needy families and others with problems. That is why these three organizations were chosen.

South Central Los Angeles Regional Center serves developmentally disabled adults. Many of these adults have been placed in my residential care facility, and have been with me for over fifteen years. My residents are very dear to me; they are a part of my family. And, I wanted to do something special for them. La-Doris and I were both happy to give back to this organization that had become such an important part of our lives.

As a black woman, I felt that it was a divine responsibility that I look carefully at a disease that affected only black people. Right in my own family were relatives stricken with Sickle Cell Disease, and I felt compelled to help find a cure. Our donation was given to Sickle Cell Disease Research Foundation.

I have always been fascinated with the field of medicine. To me, the physician is sometimes a miracle worker. I marvel at how people come into their offices feeling so terrible and leaving, most times, feeling a lot better. I thought of all the many bright students who had tremendous ability and would make excellent physicians, but lacked the funds to attend medical school. I wanted to help. Personally, I had benefited so much from the excellent medical attention I've received, especially this past year, when my own health had begun to fail. My physicians have been excellent, and that is why we gave to King Drew School of Medicine.

Once the very detailed legal arrangements for the trust fund were set in motion, my spirits were lifted. And, I felt good that I could fulfill my promise to God. I had prayed to the Lord to bless me, and I promised that I would share my life, and in making this multi-million dollar gift to charitable organizations, I was also fulfilling my commitment to the Lord. That's what we've done at this time; however, we plan to add to this list. La-Doris and I have tried to help family members, loved ones and those close to us while we are alive and well. When we pass, the estate will go to charitable organizations.

The one thing that I want to emphasize to my reader is that although I enjoy the comfort of a beautiful home, own a Rolls Royce, exquisite jewelry, furs-and have many other accumulations—none of these are as important as my relationship with God. Without Him none of those things would be possible. Knowing Him has enriched my life in every area: mind, body, and soul. My fashionable home in Holmby Hills couldn't help me when Burnie passed, neither could my luxurious Roll Royce. Only the loving arms of Jesus could comfort me and bring light to the darkness that was all around me. No riches could ease the pain in my heart. Only God could soothe the hurt, and pull me out of my misery. Only Him!

At this point in my life, I'm freer than I've ever been. I look to the future with hope—unafraid—because I know a rock that I can lean on. My God answers prayers, and He is no respector of persons. He is pure love and his arms are open to anyone. I would be happy if only one child or adult were to read this book and realize that even though they don't have the opportunity to achieve academically or economically, that by putting their trust in Christ all these things would be added unto them. Through Christ all things are possible. Any dream can be realized.

Today, I truly understand what Dr. King meant when he said he had been to the mountain top and looked over the Promise Land. As I reflect and scan the mountains and valleys of my life, a sigh of relief involuntarily escapes my lips. I realize that I didn't always make the right decisions, nor did I always do the correct thing. And I ask God for total forgiveness for any errors that I've made. The struggle has been long and hard, but God was always present, lifting me up when my own strength failed to carry me further. My life is not about what my accumulations are, although I thank God that He has blessed me. I would like to be remembered, not in terms of how much I've accumulated or what kind of car I drove, but that I really tried to help somebody else.

At this time in my life, I feel I am like the song we used to sing in church in Orion, *I am running, trying to make a hundred . . . ninety-nine and a half will not do . . . Before I leave here, I want to make my hundred in the sight of my Saviour.*

As I go about daily, with the cotton fields far behind me, I love to think about doing unto others as I would have them do unto me. I remember many times when certain situations would come up, or maybe when we were having a party, maybe one of my children would say to me, *"Oh, Mother, I wouldn't bother to invite So-and-So. We've had them for five or six times and they never invite us to anything."* And I say, *"Oh, yes, let's go on and invite them . . . we can't lose anything. Let's do unto them as we would have them do unto us. The Bible doesn't say to treat people like they treat you. It says, 'Do unto others as you would have them do unto you.' Now, let's treat them like we'd like them to treat us. Maybe one day we'll teach them something, if nothing else, and when some other person comes up in their lives, they will remember to follow our good example."*

I remember one time when Linda Hopkins stopped by with two ministers from New York. They were out here running a revival, and she wanted them to come *"and meet Momma."* They enjoyed seeing my home and talking with me, but they had to leave early to start the revival meeting. Before they left, they suggested we pray together.

"Let us have prayer here," said one. *"I just feel prayerful in this house. I just feel like this is a praying house."*

And, we all joined hands and prayed.

It was just like the time a lady that worked for me first came to see me at home. *"Oh, it's such a beautiful home,"* she said, *"that I just know God is with you, and He's going to continue to bless you. Let us join hands right now in prayer."* And, right there in the entry hall we prayed. She just jumped and shouted and tears were streaming down, and she cried for joy.

A praying home—that's truly the way I like to think of my home. I feel God is worthy to be praised at all times and any time. I feel that we should never get too cute, never be ashamed or too tired or too busy to praise God.

And now . . . all the good things keep coming, keep coming every day. To make sure I don't take it for granted, to remember who I am— just Eula—I take off my shoes and walk outdoors and let my feet be in touch with the earth God made, just as they were when I used to pick cotton and walk a dirt road to a little school shack. I have even planted some collard greens in the corner of the children's play yard on my estate, because I loved them as a child and still do. It's a funny thing—my collards are growing up here in Holmby Hills.

And now . . . I'll tell you one lovely thing God did for me when I was first thinking about writing my life story. When I lived on Beverly Drive I met some wonderful neighbors, Mr. and Mrs. Mac Presberg. Mac is now an officer and active in the McClaney Foundation. I had told him that I intended to write a book about my life, but that I just didn't know what I was going to call it. Now, Mac knew about the Voice that has guided me over the years, because I mentioned It once in a while and I always try to remind people that I believe in prayer.

One day Mac spoke to me and said that he had been sleeping and he didn't know whether he dreamed this or what, but it came to him, almost as if a Voice told it to him. It was the title for my book—*GOD, I LISTENED.*

Thank you, Lord!
I will keep on listening, always.

I would like to conclude this book by repeating the 23rd Psalm:

'The Lord is my shepherd; I shall not want.

He maketh me to lie down in green pastures;
He leadeth me beside the still waters.

He restoreth my soul; He leadeth me in the
path of righteousness for His name's sake.

Yea, though I walk through the valley of
the shadow of death, I will fear no evil:
for Thou art with me; Thy rod and Thy staff
they comfort me.

Thou preparest a table before me in the
presence of mine enemies: Thou anointest
my head with oil; my cup runneth over.

Surely goodness and mercy shall follow me
all the days of my life: and I will dwell
in the house of the Lord forever."

Epilogue

One of my mom's greatest joys was to finish this book. She felt a tremendous need to give back some of the wonderful bounty that God had so generously given to her. Even though she gave millions to charity, somehow, she did not feel that was enough. She believed that a personal testimony of her struggles, disappointments, setbacks, and ultimate incredible success (due to her complete faith and trust in God) might serve as an example to others who are without hope and in need of encouragement and direction in their lives.

On December 17, 1987, my mom (Eula *"Bie"* Hendrick McClaney) passed away, and has now gone to be with Burnie on the other side. The very last words of her book wait to be written by me, and I find them difficult to write.

As I have read and reflected upon my mother's life, I'm so grateful that I had a mom like Eula McClaney. She was my favorite teacher and best friend. I was with my mom during her final moments — she died in my arms. And despite the pain of saying good-bye, I will never forget the love, compassion and understanding she radiated even to the end.

I promised my mom that no matter what happened, I would always take care of **her** mother with the same dignity, love and in the manner to which she had grown accustomed. My devotion to Grannie is a total commitment — just as my mom requested. My mother's legacy will now be carried on by me. I plan to unceremoniously give away everything that God has so richly blessed us with. I will spend the rest of my life going around the country telling people about the goodness of God, and how wonderful He has been to the McClaney family. The Lord says, *"If I be lifted up, I will draw all men unto me."* I intend to do my best to enlighten others and help to pave the way to God's throne.

It's a lonely time for me with mom and Burnie together — and me on this side. But, I know from my mom's teachings that as long as I hold on to God's unchanging hands . . . I'll be just fine. For *I know* He will guide and see me through. So, I intend to keep on stepping!

Dr. La-Doris McClaney
Holmby Hills
Los Angeles, California

CERTIFICATES AND AWARDS

Outstanding Achievement in the Field of Philanthropy
Carson Black Heritage Association
Carson, California
1988

Statement of Condolence
The State of California
Governor George Deukmejian
Sacramento, California
December, 1987

Resolution in Memoriam
California State Senate
Senator Diane E. Watson, 28th Senatorial District
Los Angeles, California
December, 1987

Resolution in Memoriam
California State Assembly
Assemblywoman Maxine Waters, 48th Assembly District
Los Angeles, California
December, 1987

Resolution in Memoriam
Los Angeles County Board of Supervisors
Supervisor Kenneth Hahn, 2nd District
Los Angeles, California
December, 1987

Resolution of Sympathy and Remembrance
Bethune/Cookman College
Daytona Beach, Florida
December, 1987

Eula McClaney Day, in Recognition of Community and Charitable
Contributions
The City of Los Angeles
Mayor Tom Bradley
Los Angeles, California
April, 1987

Commendation for Outstanding and Dedicated Efforts in Sickle Cell
Research
Los Angeles County Board of Supervisors
Los Angeles, California
April, 1987

Ambassador Award — Good Will and Support of Higher and Higher
Education for the Youth of America
Bethune/Cookman College
Daytona Beach, Florida
February, 1987

Honorary Doctorate of Humanities
Shorter College
Little Rock, Arkansas
1987

The Madame C. J. Walker Award — Enterprise, Involvement and
Transformation of the Community
Operation PUSH
Chicago, Illinois
June, 1987

Certificate for Outstanding Achievement in Entrepreneurship
Entrepreneur Magazine
Los Angeles, California
February, 1986

Award for Unselfish Giving and Support in the Fight Against Lung
Cancer
The American Lung Association
Los Angeles, California
June, 1986

Meritorious Service Award
United Negro College Fund
Los Angeles, California
June, 1986

Award for Generous Contributions and Dedicated Service
Sickle Cell Research Foundation
Los Angeles, California
June, 1986

Award in Grateful Appreciation for Kindness and Generosity to the
American Diabetes Association
The American Diabetes Association
Los Angeles, California
June, 1986

Award in Appreciation for Generosity
King — Drew School of Medicine
Los Angeles, California
June, 1986

California State Senate Resolution
Senate Rules Committee
Senator David Roberti, Pro Tempor
Senator Diane E. Watson
Los Angeles, California
June, 1986

Award in Recognition of Outstanding Achievement
City of Compton
Mayor Walter Tucker
Compton, California
June, 1986

Eula McClaney Christian School — Civic and Community Contributions
The City of Inglewood
Inglewood, California
October, 1986

Resolution in Honor of Contributions to Eleven Local Charitable
Organizations
The City of Los Angeles
Los Angeles, California
November, 1986

Honorary Membership
Sigma Gamma Rho Sorority
Los Angeles, California
1986

Salute for Love and Support of the Students
Alpha School
Los Angeles, California
1986

Award for Interest and Support of Cardiovascular Research and
Community Education Programs
The American Heart Association
Los Angeles, California
June, 1986

Commendation for Outstanding Community Service
California State Legislature
Assemblywoman Maxine Water, 48th Assembly District
Los Angeles, California
March, 1984

Woman of the Year — Outstanding Contributions to the Community
Zeta Phi Beta Sorority
Alpha Psi Zeta Chapter
Los Angeles, California
March, 1984

Citizen of the Year Award
Omega Psi Phi
Phi Beta Beta Chapter
1984

Woman of the Year Award
Dorothy Brown School
Los Angeles, California
1984

Humanitarian of the Year Award
Los Angeles County Board of Supervisors
Los Angeles, California
March, 1983

Certificate of Appreciation— Recognition of Outstanding Citizenship,
Activities and Enhancing Community Betterment
City of Los Angeles
Councilwoman Pat Russell, 6th District
January, 1983

Humanitarian of the Year Award
Women at Work — City of Los Angeles
Los Angeles, California
March, 1983

Service to Humanity Award
Southwest Christian College
Terrell, Texas
March, 1983

N. M. M. D. F. Award
Los Angeles, California
1983

1982-1983 Award for Support of Children in the Community
Big Sisters of Los Angeles — Club 101
Los Angeles, California
1983

Commendation for Keynote Speech at Informafair
Ohio House of Representatives
11th General Assembly of Ohio
November, 1981

Honorary Citizen of Columbus, Ohio
Mayor Tom Moody, City of Columbus
Columbus, Ohio
November, 1981

State of Michigan Resolution — for Philanthropic and Humanitarian
Endeavors
Detroit, Michigan
September, 1981

City of Detroit Proclamation
Mayor Coleman A. Young, City of Detroit
Detroit, Michigan
September, 1981

Testimonial Resolution — Distinguished Recognition Award for
Courage and Perseverance and Compassion for Humanity
Detroit City Council
Detroit, Michigan
September, 1981

Entrepreneur, Philanthropist and Humanitarian Award
Afro-American Museum of Detroit
Detroit, Michigan
September, 1981

Certificate of Appreciation — Recognition of Induction into the
Schomburg Center for Research and Black Culture
The Afro-American Newspaper
July, 1981

Service to Youth Award — South Los Angeles
Weingart Urban Center
Los Angeles, California
June, 1981

Award for Outstanding Contribution in the Field of Rehabilitation
Southern California Rehabilitation Association
Los Angeles, California
1981

Certificate of Tribute — Outstanding Citizenship and Activities
Enhancing Community Betterment
City of Los Angeles
October, 1978

Outstanding Citizen of Los Angeles
Los Angeles City Council
Los Angeles, California
September, 1978

Resolution — Personal and Professional Achievements
California State Legislature
Los Angeles, California
August, 1978

Certificate of Award — Outstanding Community Services
Southwest Wave Newspaper
Los Angeles, California
May, 1978

Certificate of Achievement — High Standard of Excellence in the
Management of a Family Care Facility
Exceptional Adult Center
Los Angeles, California
December, 1974

Certificate of Appreciation
Los Angeles Junior Chamber of Commerce
Los Angeles, California
October, 1973

Commendation in Appreciation for Friendship and Generous Support of
Service to Young People
Young Men's Christian Association
Los Angeles, California
1973

W. I. S. E. Award for Outstanding Achievements as a Real Estate
Entrepreneur and Community Leader
Sponsored by Anheuser-Busch Inc.
Los Angeles, California
1981

Achievement Award for Outstanding Community Service
Women's Council, Consolidated Realty Board
Los Angeles, California
May, 1979

Participating Award — Career Day
Loren Miller Elementary School
Los Angeles, California
February, 1979

Inspirational Award
Miss Black Galaxy 1979 Contest
Los Angeles, California
1979

The Genius and Beauty of the Black Women '79 Award
V. R. Scrubb Productions
Los Angeles, California
1979

Certificate of Significant Achievement and Contributions to the State of
California in Developing Economic Independence Among Young
Adults
United States Senate
Senator S. I. Hayakawa of California
Los Angeles, California
November, 1979

Recognition for Inspiration and Example to Others
United States House of Representatives
Congress of the United States
November, 1978

Award of Merit — Outstanding Achievement in Service to the
Developmentally Disabled
South Central Los Angeles Regional Center
Los Angeles, California
October, 1978

Certificate of Tribute — Outstanding Citizenship and Activities
Enhancing Community Betterment
City of Los Angeles
October, 1978

Outstanding Citizen of Los Angeles
Los Angeles City Council
Los Angeles, California
September, 1978

Resolution — Personal and Professional Achievements
California State Legislature
Los Angeles, California
August, 1978

Certificate of Award — Outstanding Community Services
Southwest Wave Newspaper
Los Angeles, California
May, 1978

Certificate of Achievement — High Standard of Excellence in the
Management of a Family Care Facility
Exceptional Adult Center
Los Angeles, California
December, 1974

Certificate of Appreciation
Los Angeles Junior Chamber of Commerce
Los Angeles, California
October, 1973

Commendation in Appreciation for Friendship and Generous Support of
Service to Young People
Young Men's Christian Association
Los Angeles, California
1973

YMCA Outstanding Service Award
Southside Los Angeles Century Club
Los Angeles, California
1973